Global Financial Markets series

Global Financial Markets is a series of practical guides to the latest financial market tools, techniques and strategies. Written for practitioners across a range of disciplines it provides comprehensive but practical coverage of key topics in finance covering strategy, markets, financial products, tools and techniques and their implementation. This series will appeal to a broad readership, from new entrants to experienced practitioners across the financial services industry, including areas such as institutional investment; financial derivatives; investment strategy; private banking; risk management; corporate finance and M&A, financial accounting and governance, and many more.

Titles include:

Erik Banks
DARK POOLS, 2nd Edition
Off-Exchange Liquidity in an Era of High Frequency, Program, and Algorithmic Trading

Erik Banks
LIQUIDITY RISK, 2nd Edition
Managing Funding and Asset Risk

Daniel Capocci
THE COMPLETE GUIDE TO HEDGE FUNDS AND HEDGE FUND STRATEGIES

Sandy Chen
INTEGRATED BANK ANALYSIS AND VALUATION
A Practical Guide to the ROIC Methodology

Frances Cowell
RISK-BASED INVESTMENT MANAGEMENT IN PRACTICE, 2nd Edition

Jawwad Farid
MODELS AT WORK
A Practitioner's Guide to Risk Management

Guy Fraser-Sampson
INTELLIGENT INVESTING
A Guide to the Practical and Behavioural Aspects of Investment Strategy

Michael Hünseler
CREDIT PORTFOLIO MANAGEMENT
A Practitioner's Guide to the Active Management of Credit Risks

Felix Lessambo
THE INTERNATIONAL CORPORATE GOVERNANCE SYSTEM
Audit Roles and Board Oversight

Ross K. McGill
US WITHHOLDING TAX
Practical Implications of QI and FATCA

David Murphy
OTC DERIVATIVES, BILATERAL TRADING AND CENTRAL CLEARING
An Introduction to Regulatory Policy, Trading Impact and Systemic Risk

Gianluca Oricchio
PRIVATE COMPANY VALUATION
How Credit Risk Reshaped Equity Markets and Corporate Finance Valuation Tools

Andrew Sutherland and Jason Court
THE FRONT OFFICE MANUAL
The Definitive Guide to Trading, Structuring and Sales

Michael C. S. Wong and Wilson F. C. Chan (*editors*)
INVESTING IN ASIAN OFFSHORE CURRENCY MARKETS
The Shift from Dollars to Renminbi

Global Financial Markets series
Series Standing Order ISBN: 978–1137–32734–5
You can receive future titles in this series as they are published by placing a standing order. Please contact your bookseller or, in case of difficulty, write to us at the address below with your name and address, the title of the series and the ISBN quoted above.

Customer Services Department, Macmillan Distribution Ltd, Houndmills, Basingstoke, Hampshire RG21 6XS, England

---

Also by Erik Banks:

LIQUIDITY RISK, 2nd Edition

RISK CULTURE

SEE NO EVIL: UNCOVERING THE TRUTH BEHIND THE FINANCIAL CRISIS

FINANCE: THE BASICS, SECOND EDITION

DICTIONARY OF FINANCE, INVESTMENT AND BANKING

RISK AND FINANCIAL CATASTROPHE

SYNTHETIC AND STRUCTURED ASSETS

CATASTROPHIC RISK

LIQUIDITY RISK

THE FINANCIAL LEXICON

THE FAILURE OF WALL STREET

ALTERNATIVE RISK TRANSFER

WORKING THE STREET

CREDIT RISK OF COMPLEX DERIVATIVES, 3rd Edition

CORPORATE GOVERNANCE

EXCHANGE-TRADED DERIVATIVES

THE SIMPLE RULES OF RISK

E-FINANCE

THE RISE AND FALL OF THE MERCHANT BANKS

ASIA PACIFIC DERIVATIVE MARKETS

EMERGING ASIAN FIXED INCOME MARKETS

CREDIT RISK OF FINANCIAL INSTRUMENTS

OPTIONS APPLICATIONS (*Co-authored with P. Siegel*)

CREDIT DERIVATIVES (*Co-authored with M. Glantz and P. Siegel*)

PRACTICAL RISK MANAGEMENT (*Co-authored with R. Dunn*)

WEATHER RISK MANAGEMENT (*Edited and co-authored with XL Financial*)

Dark Pools

Off-Exchange Liquidity in an Era of High Frequency, Program, and Algorithmic Trading

2nd edition

Erik Banks

palgrave
macmillan

First edition 2010
Second edition published 2014 by
PALGRAVE MACMILLAN

Palgrave Macmillan in the UK is an imprint of Macmillan Publishers Limited, registered in England, company number 785998, of Houndmills, Basingstoke, Hampshire RG21 6XS.

Palgrave Macmillan in the US is a division of St Martin's Press LLC, 175 Fifth Avenue, New York, NY 10010.

Palgrave Macmillan is the global academic imprint of the above companies and has companies and representatives throughout the world.

Palgrave® and Macmillan® are registered trademarks in the United States, the United Kingdom, Europe and other countries

ISBN: 978–1–137–44953–5

This book is printed on paper suitable for recycling and made from fully managed and sustained forest sources. Logging, pulping and manufacturing processes are expected to conform to the environmental regulations of the country of origin.

A catalogue record for this book is available from the British Library.

Library of Congress Cataloging-in-Publication Data

Banks, Erik.
    Dark pools: off-exchange liquidity in an era of high frequency, program and algorithmic trading / Erik Banks.
        pages cm.—(Global financial markets)
    "Second edition" – Preface.
    Revised edition of the author's Dark pools: the structure and future of off-exchange trading and liquidity, published in 2010.
    Includes bibliographical references and index.
    ISBN 978–1–137–44953–5
    1. Capital market. 2. Liquidity (Economics) 3. Risk. I. Title.

HG4523.B364 2014
332.64′2—dc23   2014024789

Contents

Illustrations

FIGURES

TABLES

"Pools in Practice" Vignettes

Preface to the Second Edition

The marketplace for securities trading has continued evolving and growing since the first edition of *Dark Pools* was published in 2010. Specifically, following the devastating market crisis of 2007–2009, which sidelined many participants, an accelerating market recovery began to appear in 2011 and 2012, bringing retail and institutional investors back to the developed and emerging equity and fixed income markets. Their return has heralded growth in volume and liquidity, essential ingredients for dark market expansion. In addition, new technologies have been introduced in the programming, hardware, and networking sectors which have led to a new generation of increasingly sophisticated, and rapidly executed, trading strategies – including high frequency/low latency trading and algorithmic trading. Furthermore, a growing focus on cost reduction and profit maximization has caused the largest investors to find ways of employing cost-saving solutions, like low market impact trading and direct market access. These forces, combined with consolidation and restructuring in the exchange and off-exchange sector and a redrafting of market regulations, have led to a reshaping of the dark pool sector.

Against this background, dark trading remains an important financial market growth sector. By all available statistics – which are still challenging to derive in a market that, by definition, remains opaque – dark trading now accounts for approximately 40% of all U.S. turnover; the European share ranges from 8 to 15% at any point in time, while countries such as Canada and Australia have breached the 10% mark. Collectively, these are significant market shares which have helped solidify the function and legitimacy of the dark market.

Given the changes and growth in this important segment of the financial markets, it seems timely and appropriate to bring the original material in *Dark Pools* up to date and to further expand its scope. The new edition reflects current ideas on micro and macrostructure and regulations.

More specifically, this new edition incorporates the following features:

- Updates and new examples throughout the book to reflect growth and change in national markets and asset classes.
- Expanded sections on algorithms, high frequency and low latency trading, aggregators, and market structures and their interaction with dark liquidity.
- Enhancements and updates on regulatory matters, focusing on efforts in the U.S. (via the SEC and FINRA), Europe (via MiFID II and MiFIR), Canada, and Australia.
- New "Pools in Practice" vignettes which give a practical treatment of some of the topics traders, exchanges, and other market participants are dealing with.

- New concluding remarks on the future of dark pools.
- Updated appendixes featuring the latest listings of dark pool sites and authorized MTFs.
- An expanded glossary that features new and important terminology.

This new volume should prove a ready reference to those interested in one of the most interesting and important segments of the traded financial markets.

About the Author

Erik Banks is a risk management specialist who has held executive positions at Citibank, Merrill Lynch, UniCredit and in the hedge fund sector, in New York, Tokyo, Hong Kong, London, and Munich. He is the author of more than 20 books on risk, derivatives, emerging markets, and governance.

PART I

Market Structure

PART I

Market Structure

1 | Introduction to Dark Pools

A Definition

The "dark pool" – a somewhat mysterious, even ominous, term – is the name given to a market structure that has become an integral part of the traded financial markets of the twenty-first century. While on the surface the concept of a dark pool might sound threatening, reality is fortunately rather different: such pools convey a range of benefits to both buy-side investors/traders and sell-side brokers and dealers, contributing to rapid growth in a relatively short period.

Before embarking on a more detailed discussion of the subject, let us begin by removing the shroud from the term. We can do so through a simple definition:

A dark pool is a venue or mechanism containing anonymous, nondisplayed trading liquidity that is available for execution.

We can clarify this even further by parsing the definition.

Anonymous, nondisplayed trading liquidity is order flow that is submitted confidentially and is not visible to the market at large, that is, it does not appear in public order books, like those operated by exchanges. The fact that the flow is not visible has given rise to the term "dark" liquidity. Note that by extension visible trades are commonly referred to as "lit" liquidity.

A *venue* is any electronic platform that is involved either solely or partly in housing nondisplayed liquidity.

A *mechanism* is any structure within an exchange or any venue/participant in the market that houses nondisplayed liquidity.

Execution is the ability to buy or sell an asset through the submission of an order.

Therefore, we may summarize by saying that a dark pool is an accumulation of orders to buy or sell assets, but whose existence is not publicly known or advertised. This is but one way of defining the dark pool sector, but it is useful and workable for our purposes.

To put this definition in perspective, let us consider the instance of Asset Manager QRS, which owns a large position in Stock XYZ that it wishes to sell as quietly as possible – discretion, rather than speed, is QRS's priority. While it can place an order with its broker to sell XYZ on a regulated "visible" exchange in the normal manner (i.e., setting a limit or market order and having it crossed against a visible contra-trade in the market), this might attract too much attention and result in an adverse sale price. To minimize this potentially negative outcome, QRS may choose instead to place an order to "sell the block dark", meaning the broker will route the order to one or more dark pools to seek execution. This strategy of "going dark" gives QRS certain critical advantages related to anonymity and market impact, as we shall note later in the chapter.

A dark pool is actually quite similar to a conventional visible market in terms of structure and function, executing orders according to certain rules, but it features no pre-trade transparency, that is, it posts no visible prices or volume (market depth). It can thus be seen as a form of exchange or exchange mechanism that supports discreet execution of trades. Indeed, many of the world's major exchanges operate dark pools or feature dark liquidity of their own. They are joined by hundreds of major financial institutions that have also created specific dark mechanisms or ventures. Knowing this, we can take comfort that the dark sector is not negative or in some way anticompetitive or prejudicial. The dark sector is not a "wild west" marketplace, operating without rules or structure, where investors and traders can be unwittingly fleeced. In fact, the benefits it conveys are significant, and certainly a key reason why dark pools have very quickly become an important dimension of the financial markets.

* * *

Pools in Practice: A typical dark trade

Let's consider a typical trade example and how it touches the investor, broker, and dark venue as it evolves through the process. We begin by assuming that an investor is interested in submitting an order to a broker-dealer that runs a proprietary operation that is used to support its client business. In the first instance, the investor must decide whether to send the order to the lit markets, the dark markets, or both; assuming it prefers a "dark only" execution it selects the correct flag on the order entry screen of the interface provided by the broker-dealer. Since the broker-dealer is essentially operating an internal matching engine where it accumulates all of its client orders, it receives the client order and routes it directly to its engine. Assuming a match can be made against the proprietary book or other incoming client flow, the engine crosses the trade and sends a confirmation back to the investor. The dark trade is thus complete. Note that it is common within the logic of the broker-dealer's engine to rank order the matching sequence of incoming client orders, that is, match against the broker-dealer's proprietary positions or other incoming client flow first, then route to other designated dark pools if no internal match is possible, and then route to the lit markets if no dark liquidity is available *at all. Whilst broker-dealers, particularly large ones, generally opt to build their own engines in accordance with their own business, operational, and governance requirements, third party solutions are also available for purchase; this tends to be attractive to smaller broker-dealers.*

Naturally, if the investor wants to take greater control of the execution, it could use a smart order router (SOR) instead of directing the trade to the broker-dealer. In this instance, the SOR could be set up to look for dark liquidity by sending indications of interest (IOIs) or immediate or cancel orders (IOCs) to various dark pools; it would continue the process in a sequential iteration until all pools had been exhausted. At that point, if the order were to remain totally or partially unfilled, the SOR logic could be instructed to take another pass through the population of pools, or it could route the remaining order straight to the lit markets. We will discuss IOIs, IOCs, and SORs later in the book.

*   *   *

In the rest of this chapter we shall consider the reasons why dark pools exist, some of the advantages they convey, the catalysts that have led to their creation and expansion, and the evolutionary path they have taken. This will be followed by a brief picture of the regional status quo and the changing face of trading execution. We shall conclude with a brief overview of the text to set the stage for the material that follows.

It is worth noting at this early point that most of what we consider in the book relates to the global stock markets. Although the dark pool phenomenon is making its way into various nonequity asset classes, the driving force has been, and remains, the equity sector. Where relevant we shall broaden our discussion to these alternate asset classes (e.g., fixed income), but will remain primarily focused on the equity markets.

Rationale, Catalysts, and Evolution

To kick off our discussion, let us begin by exploring why dark liquidity exists and why it has given rise to myriad dark pool venues and mechanisms in recent years – which, in total, continue to gain important market share in global equity trading.

Rationale

A new financial market/product is developed by intermediaries to provide participants with advantages that might otherwise not be realizable. These advantages, which are basically drivers, can come in various forms: reduced costs, higher returns, more efficient processing, faster execution, more accurate risk management, and so forth. In the case of dark pools the primary drivers include the following:

- Confidentiality
- Reduced market impact

- Cost savings
- Profit opportunities/price improvement.

To explore these drivers, let us consider the case of an institutional investor that is thinking about buying a large block of stock, say 100,000 shares of Stock ABC. It seems reasonable to assume that if this information becomes public, other investors might try and jump ahead of the investor to buy the same stock – effectively pushing up the price of the stock in the process, and creating a market impact – or unfavorable price movement – for the investor. If, however, the investor very quietly and confidentially attempts to purchase the stock before anyone is aware, they may be able to do so without moving the price of the stock – thus avoiding a market impact. Note that this same market impact would not occur if the investor were trying to buy 100 shares of ABC, because the order would be too small to generate interest in the market. Thus, large trades, or block trades – which we may define as those in excess of several thousand shares per trade[1] – are central to the dark liquidity thesis.[2] The number of block trades in the marketplace may be small in absolute number but they account for the largest amount of volume, and often absorb more liquidity than is available on an exchange or through a dealer network.

There is arguably no benefit to be obtained from "showing one's cards" when it comes to block trades, as any such disclosure may reveal to the market a specific investment posture, the search for a certain kind of stock, a preference for a particular kind of return, and so forth. We may refer to this unwanted disclosure as information leakage, and it may seep into the market either obviously or discreetly. Preserving confidentiality can protect sensitive information from falling into the hands of competitors or others who might have an interest in such details. Once the information is leaked, confidentiality is lost and some degree of market impact will invariably follow.

Let us also consider the issue of cost savings. If any economic benefits can be derived from dealing through an alternative mechanism or venue that effectively serves as a competitor to traditional, well-established exchanges, the investor is again in a position to benefit. In fact, clients executing away from an exchange can avoid paying exchange fees – any trade that is executed off-exchange creates a savings on fees, meaning that brokers can preserve more of the spread for themselves and split the savings with their clients; alternatively, large clients that access markets directly can keep the savings all to themselves. Use of direct market access (DMA), which is an increasingly popular mechanism that links electronic trading platforms on the desks of institutional clients directly to multiple exchanges, can result in even greater savings (we shall discuss DMA later in the book). Electronic trading generally, and dark trading specifically, can generate true cost savings.

In addition, there is the potential for a profit opportunity or price improvement. Active sell-side and sophisticated buy-side institutions have at their disposal advanced technologies and analytics that they apply to a range of strategies (including high frequency trading, statistical arbitrage, algorithmic trading, and so forth) – many of which are designed to take advantage of electronic trading and pockets of displayed and nondisplayed liquidity to generate short-term alpha, or excess returns. Venues that can be used to take or provide liquidity alongside, or away from, conventional exchanges emerge as important participants in this process, and can attract a great deal of buy-side and sell-side interest. Separately, traders or investors that submit orders into a dark pool on the basis of a reference price (which we discuss below) may benefit from some degree of price improvement, which is formally defined as the savings obtained when a trade is executed at a price that is superior to the base reference price at the time the order reaches the market (typically measured in terms of ticks or fractions of ticks). Again, a venue that can interact with dark liquidity to routinely deliver price improvement will attract client and dealer interest.

We may therefore consider that any mechanism or venue that (1) brings together buyers and sellers in a confidential manner,[3] (2) reduces or eliminates market impact, (3) saves on fees, and (4) creates the possibility for alpha generation or price improvement would appear to be compelling. In fact, dark pools provide all four of these advantages, which helps explain why their market share as a percentage of total turnover has risen dramatically in recent years.

Measuring activity in dark pools is not yet an exact science, as standardized reporting is only starting to become the norm (as we shall note in more detail in our discussion on regulatory matters). Accordingly, gauging market share is based on a variety of research studies and estimates. And, while estimates vary based on definition, consensus research appears to indicate that in the U.S., up to 40% of all trades were executed through a dark pool in 2013, up from some 15% in 2010.[4] Average daily trading volume at the largest U.S. platforms ranged from 100 to 300 million shares (single counted, matched trades). Although Europe, Canada, Australia, and Asia trail the U.S., with 5% to 15% trading dark in 2013 (depending on country), all have seen significant growth over the past few years. If we assume, therefore, that 30% to 50% of the global equity markets trade on a dark basis at any point in time, then we are clearly dealing with a very important market mechanism. This becomes even more obvious when we consider projections suggesting that at least half of the U.S. market, up to 30% of the European market (depending on regulation), and between 10% and 20% of the Asian market, will trade dark within the next five years.

Catalysts

Nondisplayed liquidity has been available in some form for many years through exchange mechanisms such as reserve orders and worked orders in specialist books, and via the so-called upstairs market, effectively an off-exchange gathering of buyers and sellers of large blocks operating under the auspices of broker/dealers.[5] In recent years, various catalysts have led to the development of new venues/mechanisms to supplement the original ones. The most powerful of these forces include the following:

- Technological innovation
- Regulatory changes
- Decimalization
- Capital accumulation and mobility

Success of new dark venues has been reinforced by the willingness of buy-side investors and other clients to embrace new technologies and new business models. In fact, the benefits buy-side firms have derived from these advances have been significant enough to persuade them to direct increasing amounts of activity into the dark sector and have helped dispel the notion that a central exchange marketplace is the only, or even best, way to trade in securities. Sell-side firms and established exchanges have taken up the challenge, redesigning their technology platforms and business models in order to offer clients new execution opportunities.

Technological innovation

Technological innovation emerges as *primus inter pares* among our list of catalysts. The development, refinement, and proliferation of communications networks, mass storage, and processing speed and power have led to the creation of efficient and reliable platforms, sophisticated order routers and algorithms, standardized communications protocols, and rapid pricing/matching routines. Without these technological advancements, the off-exchange sector would surely have remained at a rather rudimentary, and potentially error-prone, stage, unable to handle large volumes of orders. In fact, it is fairly easy to correlate the development of new venues with the rise of increasingly sophisticated technologies, and we shall explore some of the essential aspects of technology in Chapter 6. Ultimately, without the essential ingredient of technological advance, no amount of regulatory change, decimalization, or capital accumulation could have created off-exchange trading and dark trading.

Regulatory changes

Regulatory changes have been fundamental to the direct and indirect development and expansion of dark pools. Such changes have come in various forms and across various jurisdictions, and we can point to several of the most significant in both the U.S. and Europe: Regulation OHR (U.S.), Regulation ATS (U.S.), Regulation FD (U.S.), Regulation NMS (U.S.), and Markets in Financial Instruments Directive (Europe), among others.[6] Similar regulatory changes have appeared in other countries as well.

Regulation OHR

In 1997 the U.S. Securities and Exchange Commission (SEC) passed Regulation on Order Handling Rules (Regulation OHR), focusing on a redefinition of quote rules and limit order display rules.

The OHR quote rule indicates that market-makers and specialists must provide their best quotes (highest price at which the dealer will buy and the lowest price at which the dealer will sell) in order to increase market transparency (rather than impact the supply/demand of securities). Market-makers and specialists can continue to trade at better prices in electronic communications networks (ECNs, or electronic trading platforms, described below), though in such cases the ECNs must publish the better prices so that they can be viewed by public investors. This essentially means that the public is informed about better prices that occur in private, off-exchange, trading platforms.

The OHR limit order display rules govern the treatment of limit orders (which we describe in Chapter 2), and require that market-makers and specialists display, in a public manner, the limit orders they receive from clients whenever the orders are better than those supplied by market-makers or specialists. The intent behind this rule is to make sure that public orders compete directly in the establishment of quotes and, in so doing, help ensure some degree of price improvement and influence supply and demand.

Regulation ATS

Regulation Alternative Trading Systems (Regulation ATS) was enacted by the SEC in 1998 as a way of defining and overseeing the new breed of electronic trading platforms that were starting to appear in the marketplace, ensuring their integration into the national market system. We shall investigate some of those platforms later in the chapter and again in Chapter 3, but for now we note that under ATS Rule 301, any alternative trading system must be registered as a broker/dealer or a self-regulated exchange and must provide to a national securities exchange or national securities association, for inclusion in the public quotation system, the prices and sizes of its best priced buy and sell orders (i.e., the best bid-offer) that are displayed to more than one person. This requirement applies to each covered security in which the alternative trading system represents 5% or more of the total trading volume. The intent of the rule is to ensure synchronicity in dealing in national market securities (approximately 5000 stocks listed on the New York Stock Exchange and NASDAQ), so that electronic platforms are not creating submarkets of their own that do not have a strict relationship with the primary exchanges. This, as we shall see later, is a vital component of proper price discovery.

Regulation FD

Regulation Fair Disclosure (Regulation FD) was introduced by the SEC in 2000 and is applicable to companies listed on U.S. exchanges. Though FD is far-reaching in its scope, its primary aim is to ensure fair and equal distribution of information by publicly listed companies to the marketplace. This is certainly a sensible way of promoting equality between buy-side investors and sell-side analysts and has been successful in eliminating the information arbitrage that once existed (e.g., the sell-side once enjoyed an information "edge" over the buy-side as a result of open access to management of companies). However, it has created unintended consequences in the electronic trading sector, including the dark sector. Specifically, with spreads compressing as a result of the vanishing "information arbitrage," at least some sell-side firms have become reluctant to commit as much risk capital to support trading of equity flows; this has moved them more aggressively toward the agency model, a logical way of handling order flow with virtually no risk. The indirect consequence of FD, therefore, has been the development of stronger agency platforms, much of that predicated on the technology dimension mentioned above. Indeed, it has become easier for sell-side firms to support low-margin equity trading business through displayed and non-displayed mechanisms, and via the use of client-based algorithms.

Regulation NMS

Regulation National Market System (Regulation NMS) was introduced in 2007 after significant discussion with industry and regulatory bodies to consolidate and strengthen the framework for trading and execution on exchanges and electronic platforms, and it formally covers exchanges, electronic communications networks, broker/dealers, and broker/dealers routing orders. In fact, NMS was an attempt to bring together fractionalized and inconsistent market practices that developed around these different participants.[7] Regulation NMS features four key streams, including

- Order protection rule
- Access rule
- Subpenny rule
- Market data rule

Under NMS's Order Protection Rule, investors must receive equal access to prices, all trades must be executed at the best price, and if the best price is a displayed price, it cannot be ignored or "traded through." In effect, the rule is designed to protect displayed prices and encourage the use of limit orders. Orders that are not displayed are not protected and can be ignored, even if the prices are better than the displayed prices. Prior to the advent of NMS, large stock blocks could be executed outside the National Best Bid Offer (NBBO)[8] – that is, the best bid and the best offer available in a security in any marketplace – making the playing field somewhat unequal for certain participants. With NMS in place, all trading must occur within the NBBO – meaning that even aggressive buyers and sellers who would otherwise trade through must rely on the NBBO as their pricing reference, a practice that has been adopted by various types of dark platforms. NMS thus sets the standards for the protected bid (offer), which is a bid (offer) on a stock displayed via an electronic trading platform and disseminated via a national market system that represents the best price available in the market. The regulation specifies handling of trade-throughs, or the purchase or sale of a stock during regular trading hours, either as principal or as agent, at a price that is lower than a protected bid or higher than a protected offer: the trade-through rule requires that the best electronically available bid or offer in each market be protected, meaning that no venue can trade through a protected bid or offer (i.e., execute an order at an inferior price), regardless of where that quote resides. Venues can thus cross orders before they get to an exchange (through whatever mechanism they choose) but the price cannot be worse than what would be available through an exchange. NMS also sets forth parameters for the intermarket sweep orders (ISO), which is a limit order designated for automatic execution in a specified venue even when a better quote is available from another venue. In order to adhere to regulations, the order must be sent concurrently to venues with better prices, but is not subject to auto-routing (we consider ISOs later in the book). The implications of the Order Protection Rule have been considerable: floor brokers on the NYSE who work orders (de facto dark orders) are no longer protected, incentives to slice up orders and sweep markets have increased, and migration to dark venues has been on the rise (where NMS only applies if the volume in a particular security exceeds a threshold, as noted below).

Under NMS's Access Rule, market centers are prohibited from executing orders at a price that is inferior to that found in another venue, quote access must come from private links,[9] access fees are capped, self-regulation organizations have to set rules to prohibit the display of quotes that lock or cross the market, and electronic platforms must display quotes (i.e., moving from dark to light) if their volume in a security exceeds 5% of average daily volume. NMS actively promotes the concept of competition from alternative platforms.[10] This has been instrumental in changing the U.S. electronic trading landscape, leading directly or indirectly to increased execution speed, greater use of common messaging, greater control by brokers and/or investors of order routing, more rapid development and use of crossing networks and other dark venues, and continued consolidation and transformation within the exchange sector. To be sure, the ability for more venues to form under NMS has almost certainly led to a greater amount of fragmentation, with attendant implications on market liquidity, as we shall discuss at various points in the text.

The NMS Subpenny Rule prohibits exchanges, market-makers, and electronic platforms from displaying, ranking, or accepting quotes on NMS securities in subpenny increments unless a stock is priced at less than $1.00 per share. This rule exists to prevent stepping ahead of a limit order based on some inconsequential amount, like a fraction of a penny. The Market Data Rule, in turn, provides for formulae and rules for revenues generated by market data feeds. Regulation NMS also provides for standardized reporting of covered order execution via its Rule 605 (which was itself created as the Exchange Rule Act 11AC1–5 in 2000); this requirement is intended to provide a degree of transparency and uniformity for all market centers that trade in NMS securities, including those executed in a dark pool; we shall consider this point in Chapter 7.

When considered in totality, the various regulations noted above have clearly been instrumental in supporting the restructuring of the U.S. equity markets and promoting the growth of electronic and dark trading. Of course, after years in force, enhancements and refinements have been made to these (and other) U.S. rules, as we shall discuss later.

MiFID

The Markets in Financial Instruments Directive (MiFID) is a pan-European legislative directive enacted in 2007 within the European Economic Area (EEA)[11] to protect consumers/investors dealing in financial instruments and to increase competition. MiFID rules center on

- Systems and controls
- Client management
- Best execution
- Reporting

Certain aspects of MiFID are macro in nature, such as ensuring that institutions in countries that participate in MiFID can "passport" financial services/products across national borders once an initial authorization or license has been obtained (this is an expansion of passporting originally included in the 1993 Investment Services Directive[12]). Others are micro-focused, such as making certain that a process of risk management, systems, and controls is properly incorporated within each financial institution, that investors are treated equitably and that proper securities execution is delivered by financial providers to all clients. Financial institutions are required to categorize their clients by degree of sophistication (e.g., retail clients, professional clients, eligible counterparties); different levels of investor protection apply to each category. In addition, an analysis of transaction suitability is required for firms that provide investment advice, centering on a "know your client" discipline.

From an execution perspective, MiFID permits trading through regulated markets (e.g., primary exchanges), multilateral trading facilities (e.g., off-exchange electronic platforms), systematic internalizers (e.g., proprietary trading desks), and over-the-counter (e.g., trades between wholesale institutions, outside of systematic internalizers). Regulated markets, multilateral trading facilities (MTFs), and systematic internalizers can match third-party buyers and sellers; regulated markets, but not MTFs, must ensure that stock issues comply with disclosure requirements. It is interesting to note that so-called broker crossing networks, or broker-operated venues able to select who is permitted to participate, were not specifically disallowed under MiFID and developed into an important part of the dark sector. Institutions dealing in the market must be authorized under one of these categories by the relevant national regulator; the full listing is maintained in the CESR's (Commission of European Securities Regulators) MiFID Database,[13] which we summarize in Appendix 2. Trading may occur via a continuous auction order book trading system, quote-driven trading system, periodic auction trading system, or through a hybrid model. Each venue must demonstrate that it has in place a best execution policy related to orders received from both retail and professional clients and that it can monitor its compliance under such a policy; best execution is primarily attributable to price, though other factors such as speed and probability of execution may also play a role.

Perhaps the most important feature of MiFID for purposes of our discussion is that member states no longer require execution of securities transactions on a regulated market or exchange (under so-called concentration rules). This leads to direct support for MTFs, or automated trading systems providing execution in the securities markets. More formally, an MTF is a multilateral system that brings together buyers and sellers of securities in an equitable manner and in accordance with rules promoted by MiFID (e.g., specific regulations, pre- and post-trade transparency). The development of various MTFs as vehicles to challenge existing exchanges in the delivery of liquidity and execution has been significant, as we shall note in Chapter 3. Importantly for our discussion, some MTFs operate dark books in parallel with their light books. MiFID also sanctions the development and use of systematic internalizers, which are essentially internal crossing books (e.g., proprietary desk positions crossing against incoming flows), but these must operate under the same pre- and post-trade transparency and best-execution rules as MTFs. MiFID, like NMS, thus promotes the use of alternative pools of liquidity, creating the potential for further growth in the sector.

MiFID's pre-trade transparency rules require that firms operating continuous order book trading systems make available for each security the five best price levels for both bids and offers, including number of shares and orders; for periodic auction trading systems the indicative auction price and volume must be displayed, and for quote-driven markets the best bids and offers of market-makers must be indicated. However, certain pre-trade transparency waivers are available for the following, which has helped build up the dark sector:

- Platforms that operate as price reference systems (the equivalent of a crossing network in the U.S.); this requires that all trades be executed at a price that is based on the primary exchange price – the European Best Bid Offer or EBBO (and in a manner that is structurally similar to the NBBO under Regulation NMS).
- Platforms that formalize negotiated transactions, subject to certain pricing restrictions.
- Orders held in an order management facility, pending display (e.g., reserve orders).
- Transactions that are "large in scale" (LIS), which are defined by certain criteria.[14] Note also that trades can be dark only if they are above minimum order sizes (which are based on the average daily turnover and market capitalization of a

stock, as defined by the Committee of European Securities Regulators). Unless a venue qualifies for an alternative price reference wavier, it must enforce the LIS rules, which means that a large order that is sliced too thinly may not qualify to go dark on a venue. In general, primary exchanges cannot qualify for the waiver.

Under post-trade rules, firms are required to print the price, volume, and time on all trades in listed shares, even those that are crossed outside of a regulated market/exchange (with some exceptions that allow for deferred publication).

Whilst MiFID has clearly been instrumental in shaping aspects of European dark trading, some elements of the original directive are being refined and restructured under a new version, so-called MiFID II. We shall consider MiFID II, and the associated Markets in Financial Instruments Regulation (MiFIR), later in the book to see how they will impact dark trading in the future.

Other regulatory frameworks

While the U.S. and Europe have progressed fastest and farthest with regard to authorizing widespread electronic trading and ensuring proper accommodation within the relevant national regulatory frameworks, other countries have also embarked on a similar process – even though they are not yet in the same state of advanced development with regard to electronic trading.

For example, Japan's Financial System Reform Law, which became effective in December 1998, makes possible the development and use of private (or proprietary) trading systems (PTSs), which are electronic trading platforms that are created by banks or securities firms and allow for off-exchange trading in stocks and bonds, including trading in the after-hours market. In fact, no off-exchange trading is permitted unless it is conducted through a PTS or through the Tokyo Stock Exchange's electronic trading interface. Though not strictly dark trading platforms, they do offer dark liquidity through the use of reserve orders, which we discuss later in the book. Over the past decade a number of venues have taken advantage of this regulatory authorization to create PTSs for the domestic marketplace. In Canada, ATSs (Alternative Trading Systems) are permitted to operate under rules set forth via Regulation of Marketplaces and Trading/ Alternative Trading Systems, issued by the Ontario Securities Commission in November 2001.[15] Various ECNs and crossing networks have established operations under the original Canadian regulations; it is worth noting that some of these regulations have been updated in recent years. Australia has emerged as another marketplace for dark trading, primarily through regulations put forth by the Australian Securities and Investment Commission. As in Canada, recent updates to the Australian regulatory framework have altered some of the country's dark trading requirements. We shall consider the consequences of Canadian and Australian regulatory changes in Chapter 7.

With all of this regulatory precedent in place, it is quite reasonable to suppose that other countries will follow suit as they move toward developing or formalizing their own electronic platforms.

Decimalization

Decimalization – or the process of moving the minimum quoted price to 0.01 from some larger amount (e.g., 0.0625 (1/16th) in the U.S.) – has had a profound impact on various global securities markets and the business models of institutions supporting such markets. The move to decimalization, introduced in various national markets at different points in time (e.g., 2001 in the U.S., 2004 in Europe, and so forth), has brought with it intended and unintended consequences. In fact, the changes were originally introduced in order to lower trading costs for investors, thereby encouraging more activity. The unintended consequences have been rather more dramatic: smaller price increments mean lower spreads, lower spreads lead to lower profit opportunities, and lower profit opportunities reduce the willingness of dealers to risk capital. In addition, liquidity formation at individual price points has been affected.

In the first instance, dealers have experienced lower profit margins. Whereas the previous minimum spread on a transaction in the U.S. was 0.0625, even on a very actively traded stock, that is no longer true – the minimum spread can be as narrow as 0.01 (though it can be wider for illiquid stocks).[16] Therefore, profits have vanished from stock trading. In fact, by some estimates the margins on trading have declined by as much as 80%, creating fewer incentives for dealers and risk-takers to commit capital to support trading activities, thus prompting a greater migration toward an agency-brokerage model of matching buyers/sellers.

Second, decimalization has led to lower liquidity at any single price point. In a theoretical sense we can imagine that under a regime of 0.0625 minimum spreads a stock features 16 price points for dollar or euro of value. This means liquidity clusters at one of 16 price points. Under a decimalized regime we now refer to 100 price points, meaning a far greater number of individual pools and a lower amount of liquidity on each point. Lower liquidity at each price point means that the market can absorb lower average trade size and cannot "disguise" large trades without creating a market impact. Figure 1.1 illustrates in a very simplified fashion 10 orders, one coming into each one of 10 price points versus all coming into 1 price point; not only are the orders diffused under the first approach (meaning less likelihood of encountering a contra-trade) but the ability to disguise is also more difficult.[17]

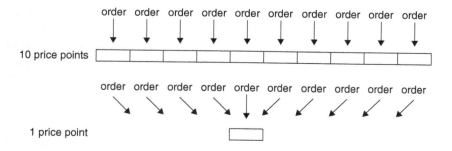

Figure 1.1 Orders coming into various price points

In fact, this point has been particularly important for the development of the dark space. In the U.S., decimalization has caused average trade size executed on exchanges to decrease by 70%, while in Europe the decline has been approximately 50%. The ability to cross block trades without "being noticed" has become increasingly difficult, which has been instrumental in driving more business away from the visible markets.

Capital accumulation and mobility

Capital, which includes the equity and debt obligations firms raise to fund their operations, represents the raw material of every economy and its financial markets. As global demand for goods and services has risen in the past decades, demand for capital financing has risen in tandem. Fortunately, such demand has been met by eager investors (equities) and creditors (debt). In fact, the amount of capital outstanding has reached record levels in the first years of the new millennium, a trend that remains intact even in the aftermath of the financial crisis of 2007–2008. Capital growth appears likely to continue as industrialized nations build on their economic bases and as powerful emerging nations enter the fray.

Capital is supplied by all manner of investors, from individuals to institutions. However, it is the growing amount of assets under management commanded by institutional investors – including mutual funds, unit trusts, hedge funds, insurance companies, trusts, and other asset managers[18] – that has radically reshaped capital mobilization, allocation, and trading. These institutional investors, which are collectively part of the buy-side, have become dominant players in the financial markets, investing on behalf of clients in a passive or active style, and becoming significant clients of banks, brokers, and other financial intermediaries. Hedge funds that pursue sophisticated, and sometimes high-volume, trading strategies are critically important to the electronic markets and dark trading; strategies such as index arbitrage, program trading, statistical arbitrage, high frequency trading, and low latency trading are key contributors in the allocation and transfer of capital.[19] The buy-side has the ability to influence markets, product trends, and microstructures; therefore, observing their requirements and behaviors is essential in understanding how electronic trading and dark trading might evolve in the future.

Naturally, capital needs to be centralized in a marketplace once it has been raised for efficient and effective trading among interested parties. The global equity markets and debt markets rely on exchanges and over-the-counter venues, some of which we discuss in this book, to foster such trading. In fact, the increased supply of capital has far outpaced the ability of any single venue to be the sole supporter of listing and trading. Although a single venue scheme may still be possible in certain smaller emerging markets, in practice virtually every national economy has such a large amount of traded capital outstanding, that a multiplicity of venues is a virtual requirement – which has certainly been instrumental in allowing new venues, including those supporting dark liquidity, to develop and expand. In fact, the experience of the U.S., UK, Germany, Japan, France, and others reflects clearly the fact that every major national market has a need for multiple venues to list and trade capital securities.

In addition to the accumulation of capital, the ability to quickly move capital across markets and national boundaries has coincided with the new breed of electronic platforms. Suppliers of capital – investors and traders, in the case of equities – can quickly buy, sell, rebalance, hedge, or transfer major amounts of capital in very short order. As this requirement expands through both deregulation and sector expansion, the need for venues capable of filling this need becomes paramount. Again, we can point to the significant efforts that have emerged in the electronic trading sector in recent years as a direct outcome. As the need to raise and trade capital on a global basis continues to increase, it seems reasonable to assume that venues that can support such activity will continue to benefit. To the extent new emerging markets also expand their demand for capital, venues that can support regional efforts should also play a leading role.

Evolutionary development

Since there are very good reasons why dark pools exist, it comes as no surprise that many supporting venues and mechanisms have developed over the years. Indeed, dark pools have existed in various forms for several decades but have, of course, become even more prominent in a twenty-first-century environment driven by the catalysts noted above. A quick snapshot of the evolution of the sector reveals that consistent innovation has occurred regularly within exchanges and across other mechanisms and venues.

Exchanges

To explore the early history of dark liquidity, let us first consider the operation of a typical exchange. An exchange is simply a marketplace where bargains can be made – bids and offers can be submitted and human or electronic interaction can cause these bids and offers to be matched and executed. The exchange permits the price of a security to be determined by the interaction of bids and offers against posted volume (or market depth). While our instincts and experiences might lead us to believe that all of the order flow that passes through an exchange is readily visible to all buyers and sellers, reality is rather different. In fact, the orders shown on an exchange screen may not be a full representation of buying and selling interest in a given security. Various global stock exchanges feature nondisplayed orders as part of their general operations and can rightly claim to be the true pioneers of dark liquidity. Most do so via

- Nondisplayed orders being "worked" by specialists or floor brokers within their order books.
- Nondisplayed orders held by the exchange, with either a small fraction displayed to the public at large and the rest remaining out of view (reserve or iceberg orders)

or with none of the orders displayed at all (hidden orders). These types of orders reside within an exchange and are not controlled by an executing broker.

These two areas of nondisplayed interest are sometimes referred to as a grey market or grey pool – they are not strictly lit and not strictly dark. While not all global exchanges operate such mechanisms, many of the largest and most prominent do, including the NYSE Euronext (now part of the Intercontinental Exchange (ICE)), NASDAQ OMX, Deutsche Boerse/Xetra, and the London Stock Exchange (LSE), among others (we shall revisit this point in Chapter 3).

Other mechanisms, venues, and participants

Although dark liquidity has been embedded in exchanges for many years, its presence in today's markets has changed and expanded dramatically. As noted, much of this progress has its roots in the advent of technology, which began with hardware in the 1980s and expanded into software, networking and communications during the 1990s. New venues emerged with greater frequency in the millennium as improvements in computing power and speed and additional flexibilities created by Internet and intranet infrastructure became available. Of course, growth in the value of accumulated capital and new regulatory flexibilities supported or accelerated the process.

Although a buy-side or sell-side institution can turn to an established exchange and try to tap into dark liquidity via working orders, reserve orders, or hidden orders, it can also turn to alternate venues, including

- Electronic limit order books (ELOBs), a type of ECN and a subset of the class of electronic trading platforms known as ATSs/MTFs, that aggregate, display, and continuously cross visible orders and, in some cases, support nondisplayed orders. ELOBs essentially serve as off-exchange exchanges, providing a degree of transparency and price discovery.
- Crossing networks, or price reference systems, which are ATSs/MTFs that aggregate but do not display orders, and cross either continuously or discretely against a given base price (meaning they do not participate in price discovery). In some cases a degree of price negotiation can occur between buyers and sellers.
- Broker/dealer desks, or "broker internalizers" or "systematic internalizers," which are desks at financial institutions that cross client flows passing internally with other client positions or with positions from proprietary trading desks; this also includes the traditional "upstairs market" on exchanges, based on crossing of large block trades between institutions away from the exchange floors. Unlike ELOBs and crossing networks, which take no risk positions at all, broker/dealer desks actively commit risk capital to support trading.
- Agency brokers, or agents that match bids and offers by operating across a range of different venues.

Each one of these is an active participant in the provision of dark liquidity, and we shall explore them, and certain other hybrid structures, in greater detail in Chapter 3. It is worth noting that some industry definitions classify dark pools more narrowly, including only crossing networks. However, this definition is in our view too restrictive. Any examination of dark liquidity must focus on all locations where nondisplayed orders can gather, which includes all of the mechanisms and venues just noted. Figure 1.2 summarizes the various exchange and off-exchange venues where dark liquidity may exist.

The electronic era

Let us now consider several seminal events in the evolutionary path of the dark pool sector – with a focus on the technological dimension of the marketplace – to gain some appreciation for developments over the past few decades. Although the nomenclature and typology of the sector can be a bit confusing, we can generalize by again noting that ATSs/MTFs represent a generic form of electronic trading platform; within that general category we find two important subcategories, namely ECNs (including ELOBs) and crossing networks.

Electronic stock trading in the U.S. dates back to 1969, when Instinet (then known as Institutional Networks) was created as a de facto ECN to match incoming orders – though it obviously was not considered an ECN until years later. NASDAQ was created shortly thereafter, in 1971, as an all-electronic, quote-driven marketplace based on a system of market-makers, making it another pioneer in the electronic trading sector. The NYSE, which was founded as a physical, order-driven, auction-based market comprising of specialists, entered the electronic sphere in the early 1970s with its DOT computerized order router, which allowed it to pass orders electronically from members down to the trading post for execution by specialists. The open automated reporting system of the time also helped specialists determine market clearing prices. The first electronic trading montage screen, showing quotes on NYSE stocks, went live in 1977 through Instinet's efforts. Investment Technology Group's (ITG) POSIT (Portfolio System for Institutional Trading) emerged as another pioneering platform in the late 1970s, crossing block trades electronically away from the exchanges on a scheduled basis – though still in a visible fashion.

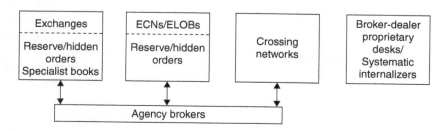

Figure 1.2 Sources of dark liquidity

And, even though ITG proved ultimately to be one of the success stories of the sector, its success was many years in the making – achieving a true critical mass of block flows took years to achieve.

During the 1980s, brokers/dealers supplemented their upstairs market activities by actively crossing trades for clients internally through their own electronic proprietary trading systems. Execution success in this instance depended on having enough flow to be able to match both sides – houses with big retail and institutional franchises were the most successful in this endeavor. Rapid growth in index arbitrage and portfolio trading during this period led to further advances in computerized order entry and routing, as large baskets of trades needed to be input and executed with as little delay as possible. In another pioneering move, Instinet rolled out its first after-hours crossing platform in 1986. Further changes appeared in the aftermath of the 1987 Crash, as regulators mandated a reinforcement of liquidity and more equitable handling of retail orders, which led to the development by NASDAQ of the Small Order Execution System (SOES)[20] – essentially an automatic order execution platform designed expressly for small size lots.

Naturally, electronic efforts of this period were not confined to the U.S. markets, but also emerged in certain key international markets. For example, the Paris Bourse (now part of NYSE Euronext), developed a leading-edge electronic trading platform for the French stock market as early as 1989 – which had the immediate effect of reversing the migration of French stock trading from Paris to London, eventually bringing it back almost entirely to home shores. In fact, the technologies developed by the Paris Bourse were ultimately licensed to other global exchanges. Interestingly, most of the European exchanges that converted from physically traded floor operations to electronic open order books by the late 1990s were operating as quasi-ECNs before the turn of the millennium; in fact, this is at least one reason why the "new" ECN model did not gain much traction in the European markets in its earliest phases.

Though advances were clearly occurring in electronic trading during the late 1980s and early 1990s, it was not until the late 1990s and the early part of the millennium – as technology, communications, and networking took a quantum leap forward – that ATSs emerged as a viable force. This was especially evident in the U.S. markets, which embraced new business models. Various ECNs set up operations to try and capture growing equity trading volumes through their new technology platforms; key ECNs of the period included Island, Archipelago, Brut, Attain, Bloomberg Tradebook, Track, Redibook, NexTrade, and MarketXT, among others. NASDAQ itself improved the sophistication of its platform, introducing different levels of client access (e.g., so-called Level I, Level II, and Level III services).[21] The rising stock market (built largely atop the dot-com/Internet wave) and lower executions costs helped fuel interest and growth in electronic trading. However, not all of these early electronic trading efforts were successful, in part because interfaces were still evolving, the platforms suffered from technical complexity, and gaining a sufficient critical mass of liquidity was very difficult. In the U.S., for instance, OptiMark and Harborside were early casualties. In Europe, a series of pre-MiFID platforms appeared but soon stalled, in part because of significant national market differences in the pre-Euro period. ECNs such as Tradepoint, Jiway, MTA International, and others failed to make a meaningful mark, though certain crossing platforms were more successful, as were certain bond-related ECNs (such as EuroMTS). And, although technology was needed to enter the marketplace, sustainability came from gaining and maintaining sufficient order flow. Liquidity was, and remains, the lifeblood of any electronic venue – including dark ones – that seeks to be viable. In fact, many of the platforms of this period were simply unable to gain or hold market share.

Not all aspects of the financial markets could be freely accessed via electronic platforms at this point. For instance, before 2000, the NYSE remained a "closed shop," with member specialists holding a firm grip on all operations. ECNs were not allowed to tap into the NYSE's liquidity because of Rule 390, which indicated that dealers trading NYSE stocks over-the-counter (rather than on the exchange floor) could not be members of the NYSE – an effective way of keeping ECNs out of NYSE's flows. This rule was eliminated at the beginning of the millennium and stripped the NYSE of its protected status, opening up the market for trading via ECNs dramatically, at which point the NYSE began losing market share to other venues and commenced a multiyear plan to change its own business model.

The dark pool phenomenon and crossing network structure came more formally into focus in September 2002, when INET, the product of a merger between the Island ECN and Instinet, indicated that it would stop displaying order book limit prices to avoid connecting to the relatively slow Intermarket Trading System (ITS); ITS was introduced in 1978 as a platform to disseminate trading prices on nine U.S. exchanges so that investors could select from the best prices, but gave the primary listing exchange of a particular stock up to 30 seconds to respond with a new price (giving them de facto priority). Through this action, INET effectively "went dark," meaning limit orders were no longer visible to market participants; a formal dark pool platform, Instinet CBX, followed in 2003. At the same time, decimalization contributed to the need for split orders, while the creation of algorithmic trading (trading rules coded into the order management or execution systems) gained widespread footing within the institutional community. Both of these factors led to increased demand for the services provided by electronic platforms generally, and crossing networks specifically. By 2003, seven crossing networks had been established as dedicated providers of nondisplayed liquidity, and just five years later the number had surpassed 40; the number has expanded even further since that time, as we shall note later in the book. While crossing networks increased in size and scope, the number of independent ECNs gradually declined through consolidation. Though ECNs are no longer the dominant, independent players they were in the early part of the millennium, their business models and technologies have been absorbed into other institutions, making them an integral part of market trading. Whether the more popular crossing networks go through a similar evolution is a matter we shall discuss later. In the meantime, it is important to note that such platforms have already dramatically changed the microstructure and macrostructure of trading and execution, to the point where it is likely their contribution will be enduring.

Developments on the sell-side have been accompanied by parallel evolution on the buy-side. While buy-side clients of the late twentieth century had traditionally been rather passive, simply accepting a range of services from the sell-side and conducting their transaction executions through normal market practices, their approach began to change in the early part of the millennium. The advent of a larger number of increasingly influential hedge funds and institutional asset managers with a more aggressive approach to trading and execution began shifting the balance of power. These buy-side clients began demanding better analytics and algorithms, and better interfaces with which to execute electronically. In addition, as they began moving larger blocks of stock, they became far more sensitive to the advantages of confidentiality, the negative price effects of decreasing execution size on block trades, and the perils of information leakage. Similarly, those engaged in "black box trading" (such as high frequency trading, statistical arbitrage, and so forth) demanded faster execution. Together, they helped support the nascent electronic platforms that operated partially or totally "in the dark."

In fact, the sum of the evolutionary changes in the electronic sphere has led to a radical change in the business model for delivering and accepting securities execution. The "high touch" model that defined the financial markets through the 1990s – built atop sales desks, high barriers to entry, and very controlled information dissemination – has evolved into a much more flexible and adaptable structure that has placed greater power in the hands of clients; the use of crossing networks, direct market access, algorithms, and other innovations (in both the visible and dark sectors) has led to falling commissions and fees, better execution, and more efficient and automated processes. Of course, it has also placed enormous pressures on the global IT infrastructure and the data handling capabilities of networks and storage repositories; it has also made it difficult for institutional players to use traditional venues to execute trades without leaving a footprint, and has created some degree of fragmentation and liquidity gaps – important issues which we shall consider later.

Regional Marketplaces

With some background on the electronic trading sector and dark pool sub-sector in hand, let us briefly consider the state of play on a regional basis. As we might imagine, the dark pool movement is expanding on a global basis, albeit with speed and depth that varies by country.

North America

The U.S. has been a clear leader in the equity dark pool sector, running several years ahead of European markets, and perhaps a decade ahead of the Asian markets. The U.S. markets feature very strong representation in terms of exchanges with dark mechanisms (to wit, NYSE, NASDAQ, BATS, and others), ECNs/ELOBs, and crossing networks (described in Chapter 3). In fact, by late 2009, the U.S. featured more than 40 venues partly or wholly dedicated to the provision of dark liquidity; this figure increased to 45 in 2013. The U.S. is also home to banks and broker/dealers which operate dark internalizers, with dozens in operation in 2013. In fact, the largest banks, including JP Morgan, Goldman Sachs, Morgan Stanley, and Bank of America Merrill Lynch, are significant players in this segment of the dark market. A well-established network of agency brokerage supports much of the client access. The Canadian markets, while obviously much smaller than the U.S. markets, feature several ATSs that provide dark capabilities, including Chi-X Canada, TriAct Canada, Perimeter BlockBook, and Liquidnet Canada.

Of course, all of this sell-side capability is valuable only if there is a buy-side to take advantage of the services being offered. In the case of the U.S. marketplace it is fair to say that the equity capital markets are deep and broad, with thousands of listed companies comprising trillions of dollars of market capitalization. Investor participation is active and includes both retail clients and institutional investors. The institutional base, in particular, is large and well established, and exhibits sophistication and willingness to trade, sometimes aggressively. Insurance company investment funds, corporate pension funds, mutual funds, exchange traded funds, hedge funds, and other trading/investing vehicles are all users of dark liquidity, to varying degrees. Therefore, the demand side of the equation is properly developed and able to support the myriad venues and mechanisms that house dark liquidity.

Importantly, the U.S. marketplace features two other well-developed sectors that cater directly and indirectly to innovation and expansion in the dark sector: technology companies and private equity/venture capital firms. The contribution of technology companies, including those that are specialized in the development of tools, analytics, algorithms, networking, and infrastructure that are used by the major providers of dark liquidity, is vital to the success of the sector; without these rather significant efforts, the marketplace would not be in its current state of advancement. It is also worth noting that much of this technology is portable across borders, meaning it can be, and is, applied in other regional settings – Europe, Asia, and other developing markets can avail themselves of this work (to be sure, strong technology efforts also exist in other countries, such as France and Japan, and these also contribute to the overall effort).

Private equity and venture capital firms had, and continue to have, an important role to play in sector development. In fact, such firms have provided capital to some of the independent trading/execution ventures that have developed over the years to challenge established exchanges and to promote new business models. Firms such as Archipelago, Island, and Brut, who might be regarded as pioneers, benefited from such start-up funding in the earliest days of the market's migration to dark trading.

Growth in U.S. dark trading has expanded steadily since markets recovered from the 2007–2008 financial crisis. Specifically, between 2009 and 2013 dark trading volume rose nearly 50% to reach 31% of all U.S. equity trading. The migration from light to dark continued in 2013, with dark trading reaching 40%, a truly remarkable achievement in a relatively short span of time. Not surprisingly, as off-exchange market share of dark venues increased, market share at NYSE, NASDAQ, and other regional exchanges declined, posting a 30% drop over the past few years. Average trade size continued to decline, with traditional large institutional blocks being joined by an increasing amount of small size retail tickets. Indeed, broker-dealer internalizers, which continue to handle all marketable retail flow, were increasingly seen as offering price improvements to the best bid offer. Investor confidence in the dark sector also continued to improve, with more than 70% of surveyed institutional investors citing comfort with dark pool practices, up from about 50% in 2008. Whilst the usual concerns remain in the U.S. market (e.g., access, transparency, competitive landscape) it has become increasingly obvious to a growing number of participants that better quality execution is possible when dark liquidity is part of the overall mix of execution options.

Europe

Europe has quickly become the second largest regional player in the sector, featuring a broad range of venues focused on electronic trading and algorithms. Though electronic trading and dark trading institutions date back several years through broker pools, reserve order facilities on various exchanges, and various crossing networks (e.g., POSIT Match arrived in Europe in 1998, while Liquidnet set up a platform in 2002), additional impetus came via passage of MiFID – which, as we noted, allowed for the further development of MTFs as off-exchange competitors capable of delivering best execution.

In fact, MiFID has given established exchanges such as the LSE, NYSE Euronext, NASDAQ OMX, Deutsche Boerse, and others additional competition, causing them to reformulate their own business models. By late 2009, Europe featured several dozen venues supplying dark liquidity in large-, mid-, and small-cap stocks, including exchanges (via reserve and hidden orders[22]), crossing networks, and systematic internalizers. As in the U.S., this number has grown steadily since then. Representative players include exchanges such as LSE, Deutsche Boerse/Xetra, Milan Stock Exchange, Euronext, Madrid Stock Exchange, as well as electronic exchange platforms such as Equiduct-Berliner Boerse, NASDAQ OMX Europe, BATS Chi-X Europe, and NYSE SmartPool,[23] among others. Given the somewhat uncertain operating environment and the potential for future consolidation, some financial institutions have opted to enter the MTF/crossing network marketplace through the consortium structure – a sound way of diffusing risk and backing multiple, nascent platforms to see which one(s) ultimately prove viable. For instance, in 2008 ten institutions participated in the development of the Burgundy MTF (specializing in Nordic equities), while nine major banks[24] launched the Turquoise MTF (specializing in pan-European equities). Both have since been subsumed by other exchanges, as we shall see later in the book. Major UK and European banks (and the subsidiaries/branches of U.S. banks) also run internal crossing books of their own to support light and dark flows (e.g., UBS, Credit Suisse, BNP Paribas, Deutsche Bank, Societe Generale, Barclays, and so on).

Like the U.S., UK and Europe feature large equity capital markets and very significant institutional investor bases that include many of the same vehicles noted above – hedge funds, unit trusts (as mutual fund equivalents), pension schemes, and sovereign wealth funds. While many of these may run passive portfolios (and are thus more likely providers of latent liquidity), some are aggressive and trade the markets actively. In addition, the UK and Europe have a tradition of block trading which is well established, meaning another driving force of activity is in place.

Given all of these factors, it comes as no surprise that growth in the dark sector has accelerated rapidly in recent years. While continued consolidation is likely over the coming years, the market appears capable of supporting the dozens of venues and institutions that have committed themselves to providing dark liquidity. As we have noted, approximately 11% of all equity trading occurred in the dark in 2013 (based on data from reporting platforms plus estimates from non-reporting ones), up from about 8% the year before and 5% a few years before; some 2100 European stocks had some form of dark activity, with the large capitalization names featuring most turnover (e.g., Vodafone, Nestle, Sanofi, Roche, Novartis, HSBC, Glaxo, SAP). Interestingly, virtually all institutional investors active in European markets made use of dark pools in their trading (e.g, 85% by 2011 and 94% by 2012).

The rapid growth of European dark trading has caught some off guard. Whilst MiFID set the stage for alternative trading solutions, the expansion actually achieved in the past few years has been dramatic, bringing with it interesting consequences. For instance, the expansion of alternative venues has given institutional investors in European equities the ability to be less dependent on long-standing relationships with broker-dealers executing through traditional exchange-driven mechanism – ultimately creating more opportunities for trading flexibility and improved pricing. Buy-side investors have also become much more sophisticated and aggressive about controlling the quality and pricing of their execution. In addition, as in the U.S., there is evidence that retail flows are being channeled through institutional money managers for dark execution. This places some additional burdens on institutional managers to demonstrate that they are approaching the dark market with a thoughtful and measured approach; ultimately, good execution plays a central role in performance comparisons of money managers.

Naturally, not everyone has been in favor of this "move to the dark." Argumentation is similar to what has occurred in the U.S., with banks and brokers supporting dark activity but exchanges (particularly those that have not adapted their business models and which face higher compliance and technical costs) complaining about lack of transparency, absence of rules-based level playing field and potential for systemic dislocation and other market disruptions. Some regulators argue the same.

Asia

Developments in the Asian market have proceeded at a slower pace than in the U.S. or Europe, for at least three reasons. First, the underlying equity markets are in an earlier stage of development. Apart from the equity markets of Japan, the Hong Kong portion of China, and Australia/New Zealand, the rest of the region is still in the process of equity market growth and development. Overall market capitalization and turnover are relatively small in these developing markets, which means that the supply of tradable shares is rather modest compared with the U.S. and Europe; indeed, many listed stocks are quite illiquid. In addition, the number of block trades is rather modest compared with other parts of the world. Second, the markets are quite heterogeneous, meaning that it does not necessarily make sense to apply a "one size fits all" solution to trading in the sector. Each country has investors with unique requirements; separate currencies; and specific trading, clearing, and settlement standards. The characteristics and needs of investors in Korea or the Philippines are different from those in Indonesia, Thailand, India, Singapore, New Zealand, and so forth, so it may be inaccurate to suggest that dark trading is necessary or desirable in every national marketplace. (Note that while the same might be said in a European context, movement toward commonality in financial market affairs, via, for instance, directives from the European Union, MiFID, a common currency, and so forth, creates a greater amount of homogeneity with regard to trading). In addition, some Asian markets still bar or limit free access by foreign investors, meaning that a potential source of liquidity is restricted. Third, the characteristics of the institutional marketplace are different than they are in the rest of the world. At the risk of generalizing slightly, we may state that the Asian markets feature larger pools of passive institutional investors, including postal insurance funds, pension funds, and sovereign wealth funds. Though large investors exist, they are not necessarily active ones – meaning they may be a good source of latent liquidity but may not be aggressively trading their books. Active institutional traders such as hedge funds exist, but are not particularly large. Absence of the same level of active liquidity can create some complications in effectively delivering the dark mechanism, as we shall note later in the book. That said, the level of information leakage in many of the regional markets tends to be high, so dark mechanisms can, at least theoretically, prove useful.

For all of these reasons, it comes as no surprise that the Asian dark sector is still quite small, featuring a relatively modest number of dedicated dark venues. Some established exchanges, such as the Australian Securities Exchange, allow for hidden orders, and a number of crossing networks/electronic agency brokers have been established in countries such as Korea, Hong Kong, Singapore, and Australia. Major global firms, including Nomura/Instinet, ITG, Liquidnet, CLSA, and BNP Paribas, among others, operate some of these platforms. Japan itself features a number of domestic PTSs, such as Monex Group's Nighter, and SBI Japannext, as well as platforms operated by several major U.S. and European firms. Pan-Asian cross market efforts which can handle stocks from multiple countries have also developed through ventures such as TORA Trading and BlocSec, among others. Another promising structural approach centers on dark aggregation, the de facto linking of pools that support trading in individual national markets. For instance, well-established venues such as Instinet and ITG have created linkages between regional dark pools that are effectively broker-dealer internalizers (rather than MTFs). Instinet has also teamed up with US bank JP Morgan in linking up 22 Asian pools. High frequency/low latency trading that taps into dark liquidity is also in its early stages, but will ultimately depend on expansion of a regionally robust technological infrastructure, which is not yet found throughout Asia. Thus, while all of these efforts are still in the initial stages, they are indicative of potential future growth opportunities in a marketplace that is somewhat fractionalized.

Changing Market Trends

Dark trading has been subject to changing market trends in the past few years, the most important of which include:

- continued migration to dark markets;
- changes to the location of execution;
- decline in trade size;
- improvements in technologies; and
- adaption of the business model.

Let us consider each of these in turn.

The first primary trend, and a major theme of this work, centers on the continued migration of trading from light to dark. As we have noted, in the U.S. dark trading accounted for up to 40% of all equity turnover in 2013, while in Europe it reached between 8% and 11% (depending on the estimates and included population). Even smaller markets, such as Canada and Australia, managed to cross the 10% threshold for the first time (though both may face future growth uncertainties as a result of the regulatory changes we discuss in Chapter 7). When markets are in retracement or volatility is high, activity appears to trend toward aggressive bids in the lit market rather than passive and active routing to dark markets. Accordingly, during the period of 2011 onwards, which saw a strengthening of global stock markets and a reduction in volatility, participants redirected flows back to dark pools. Note that a portion of this increased volume was not executed electronically but via the upstairs market (which remains strong in certain marketplaces, including the UK, Canada, and Australia). Price improvement has certainly been part of the value proposition: even after commissions the price improvement makes participation economically attractive (particularly for institutional investors). Certain services (such as Liquidmetrix) estimate that improvement can range from 3 to 10 basis points per trade, providing compelling motivation. In fact, there is also at least some evidence that rising dark volumes may lead to wider spreads and higher costs in lit markets. This, however, may depend on the breadth and depth of each individual national market and the degree to which dark pools either foster competition or fragmentation.

The second, and associated, change has been the erosion of market share by "home exchanges" in their own listed stocks – in other words, the location of trading execution has moved from the original sponsoring exchange to multiple venues (e.g., Apple is no longer traded only on NASDAQ, but also on the NYSE, BATS, and others, just as Procter and Gamble is no longer traded solely on the NYSE, and so forth). Regulatory changes related to free competition and technology have made it possible for traders and investors to execute transactions away from exchanges, on alternative platforms that offer light and/or dark pools of liquidity. While the major exchanges of the world once handled the lion's share of trading in their own listed issues, such is no longer the case – in most instances execution has migrated to multiple locations, some light, some dark, and some integrated. The monopoly power once held by the "traditional" exchanges has thus eroded and given way to new realities. For instance, as we have noted above, at the end of 2013, dark pools (including internalizers) accounted for 40% of US stock trading, followed by NYSE Arca/Big Board (17%), NASDAQ (15%), Direct Edge (11%), BATS (10%), and then a host of smaller regional exchanges. The monopoly once enjoyed by the NYSE and NASDAQ has clearly disappeared.

Electronic platforms and internal desks have demonstrated their collective ability to take market share from the established exchanges because of the catalysts mentioned earlier. Of course, this phenomenon is not limited to the U.S. Similar erosion has occurred within the pan-European space, for example, where leaders such as the LSE, Deutsche Boerse/Xetra, and NYSE Euronext have ceded ground to the light/dark electronic platforms and internal desks. As an example, during 2013 European dark venues accounted for between 8% and 11% of trading, while the lit market was split between the LSE (21%), BATS Europe (20%), NYSE Euronext (15%), Xetra (10%), Turquoise (7%), Swiss Exchange (6%), and NASDAQ OMX (6%), followed by various other small regional exchanges. Again, the national monopoly power long held by the leading exchanges has given way to a new competitive landscape.

We must, of course, be careful about drawing too many conclusions from single data points. However, a review of the historical trends of matched market share on the primary exchanges reflects a consistent theme: exchanges have lost market share to other venues operating light and dark books. We should also stress again that not all of the volume ceded to alternative platforms is purely dark; equally, not all of the volume matched on primary exchanges is purely light.

A third major trend centers on trade size. Although key markets, such as the U.S. and Europe, now feature more dark pools and more participants than ever before, it is still true that if large blocks of stock entering cannot be crossed immediately, they will almost certainly be sliced up and routed into multiple pools. That said, block trading (whole or sliced) has become a smaller part of the dark pool market over the past few years. Smaller sized outright trades, coming from institutional or retail clients, are becoming more prominent – suggesting at least some "mainstreaming" of the sector. Indeed, dark trading is no longer the exclusive domain of the influential buy-side investors with large blocks of stock to buy or sell. At least one reason for a decline in average trading size appears to be centered on the fact that some institutional investors are less willing to post large resting orders for fear that they may be subject to information leakage. The influx of smaller (retail) trades raises the issue of whether such trades should be executed in the dark if they can be done in the lit market without risk of information leakage. This is particularly applicable in smaller markets or with less liquid stock, where each incremental trade executed dark rather than light can lead to fragmentation and cloud the price discovery process. While perhaps an important issue, it may also be somewhat academic – small trades, including those from retail investors, have become an important part of dark trading.

A fourth observation relates to technology, which has been so central to the development and expansion of dark trading. Advances in processing technology, data management, and network communication have led to faster execution times and greater ability to route into pools of liquidity. Algorithms have become ubiquitous within the professional investing/trading sector, and technology-reliant high frequency trading and ultra low latency trading platforms (all of which we discuss later in the book) have directed important order flows into the dark. Smart order routers are by now relatively advanced and capable of dealing with orders across various markets. Specialized versions are quite capable of targeting dark liquidity and broker-dealers, who have been the pioneers in developing dark SORs, often use their proprietary versions to cross order flows initially with their own dark liquidity and ultimately with liquidity resident in other pools. Some SORs allow for shadow orders, which essentially leave a client order resident in a broker-dealer's internal book with a duplicate that can access external pools; execution of either order leads to an instantaneous cancellation of the second order. While technology is obviously critical to both dark pool operators and to participants who make use of dark pools, it is worth emphasizing that the established exchanges, which are the source of pricing for virtually all dark transactions, face the largest cost burdens. After all, exchanges must feature fast, sophisticated matching engines, communication hubs and data processing to provide lit quotes which are used by dark players. Such technology does not come cheap, and is sometimes the source of friction between lit and dark venues.

A final trend worth observing centers on the business models related to trading and execution, which have evolved considerably over the past decade as a result of the forces we have mentioned. Exchanges and financial institutions that are active in the lit and dark markets continue to refine their offerings, either by adding, consolidating, or spinning off portions of their dark business; the process is a dynamic and evolutionary one. One key business model topic centers on the fate of "traditional" market makers – the suppliers of risk capital standing ready to fulfill positive obligations of quoting two way markets in particular stocks in all market conditions. Prior to decimalization, risking capital in support of sometimes attractive market-making spreads was considered a worthy endeavor, and certainly well balanced from a risk/return perspective. In the post-decimalization era starting in 2001 (and in a post-crisis regulatory environment where capital hurdles are much greater) the issue is less clear-cut. Many market makers have decided that it is no longer worth risking capital in that manner and have pulled away from these duties – either abandoning business altogether, shifting to pure proprietary business without quoting obligations, or morphing into an agency role. Taking their place, to some degree, is the new breed of high frequency traders. These traders, which we discuss at greater length at various points in the book, post and take liquidity on a continuous basis through their high speed trading algorithms. Though their overarching strategies are meant to capitalize on small price discrepancies that can be exploited through rapid execution (generally by taking liquidity), further revenues are generated in the form of rebates from posting liquidity. This means they are often quoting on both sides of the market, as any normal market maker is obliged to do. However, a key difference exits: while traditional market makers are obliged to quote prices on both sides, in all market conditions (and are subject to regulatory review and scrutiny as a result), high frequency traders face no such obligations – their participation is purely voluntary.

So, decimalization has changed the trading landscape, bringing the breed of high frequency traders into the breach to fill a role that was once the domain of traditional market makers. The quality of the market-making, however, must be seen as perhaps less robust, particularly in volatile and rapidly declining markets.

Concerns and Threats

Any growing marketplace is likely to be scrutinized by competitors and regulators for potential concerns or threats that could create competitive disadvantages or systemic problems. The dark market is no different, and has been the focus of regular commentary, analysis, and inspection by a number of third parties. Let's consider some of the most common concerns/threats.

In the first instance we note issues arising from incomplete post-trade disclosure. While the essence of the dark market is to shield as much information as possible, post-trade reporting to a trade reporting facility and from there to the consolidated tape is seen as an important gauge of what is going on in the marketplace. Unfortunately, there is no uniformity in such reporting and compliance through 2013 was not mandatory – meaning the true picture of what is happening is not available, either to market participants or to regulators. Consider, for instance, that the largest U.S. dark pool, Credit Suisse's CrossFinder, stopped reporting data in April 2013; a further dozen venues followed shortly thereafter, suggesting that the trading and execution picture emerging post-trade has been incomplete (with gaps filled in through reasoned estimates). Naturally, a distinction has to be made regarding post-trade transparency: while uniformity and consistency across all participating venues can be considered an important and worthwhile goal, near-real time post-trade transparency could be considered a threat to the market and its participants. Any such disclosure could result in greater market impact, poorer execution, and a shift of liquidity into perhaps more manual forms of crossing (e.g., the upstairs market). Accordingly, some form of delay (certainly hours, if not days) has to be an elemental part of the market construct.

Another concern centers on the fact that significant expansion in the number of dark venues can lead to fragmentation (making price discovery more challenging) and increase the odds that buyers and sellers will fail to cross trades (e.g., the "ships passing in the night" phenomenon). If true, this means that guarantee of best execution is no longer possible. Although the increasing use of algorithms, which we consider later in the book, can partially alleviate this problem, the fact remains that the greater the number of dark venues, the greater the number of locations to which orders can be sent, and the lower the chances that crosses will occur.

A further issue that has proven concerning, particularly for regulators, has been the expansion in trading mechanisms and styles that often make use of dark liquidity – but which are difficult to sometimes understand (and control). In particular, areas such as high frequency trading, ultra low latency trading, algorithmic trading, and direct market access (to be discussed later) have become increasingly popular and widespread – in some cases even reaching the "financial mainstream." Concerns center on the potential negative feedback loop each one of these trading mechanisms might deliver at any point in time – creating systemic weaknesses and exacerbating any downward market movements (such as was experienced during the "Flash Crash" of 2012). Since these trading strategies are very fast moving and often tap into the dark markets, their ex-ante (and even ex-post) impact on markets is uncertain.

Given these (and other) concerns, it is not surprising that regulatory authorities took the opportunity, starting in 2011, to consider new regulatory checks on both markets and venues. The early focus of such discussions centered on improving transparency (including clarifying how broker-dealer internalizers manage crosses between retail and proprietary flows), enhancing disclosure, understanding how dark pool trade information is disseminated to third parties, and potentially requiring price improvement for retail crosses. We shall consider these and other, regulatory, issues at greater length in Chapter 7.

Overview of the Text

In order to set the stage for the balance of the text, let us review the scope of the remaining chapters. In Chapter 2 we continue our discussion of market structure by introducing the concept of market liquidity, considering the formation of displayed and nondisplayed orders and the resulting creation of dark liquidity. Chapter 3 extends the discussion by describing how dark pools exist and function from a structural perspective, considering in more detail the key players and their interactions with one another and with established exchanges. In Part II we turn to "micro" issues, starting with an examination of topics related to pricing and execution in both the visible and dark spaces in Chapter 4. Chapter 5 continues with the "micro" theme by examining trading strategies employed by participants, including block trading, program trading, algorithmic trading and benchmarking, high frequency and ultra low latency trading, and gaming. Chapter 6 investigates (in nontechnical terms) certain technology issues surrounding order routing, matching and execution in both the visible and dark sectors. In Part III we shift our focus to consider the future of the sector. Chapter 7 examines the framework of regulations/control surrounding dark pool activities, with a special focus on new regulatory changes that have been implemented in certain regions. We summarize our discussion, in Chapter 8, by considering the future of dark pools in light of pros/cons, consolidation, and technological advances.

2 | Market Liquidity and Structure

In Chapter 1 we introduced the concept of dark liquidity and the reasons why it has expanded and developed in recent years. But dark liquidity does not exist on its own – it is part of an entire spectrum of trading liquidity which is built atop specific market microstructures. In this chapter we take a broader perspective on the topic of liquidity and secondary trading in securities, starting with a review of the need for market liquidity and the issues of market impact and information leakage in relation to block liquidity. We will then explore market microstructure, focusing on orders as the fundamental instructions to buy and sell securities and markets as the forums that combine these orders and match buyers and sellers. We will conclude with a discussion of liquidity supply and demand, considering key parameters such as immediacy, depth, breadth, and resiliency. Note that some of these topics will contribute to our discussion of pricing and execution in Chapter 4.

Aspects of Market Liquidity

Trading liquidity is a fundamental feature of every advanced financial market. While the sum of liquidity encompasses both large and small trades, it is the large trades, as noted in Chapter 1, that feature interesting characteristics that affect market dynamics.

The need for liquidity

Liquidity is the central ingredient of an efficient financial marketplace. While capital-raising exercises (e.g., initial public offerings, secondary offerings, rights issues, and so forth) supply the markets, and by extension investors, with the necessary "raw material" to make trading and investment decisions, the presence of liquidity makes it possible to execute initial and ongoing decisions in an economically sensible manner. Indeed, it is of little use having access to the raw material of securities if the cost of subsequent buying or selling is excessively large. While this may be acceptable for long-term "buy and hold" investors, it is not particularly helpful to the retail or institutional investor with a shorter time horizon, and erodes severely the economic returns that can be obtained; in fact, it calls into question the rationale for allocating risk capital.

Robust secondary liquidity allows the reallocation of risk capital at a moment's notice, and helps buyers and sellers achieve specific goals at reasonable cost. When liquidity is disrupted or unavailable, markets become difficult to trade and the pursuit of financial goals becomes complex and costly. Indeed, there is plenty of evidence to suggest that during times of market stress (e.g., 1997, 1998, 2001–2, 2007–9) liquidity can disappear rapidly (and for an extended period) as investors become risk averse and move to the sidelines; this is true even for actively traded securities like government bonds and large capitalization stocks. Such thinly traded markets make it difficult to establish price transparency, and introduce price-gapping (i.e., a discontinuous price movement) and volatility, all of which can have a negative impact on investors. A steady supply of liquidity is therefore essential in promoting efficient markets. As we will note in this chapter, the combination of displayed liquidity and nondisplayed liquidity is an integral part of the equation; each one is a necessary, but not sufficient, condition for establishing the overall picture of market liquidity.

In a theoretical sense the search for liquidity in a specific security may be unilateral – one party seeking to fill an order – or it may be bilateral – two parties on opposite sides seeking to fill their orders. A unilateral search involves a sequential search for the best price available, which can continue for an indefinite period – one can never be totally certain, in a market comprised of visible and dark activity, that the price available in a particular location at any point in time is, in fact, the best one achievable. At some point the cost of searching, and the opportunity cost of not executing, becomes difficult to justify. The bilateral search for liquidity is somewhat more complex, as two parties (a buyer and a seller) will conduct their own searches independently on an active or passive basis; at some point the two must stop and fill their trades. If the parties have encountered each other at some point during the search, but opted to continue their searches, there can be no guarantee that one or the other party will still be present at the end of the search. Taken against this theoretical background, it is clear that any mechanism or process that helps achieve a search for liquidity so that an order can be filled is a necessary and practical requirement. Different types of orders, different market structures, and different forms of technology are all integral to this effort.

* * *

Pools in Practice: Traderspeak....

It is by now well known that the trading community speaks a language all its own, developing jargon that becomes part of daily activities – and which, in some cases, even enters the financial mainstream. Whilst an understanding of the jargon isn't essential to an understanding of trading or even dark pools, some familiarity with "traderspeak" can be a good thing and provides a glimpse into the real world of trading. Let's take a look at a handful of common terms.

When a trader speaks of a "cross" it means to match and execute a trade; thus, "crossing a block" means to match and execute a block trade or "crossing a board lot" means to match and execute against the minimum preferred dealing size in a venue (which varies, from 10 shares to 1000 shares, depending on market); "crossing an odd lot" means to match and execute any amount that is smaller than a board lot. Once an order has been crossed it is referred to as a "fill." The "contra" is the opposite side of the trade needed to make a cross. Of course, not all orders cross, particularly in the dark, where it is difficult sometimes to detect contra and orders can miss each other – a phenomenon known a "ships passing in the night."

More broadly, when a trader or a marketplace refers to the "top of book" it means the best bids and offers available in a stock at a particular time – say, the top five best bids/offers, which tend to be the focus of liquidity and activity. When a trader or an algorithm starts "walking the book" it relates to filling a large order at increasingly worse prices (e.g., more expensive buys or cheaper sells).

On a slightly more descriptive note, "shotgunning" and "spraying" relate to the practice of sending in multiple orders into multiple venues in hopes of finding contra to make a cross. Similarly, "sweeping" means to take an order and try to cross it against the book (e.g., walking the book) or against contra in multiple markets (e.g., sweeping the market) – the intent, of course, is to try to cross as much as possible.

When a trader "rests" an order, it means to leave it passively in a market awaiting contra. So, logically, resting orders don't typically reside in the top of book (as they would cross rather quickly), but somewhere just outside. A big order can be "sliced" into various "children" and routed or swept in order to find contra. A large order that has both a long and a short position (e.g., as in a pairs trade or a program trade) is often "legged" into the market, meaning it is executed in long/short increments, rather than all long and then all short (which generates too much market risk).

On to pools: we already know about dark and lit, but there is also "grey," which is a market (or strategy) that features both lit liquidity and hidden liquidity (like "icebergs," which are orders that are lit on top and dark on the bottom). A "twilight" pool is mostly dark but exposes some general details of its order book at select times; on a micro level a "sunshine trade" is a dark trade that is exposed at a particular point as an invitation to deal. And, when a pool is "toxic" it means that the price of execution is generally worse than in other venues, primarily because the pool hosts very aggressive traders with rapid crossing strategies. A "blotter scraper" is a pool that is authorized to look at the trading blotters of participating broker/dealers to find dark contra for crossing.

Of course, there are some nefarious (but legal) goings-on in the market as well, perpetrated by "sharks" (sometimes "fishers," traders who try to identify trading strategies particularly in the dark) by using "sniffers" (algorithms that can spot trading trends through various "gaming" devices). One common gaming method is "pinging," where a trader or algorithm sends small immediate-or-cancel orders into a dark pool to see whether they cross – if they do, there is a chance that a much larger order is resting, something the shark can capitalize on.

There is, of course, lots of other jargon, but this should give a little flavor.

* * *

Block liquidity, market impact, and information leakage

A marketplace is comprised of all forms of liquidity, including liquidity from both small and large trades. However, we have a particular interest in large trades, or block liquidity, because they can create important financial and behavioral impact.

More specifically, we know that buying or selling a block of shares has the potential of moving the market price of the underlying security in an unfavorable manner – that is, creating a negative market impact. If a trader advertises a desire to buy 10,000 shares of Stock QRS (where 10,000 shares represent a relatively meaningful fraction of the day's trading activity), it is almost certain that the order will cause the price of QRS to rise in advance of execution as sellers adjust their offers to reflect the large visible buying interest. In short, in a market with pre-trade transparency, one look at the trading screen will reveal the QRS bid of 10,000 shares and will cause participants to react accordingly. This is a form of direct market impact. The same would occur, in reverse, if the trader emerged as a seller of a block of QRS, where the fill price would be negatively impacted. Of course, if only 100 shares or 500 shares is at stake, market impact would be negligible – hence our focus on blocks.

As we know, mechanisms that can shield block liquidity from the markets (i.e., removing the pre-trade transparency) have the potential of reducing market impact. Obviously, this should be of interest to the trader in QRS, and any other investor that actively buys and sells large blocks. In fact, block liquidity can be protected through one of two major mechanisms: disguising the trade in its entirety through a dark mechanism, or breaking up the large trade into a number of smaller slices before submitting for execution in the light or dark markets. Either can help the trader achieve a better execution level than an undisguised display in the market.

However, care must still be taken with regard to information leakage. A block trade that is sliced into a number of different visible orders which are routed to multiple venues for execution can leave a trail that clearly indicates the activity that is occurring. Thus, if the trader slices the 10,000 shares of QRS into 10 trades of 1000 each and routes them to several platforms, clever electronic mechanisms may pick up on the trail and re-position to take advantage of the aggregated purchase interest in QRS. A trader sitting in front of a multi-paned trading screen may not necessarily detect this, but certain algorithms can. In addition, if several slices of the order remain within a venue for a period of time (instead of executing immediately), they may again leave "digital fingerprints" that can be used by swift operators. The same may occur if the trader in QRS decides not to break the trade up, but simply place it into a dark venue for execution – and either keep it there until it fills or route unfilled portions to other dark venues until it is completed. Such a strategy can invite manipulation as individual sites are "pinged" by those looking for dark blocks, or as unfilled portions are tracked as they route from venue to venue. In addition, there is a tradeoff between speed of execution and potential for information leakage. A trade that is crossed as a matter of urgency in the dark and light markets, or exclusively in the light markets, will create some amount of market impact. A trade that is crossed strictly in the dark and is never represented visibly in the market may take longer to fill, but should remain shielded from information leakage and thus avoid market impact. We may think of visible liquidity as providing the greatest opportunities for information leakage and thus market impact, and dark liquidity as protecting against that information leakage and minimizing market impact. Equally, we may state that small orders create less market impact than block orders.

Of course, not all dark pools are "equally dark." Those that are truly able to eliminate any possibility of information leakage are absolutely dark. But any pool that takes order flow from a public source might be susceptible to information leakage, as a trail can be created in moving from light to dark. In practice, some information leakage can appear from time to time in almost any venue, generally based on the construct of the pool, the degree to which block orders rest inside the venue for a period or are routed to, or received from, other venues, the degree to which "sharks" enter the pool and take advantage of large orders, and so forth. Such pools are not, of course, bad – in fact, they may appeal to some traders who are more aggressive in seeking a match. However, it is incumbent upon traders and investors seeking or taking liquidity in the dark space to know whether a pool is truly dark.

* * *

Pools in Practice: Twilight pools

We have already introduced the concept of lit and dark venues. Now consider a new-comer on the scene: the "twilight pool." Despite its slightly haunting moniker, the twi-light pool is a seemingly practical "middle ground" that straddles light and dark. The pool, which is a new structural entrant to the marketplace, works by conducting most of its business in the dark, as per usual, but then exposes its book to the light at certain times of day or when certain conditions are met. The twilight pool's specificity is still not the same as in a lit market, that is, the pool won't expose a full set of bids and of-fers or market depth as in an electronic limit order book, but it does provide a glimpse into the stocks being traded, so that participants have a sense of where to direct their orders. The pool may be motivated to temporarily and periodically display some high

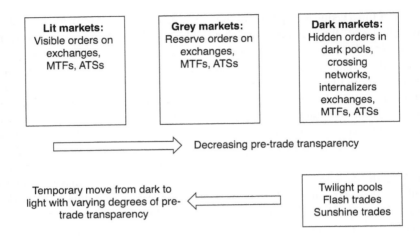

Figure 2.1 Twilight pools in the lit/dark market

level information about its activities to attract additional liquidity. By giving traders or investors an indication that certain stocks are being bid or offered, the pool hopes to draw in more buying and selling interest, thus improving the chance of crossing orders – all without revealing too much and giving away the advantages that dark trading conveys. We consider the twilight pool and two of its "structural cousins" – the flash trade and the sunshine trade, both considered later – in relation to the dark/light spectrum, in Figure 2.1.

*   *   *

Market Microstructure

Our review of market microstructure begins with order types, the basic instructions for the transfer of liquidity, and migrates to markets, the conglomeration of all such orders. Both are essential in creating and transferring visible and dark liquidity.

Order types

The supply of, and demand for, financial securities (and other assets) is driven by orders that are submitted by prospective buyers and sellers; this is true regardless of the specific construct of a market. Orders are simply instructions which indicate how and when a particular purchase or sale of securities should occur, and can be broadly classified as follows:

- Market orders

- Limit orders
- Peg orders
- Complex/hybrid orders

Within these broad classes we may also attach certain additional parameters that specify or refine actions to be taken; these may include display parameters, quantity parameters, and time in force parameters.

Different order types are available to let buyers and sellers achieve one or more goals, including

- Speed of execution
- Price improvement
- Risk limitations
- Method of display
- Time to market

In this section we will describe the major types/subtypes of orders and then categorize each one by the primary goal it is intended to accomplish. Before doing so, let us briefly review the common nomenclature of the trading world as related to order types. Specifically, we can define the following:

- Bid: the price at which one party will buy a security
- Offer: the price at which one party will sell a security
- Best bid: the highest bid price in the market at any time
- Best offer: the lowest offer price in the market at any time
- Inside spread: the difference between the best bid and best offer

We will reference these terminologies at various points in the book.

Market orders

A market order is an order to buy or sell a specific number of securities at the current available market price. It is the simplest of all orders as it sets no specific price conditions – in fact, it is sometimes referred to as an unpriced order. For example, an investor may submit a market order to buy 10,000 shares of Stock QRS at market. If the market is bid at $24.78/share and offered at $24.80/share and sufficient volume exists, then the investor receives the 10,000 shares in exchange for $248,000 (plus commissions and any attendant fees). Market orders can be filled very quickly, but may suffer from "inferior" pricing as the tradeoff for execution speed (discussed later in the chapter as the price of "immediacy.") The market impact of a market order increases with size; indeed, a large buyer of a block of securities may be forced to pay a premium, while a large seller may have to accept a discount – these are commonly known as price concessions. That said, there may be an "expectation" among at least some participants submitting market orders that the fill price will be at, or near, the midpoint of a base reference price, such as the NBBO or EBBO. That may or may not be the case, depending on the depth of trading in the stock.[1]

There exist, of course, certain idiosyncrasies across national borders. For instance, some countries (e.g., Hong Kong, Brazil, Turkey, among others) feature no market orders during continuous trading, opting instead for limit orders or marketable limit orders (which are de-facto market orders with floor or ceiling prices). In the US markets, an exchange receiving a market order needs only to honor displayed liquidity at all lit exchanges, after which dark execution is possible. In some markets, a market order sweeps only a specific venue and does not automatically route to other markets if left unfilled; thus, if a complete fill is needed (especially on a large order), the order must be accompanied by routing instructions. In still other markets, especially in Europe, a market order sweeps only the top of book and then cancels any unfilled portion (as a form of immediate or cancel, discussed below). Finally, in other markets the order sweeps the top of book and then converts into a limit order at the last executed price. As we can see, even the "vanilla" market order can take on different forms.

Despite these nuances, we can still safely categorize market orders by subtypes, including

- Stop order
- Trailing stop order
- Market-to-limit order
- Market-if-touched order
- Market-on-close order
- Market-on-open order
- Uptick/downtick order
- Sweep-to-fill order

A stop order is an order that creates a market order to buy or sell some quantity of securities if a trigger price is attained. In practice, a sell stop order is placed below the current market price (e.g., if QRS is trading at $24.80, then any amount below that), while a buy stop order is placed above the current market price (e.g., any amount above $24.80). It should be noted, however, that even if the stop is triggered and converts into a market order, a fill cannot be guaranteed if there is insufficient volume. Though a stop order may appear similar to the limit order discussed below, in reality it is just an instruction to create an order.

A trailing stop order is similar to a stop order except that the order carries an attached trailing amount that moves with the market price of the security. Thus, a sell trailing stop order sets the stop price at a fixed amount below the market price with an attached trailing amount that causes the stop price to rise as the security price rises, but remains unchanged if the security price falls; once the stop is hit, the market order is created and submitted. A buy trailing stop order works in reverse. In either case, the investor is able to take advantage of favorable market moves and remain protected against unfavorable ones. We consider a variation of this structure, along with an example, in the section on trailing stop limit orders below.

A market-to-limit order, as the name suggests, is an order that is submitted in the first instance as a market order; if it can only be partly filled, the balance of the order is automatically cancelled and resubmitted as a limit order, where the limit price is equal to the price of the original fill. Since the order becomes a de facto limit order, there is no guarantee that it will be filled in its entirety.

A market-if-touched order is an order to buy a security below the current market or sell a security above the current market, which is held back until a trigger (or touch price) is reached; once touched, it is submitted as a market order. In fact, the market-if-touched order is similar to a stop order, except that a sell is placed above, rather than below, the current price, while a buy is placed below, rather than above, the current price. For instance, an investor may submit a market-if-touched order to buy 1000 shares of QRS, currently trading at $24.80, if a touch price of $24.75 is hit; the order will execute at the existing market price once the touch price is hit – in all likelihood this will be very near, or at, the touch price, depending on speed of execution and the composition of the QRS order book across all venues.

A market-on-close order is an order submitted to execute as close as possible to the closing price, though there again is no guarantee of a fill. Similarly, a market-on-open order is an order submitted to execute as close as possible to the opening price.

An uptick (downtick) order is an order that leads to the purchase or sale of securities if the market moves up (down) by a tick. In practice these types of orders are now relatively uncommon since most major markets operate on a decimalized basis, where the value of a tick is worth a penny; not surprisingly, they were more widely used when tick increments were larger.

A sweep-to-fill order is an order that seeks to execute as quickly as possible at the best available prices, regardless of venue. The order is submitted to the first location with the best price and is filled to the extent possible; it then sweeps to the next venue with the next best price and any remaining portion is filled at that point, and so forth. In fact, the cycle is repeated as many times as is required in order to complete the order, typically resulting in "less favorable" price terms with each sweep. For instance, an investor can submit a sweep-to-fill order to buy 5000 shares of Stock QRS, currently trading at $24.80; as the order sweeps, it may get fills of 1000 shares in Venue A at $24.80, 2000 shares in Venue B at $24.82, and 2000 shares in Venue C at $24.83.

Limit orders

A limit order is an order to buy or sell a particular number of securities at a desired price or better. For instance, our investor may wish to buy 10,000 shares of QRS stock at a price of $25.00/share through a limit order. If the stock is offered at $25.01, the order will not be executed. If it is offered at any price equal to, or less than, $25.00, it will execute in whole or in part, depending on available volume. For instance, if 5000 shares are available at $24.99 and 5000 shares are available at

$25.01, then the investor will receive only a fill on the 5000 shares at $24.99. An unfilled limit order is known as an open, or standing, order, and is placed in the exchange's or ECN's limit order book (e.g., the ELOB) for future execution; some of these can, of course, be dark orders. While it is in the process of being filled, it is considered to be a working order. As we might expect, the more "aggressive" the limit order – that is, the closer the limit price to the market bid or market offer – the greater the probability of execution. Such orders are considered to be "top of book" and are almost certain to be filled in the short-term. A marketable limit order is an order that can be executed immediately; a buy order is at or above the best offer, while a sell order is at or below the best bid. These marketable limit orders look very much like market orders, except that they have limits on the price concessions at which they can be filled.

Limit orders that buy at the best bid or sell at the best offer are said to be "at the market," while those that are away from these best levels are said to be "behind the market"; specifically, a buy order with a limit price that is less than the best bid, or a sell order with a limit price that is above the best offer are behind the market. Figure 2.2 illustrates a range of bids and offers on limit orders for a given stock.

Limit orders are interesting because they effectively give other traders an option to trade. For instance, an open sell limit order is akin to a free call option for a trader to buy when desired, while an open buy limit order is similar to a free put

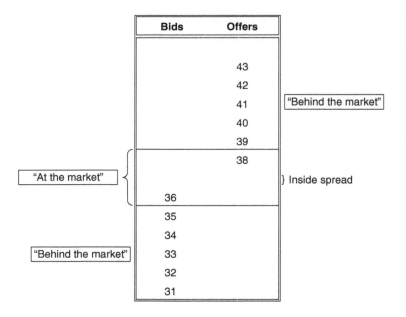

Figure 2.2 Limit bids and offers

option – in both cases the strike price is equal to the limit price. Using limit orders is situational and depends on the goals of the investor/trader – the degree to which immediacy is or is not a factor, the extent to which the investor is a liquidity taker or provider, the need for a specific risk reduction or investment gain, and so forth.

Once again, certain limit order subtypes exist, including

- Stop limit order
- Trailing stop limit order
- Limit-if-touched order
- Limit-on-close order
- Limit-on-open order
- Discretionary order
- Intermarket sweep order

A stop limit order is similar to the stop order described above, except that a limit order (rather than a market order) is submitted if a trigger price is attained. Similarly, a trailing stop limit order is identical to the trailing stop order, except the investor or trader substitutes the market order plus trailing amount with a limit order plus trailing amount; the limit price used in the limit order is computed as the stop price minus the limit offset. Consider a simple example: an investor wants to sell 1000 shares of Stock ABC trading at $80.03 and creates a sell trailing stop, with a trailing amount of $0.15, a stop price of $80.00, and a limit offset of $0.10, to yield a limit price of $79.90. Assume first that the price of ABC rises to $81.00; this causes the trailing stop price to rise to $80.85 (e.g., $81.00–$0.15), meaning that the limit price becomes $80.75. Assume next that the price of ABC declines to $80.90; in this case the trigger remains unchanged at $80.85. If, however, ABC drops further, to $80.80, the trigger is breached and a limit order to sell 1000 shares of ABC at $80.75 is submitted.

A limit-if-touched order is an order to buy or sell a security at a limit price, which is held until a trigger is touched; once touched, it is submitted as a limit order.

A limit-on-close order is a limit order submitted to execute at the closing price if it is at, or better than, the specified limit price, or else the order is cancelled. Similarly, a limit-on-open order is a limit order submitted to execute at the opening price if it is equal to, or better than, the limit price.

A discretionary order is a limit order that features a working visible price and a hidden discretionary price, which increases price flexibility in order to improve the chances of execution. The discretionary price spread may be triggered by a broker or through an order management system or trading interface. A market-not-held order is another way of defining a discretionary order. Note that discretionary orders are effectively a form of dark liquidity, as we will note through an example later in the chapter.

As noted in Chapter 1, the Order Protection Rule of Regulation NMS (known as the "trade-through rule") is designed to prevent orders on one exchange from being executed at prices that are inferior to "protected" quotes (e.g., the inside spread of the NBBO) at another exchange. An exchange must therefore reject marketable orders or route them to the market center displaying the best price. In effect, this prohibits exchanges from executing trades that can be filled at better prices at away markets and reinforces the concept of the NBBO. There is, however, an exception to this rule, conveyed via the intermarket sweep order (ISO): the SEC has allowed an exception for institutions that need to sweep through multiple levels of the order book. While normal orders routed to a venue not displaying the best price would create a trade-through and force an exchange either to reject or to reroute an order, limit orders that are marked "ISO" are executed by the exchange without any requirement to check away market pricing or to apply trade-through protections; in effect, the exchange can immediately execute ISOs against orders on the book without checking protected quotes in other markets. It should be noted, however, that the order originator still takes responsibility for sending orders directly to the other market centers to clear protected orders. For instance, if a trader wants to cross a large block, it can send in an ISO and, after clearing protected quotes in any other market, fill the order in its entirety at decreasing sale or increasing buy prices (e.g., sweeping the book).

Peg orders

A peg order is an order to buy or sell a particular number of securities based on a price that is pegged to a recognized base reference, such as the NBBO or EBBO, and is very commonly used in crossing networks/price reference systems. Within this general class of orders we can distinguish between

- Primary peg order: a peg order that pegs to the same side of the base reference (e.g., a buy is pegged to the best bid; a sell is pegged to the best offer).
- Market peg order: a peg order that pegs to the opposite side of the base reference (e.g., a buy is pegged to the best offer; a sell is pegged to the best bid).
- Midpoint peg order: a peg order that pegs to the midpoint between the bid and the offer of the base reference (see Pools in Practice below).
- Alternative midpoint peg order: a peg order that pegs to the "less aggressive" side of the midpoint by a small fraction, such as a single tick.

For instance, if an investor now wants to sell 5000 shares of TUV stock, it may choose to do so by submitting a midpoint peg order based on the NBBO. If the NBBO is quoted at $70.01 (bid) and $70.03 (offer), then the trade will execute at $70.02. If the peg had been submitted as a market peg, it would execute at $70.01. Note that we can consider this to be an aggressive form of order, designed to be executed – that is, the investor is willing to accept only $70.01 per share, instead of the midpoint or the offer side of the market, and in this sense the market peg looks quite similar to a market order. The primary peg is, of course, far less aggressive and is less likely to be executed than its peg counterparts. It is important to note that regular peg orders (e.g., primary or market) have a higher priority than midpoint peg orders ranked at the same price; in addition, in the U.S., peg orders may execute at subpenny increments.

*   *   *

Pools in Practice: The midpoint match

The International Securities Exchange (ISE), discussed in more detail in the next chapter, has been a dark market pioneer, creating one of the first exchange-owned dark pools as early as 2006. Part of its success can also be linked to the midpoint match (MPM), a special order type it created. As the name suggests, the midpoint match order always executes at the midpoint of the NBBO, providing the trader or investor with price improvement, anonymity, order precedence in the queue and exposure to dark or light liquidity. Brokers can submit anonymous MPM market or limit orders on behalf of their clients which are then direct routed to the ISE for execution (note that the market is open to ISE members or broker dealers who are members of the ISE Stock Exchange). In particular, market orders execute at the midpoint whenever a contra order is available for matching. Limit orders, in contrast, are executed when the midpoint price is better than the limit price. For instance, assume an investor wants to execute a 5,000 share market buy in Stock ABC (trading at $20.22–$20.24) at the midpoint rather than on the offer side (e.g. at $20.23 rather than $20.24). Through the electronic order slate on the trading platform offered by its broker, the investor flags a 5,000 share market MPM buy in ABC, with a routing destination of ISE and submits. If contra is available, the order will be executed immediately at $20.23. Naturally, an MPM order can rest in the pool, awaiting contra flow, if immediate execution isn't possible. Alternatively, the MPM order can be further paired with routing designations, including IOC, FOK, or IOC minimum quantity.

*   *   *

Hybrid and complex orders

Many other kinds of orders can be created by combining one or more of the structures noted above. We may consider these to be hybrid orders, all of which are designed to yield even greater execution specificity. Common hybrid/complex orders include the following:

- Cross order
- Derivative order
- Conditional order
- Benchmark order
- Do-not-route order
- Pass-through order

This is but a small sampling of hybrid/complex orders – many others also exist.

A cross order is an order to buy and an order to sell the same security at a specific price that is better than the best bid and offer on an exchange, and equal to or better than a base reference price. Various forms of cross orders can be submitted, such as a midpoint cross, opening cross, closing cross, ISO cross, cross with size, and so forth, which incorporate features of the relevant orders described above.

A derivative order is any type of limit order where the limit price is derived from, or related to, a particular variable, such as the midpoint of the bid and offer, the last sale, the last sale less one tick, and so forth.

A conditional order is any type of order that is submitted for execution (in limit or market form) once a specific event occurs. The named condition can relate to price, volume, time, and so forth (see Pools in Practice below).

A benchmark order is any type of order that is submitted for execution at a price that is different than the base reference price, but which is still permissible under regulatory rules.

A do-not-route order is any type of order that is submitted for execution in a single exchange or venue and cannot be sent to any other exchange or venue should a fill not occur. In such cases the order rests in the order book as a working order until it is filled or specifically cancelled. A post only order, which is similar, is an order that is not routed and is cancelled if it is marketable against a contra order in the venue; post only orders are intended to amass liquidity in a particular pool.

A pass-through-order is any type of order that remains in a designated venue for a single matching cycle (where a matching cycle may be continuous, discrete, or end-of-day), after which any unfilled portion is re-routed to alternate venues.

Though the number of combinations is potentially quite large, we can speak of common hybrid orders such as hidden peg orders (e.g., NYSE Arca's Post No Preference Blind Order, which is a hidden order priced at the NBBO or better), grey peg orders (in particular, ConvergEx's grey order, which pegs passively to the displayed market but recalibrates to the dark market as volume becomes available), nonroutable immediate-or-cancel orders (which may or may not be an ISO, and which are often used to ping a venue in search of liquidity), primary before/after orders (which are orders that reside in the primary exchange and then revert to an exchange's ELOB if they are unfilled, or which remain in the ELOB and then revert to the primary market if unfilled), and so forth. In fact, the most complicated types of orders are known as algorithms, which often contain many individual parameters that define precisely how a buy or sell order is to be created and filled. We will consider algorithms separately in Chapter 5.

Display parameters

In addition to the price specification, the orders described above may also contain a display parameter. In most marketplaces an order is assumed to be visible to the public unless specifically tagged with a "do not display" instruction. When anonymity is needed on any trade that is flowing through an exchange or ECN (rather than through a crossing network, which by definition displays no orders), then a "do not display" designation can be applied to all (hidden) or part (reserve) of the order. As noted in Chapter 1, such orders form a key pillar of dark liquidity.

A hidden order is an order that is not exposed to the market, but which is embedded in a venue's dark book. In general, a hidden order is a limit order that assumes a lower priority than visible orders that have the same price level as well as the nondisplayed portion of reserve orders described immediately above. For instance, if an investor submits a hidden order to sell 10,000 shares of XYZ at $70.00, it will remain hidden within a venue and cross against a buy order entering the same venue once its turn in the queue has arrived; alternatively, it may be routed to other venues, remaining hidden until filled or cancelled.

A reserve order (often referred to as an iceberg, and forming the essential element of the grey market) is an order that is only partly exposed to the market. The reserve therefore combines aspects of a visible limit order and a hidden order and, while the total amount is available for execution, only a portion is visible at any point of time; as each visible portion is executed, the next portion becomes visible, and so forth, until the order is fully executed. From a priority perspective the reserved (e.g., dark) portion of the order ranks behind visible orders and ahead of hidden orders; the tip of the iceberg is, of course, visible and ranks with other visible orders in the queue. Continuing the example above, our investor may submit a reserve sell order on 10,000 shares of XYZ at $70.00, exposing 1000 share increments to the market. The order will cycle through the price queue in its proper priority as each 1000 share block is exposed and executed.

Figure 2.3 summarizes the iterative execution process of a reserve order of 10,000 shares in Stock XYZ against the tip of the iceberg, which is defined to be 1000 shares. Figure 2.4 reflects the same 10,000 share execution in Stock XYZ described immediately above, but this time submitted as a hidden, rather than reserve, order.

Since reserve and hidden orders are critical to dark liquidity formation, we will revisit them in the next chapter.

*　　*　　*

Pools in Practice: The slow death of flash trading?

An interesting, if somewhat controversial, U.S. trading practice centers on so-called flash trading, in which an outstanding marketable order that has not been executed is exposed to certain market participants (i.e., those that have paid a fee to have access to the flash data) for some milliseconds so that they can determine whether or not to cross the order. The flash thus has the potential of tapping into dark liquidity.

Flash trading traces its roots back to 1978, when floor brokers on the exchanges were allowed to verbally announce price improvements to those on the floor in the hopes of generating additional trading interest. As exchanges migrated to electronic platforms, flash trading was made permissible through an exception to NMS Rule 602. During the first decade of the millennium a number of exchanges introduced flash trading to their clients, generally to strong interest. At its peak in 2009 flash trading accounted for about 3% of U.S. equity trading volume.

Let us consider the following simple example of a flash trade (also known as a pre-routing order or a step-up order): an investor seeking good execution submits a limit order to sell 10,000 shares of XYZ, noting on the order that it is a flash (if it is not so designated, then the exchange cannot expose the trade). As soon as the trade enters the exchange system, 6,000 shares are matched within the NBBO instantly, but the remaining balance remains unfilled due to lack of depth in the lit book. At this point the exchange flashes the 4,000 share sell order to the flash participants for less than half a second. One participant, a high frequency trader, is a willing buyer of the block and actually improves on the available exchange price, giving the selling investor a fill on the rump of the order. In this instance the flash trade has tapped into dark liquidity to the advantage of both the selling investor and the flash trader. Of course, not every flash trade will result in a match and cross; in such cases, the balance of any unfilled order will re-route to another market venue for possible execution.

Whilst flash trade would seem to be beneficial to all parties – that is, the selling or buying investor gets a chance to source dark liquidity at a potentially improved price and the flash investor or trader can see a potential trade before it hits the lit book – the practice has generated debate in recent years. The key concerns of regulators (e.g., the SEC) center on whether the practice is essentially a form of "front running" (i.e., trading ahead of the public order book) and whether it leads to a "two tier" market, comprised of privileged traders (such as large financial institutions and aggressive and sophisticated buy-side players, including high frequency traders that can "pay to play") and the public at large (which gives up these profits). High frequency traders, in particular, have been significant flash participants in the past few years, paying fees to access these orders to feed their automated market-making businesses. The SEC led investigations into the matter in mid-2009, eventually recommending that flash trading should cease through an affirmative vote to suspend the Rule 602 exemption; the SEC then opened the topic for comment, meaning the mechanism is still technically permissible. Whilst no formal "cease and desist" mandates are in force, a number of large exchanges, such as NASDAQ OMX and BATS, have voluntarily given up their flash programs. Others, however, such as DirectEdge and the ISE, have continued to offer the capabilities (either in equities, options, or both). The advantages cited include giving investors/traders the chance to access dark liquidity when an order cannot otherwise be filled (with the possibility of getting a price better than the NBBO), letting investors/traders with large orders avoid "walking the book" (i.e., executing at increasingly bad prices), allowing them to eliminate re-routing fees that would otherwise accrue to any unfilled order and improving execution speed by increasing chances of a fill rather than a re-route. DirectEdge in particular has remained a vocal proponent of flash trading. Registered as an exchange (whose market share has increased from 1% to more than 12% since 2007), DirectEdge's management noted as part of U.S. Congressional testimony that "DirectEdge pioneered the use of flash order technology in the equities markets precisely to give retail and other investors access to dark pool and other off-exchange liquidity they never had access to, and our data shows investors receive better prices on their trades as a result."[2] Whether DirectEdge will continue to offer flashes following its acquisition by BATS remains to be seen.

The efforts of a small number of venues like ISE and DirectEdge notwithstanding, we must wonder whether all U.S. flash trading will eventually fade away, either through direct regulatory change or through moral suasion – its future is uncertain. It is worth noting that flash trading does not feature in Europe – there are no identical mechanisms (the closest being NASDAQ OMX's Blink offering, which is a non-discriminatory structure that offers a 25 millisecond flash to all market participants).

* * *

Quantity parameters

Many of the orders described above can be further refined through a quantity parameter which specifies the course of action to be taken if the full amount of an order cannot be filled immediately. The most common quantity designations include

- Fill-or-kill (FOK) order: a designation indicating that the entire amount of the order should be filled and, if it cannot, it should be cancelled.
- All-or-none (AON) order: a designation indicating that the entire amount of an order should be filled or else not at all; the order remains in force pending future execution (e.g., resting, awaiting arrival of the full amount of the contra-trade) unless it is specifically cancelled. It is thus similar to the fill-or-kill, except that it remains in force until it is withdrawn.

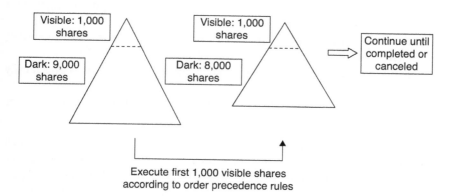

Execute first 1,000 visible shares
according to order precedence rules

Figure 2.3 Reserve order execution in Stock XYZ

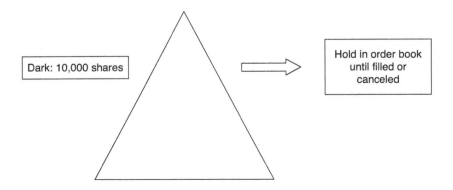

Figure 2.4 Hidden order execution in Stock XYZ

- Immediate-or-cancel (IOC) order: a designation indicating that any unfilled portion of an order that exists shortly after it has been submitted is to be cancelled (and where "shortly" is considered to be a matter of seconds).
- Minimum acceptable quantity (MAQ) order: a designation indicating that at least a minimum amount out of a full order size must be filled.

It is worth noting that the fill-or-kill and immediate-or-cancel orders have a time dimension as well, and might also be correctly categorized in the following section.

Time in force parameters

Some of the orders described above – primarily limit orders, though unexecuted market orders can also be included – allow for so-called time in force parameters, which permit certain duration limitations or extensions around the order. Common time in force parameters include

- Day order: an order that is valid until exchange closing, e.g., 4pm, at which point any unfilled portion is cancelled.
- Good till date order: an order that is valid until the end of a specified business day, at which point any unfilled portion is cancelled.
- Good till cancelled order: an order that remains valid until it is specifically cancelled.
- Good after date order: an order that comes into force after a specified time or business day.

As a final point, let us mention the indication of interest (IOI), which is a tool that is used in certain dark venues. The IOI, as the name suggests, is a form of message conveyed by an investor to a broker or dealer (or vice versa) that reflects interest in, or possibility of, executing a trade under certain size and price parameters. IOIs are used by some platforms as a way of confidentially gauging buying/selling interest in a security, but are not generally considered to be actionable instructions in the manner of the orders described above (though some IOIs can be constructed as "actionable order messages"). In fact, an IOI that generates a positive response between a buyer and a seller will lead to the creation of an order to satisfy that positive response. However, IOIs must be used with care, as the dissemination of price information through messaging could be construed as a "quote" for purpose of pre-trade transparency, and thus bring platforms using the IOI mechanism under stricter regulation.

* * *

Pools in Practice: The rise of the conditional order

We've noted, immediately above, the concept of the IOI, a non-binding invitation to deal. While it can be used in various ways, it also forms the backbone of the conditional order, a special type of instruction that is on the rise in dark pools. While this has been primarily a U.S. phenomenon, it is now starting to expand into other markets, primarily because the order structure has some distinct advantages. In its simplest form, the conditional order comes from an algorithm or smart order router initially in the form of an IOI with relevant trading parameters (e.g., stock, price, size) sent into a dark pool. At this point the IOI is not a firm order, simply an invitation to display interest. If the parameters designated in the IOI can be met, the pool requires a confirmed order to be submitted via the algo or SOR within a period of time, generally less than 1 second, or else the transaction is considered to be cancelled.

The advantage of the conditional order is that a trader or investor (and particularly one dealing in a large block), can post the IOI into various pools simultaneously, thereby increasing the likelihood of a cross – without otherwise creating a binding order. Once the IOI parameters are met within a pool, the algo or SOR can simply cease to confirm any subsequent confirmations from other pools within the 1 second time window, rendering them null and void. The disadvantage of this approach is that the risk of information leakage can increase when submitting multiple conditional orders at the same time. Smart sniffers may be able to track the submission of IOIs into multiple pools, allowing for gaming. So, while the conditional order can bring with it better probability of execution, it also carries higher risk of leakage and market impact.

* * *

The list of order types we have described above is not exhaustive; certain other variations on the theme exist, but most of these are simply subtle changes to the major types we have described above. The main point to stress in this discussion is that orders drive market activities and have very specific ways of building, withdrawing, and otherwise influencing liquidity. The interaction of displayed and nondisplayed liquidity through order books is also of interest to our discussion, as it sets the stage for what can, and cannot, be accomplished by institutional investors with big blocks of securities that need to be purchased or sold.

Figure 2.5 illustrates major classes of orders.

Table 2.1 summarizes the primary goal each order is intended to address.

With this background in mind, let us now consider two simple examples that show how visible and dark market and limit orders might interact to establish the best bid and offer and to clear orders on the book.

Table 2.2 highlights the opening order book in Stock EFG with a range of prices ($19.80 to $20.30) and a best offer ($20.10) and best bid ($20.00); all bids and offers are visible. In the first step no matches can be made, since no order crosses the best bid or offer. In the second step a new visible offer enters the market that crosses the bid and executes. In step 3 we see the book after the cross, reflecting a new best bid of $19.90. Step 4 sees the arrival of a dark bid at $20.00, which does not cross the offer, meaning no match can occur. In step 5, a new visible order enters the pool at $20.00, which crosses half of the dark offer on an improved price basis of $19.90. Step 6 reflects the new book structure after the cross, with a $19.90–$20.10 inside spread and a combination of dark and light orders awaiting the next order submission so that further crosses can be made.

Table 2.3 illustrates a new order book in Stock EFG, which includes a working discretionary bid order at $20.10 – the discretionary order is dark, since it is being worked at the discretion of the broker. In step 1 no matches can occur as no order crosses the best offer of $20.20 or the best bid of $19.90. In step 2 a new visible offer at $19.90 appears, which crosses against the best visible bid. In step 3 we see a new visible offer enter the pool at $20.00, which can execute against the dark discretionary bid of $20.10. Step 4 reflects the book after the cross and with a new inside spread of $19.90–$20.20.

These simple examples demonstrate how different types of light and dark orders can interact with each other. They are slightly misleading, of course, because we can "see" the dark orders in the examples below. To make this more realistic we can imagine removing the dark bids and offers from the figures – the result would

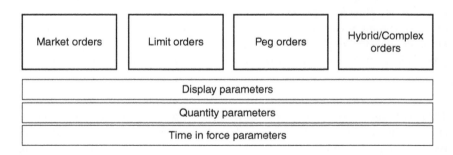

Figure 2.5 Order types

Table 2.1 Major classes of orders and primary motivations

Order type	Primary motivation
All-or-none	Time to market
Benchmark	Price improvement
Discretionary	Speed of execution
Fill-or-kill	Time to market
Immediate-or-cancel	Time to market
Good-till-cancelled, good-till-date	Time to market
Hidden	Display
Limit	Price improvement
Market	Speed of execution
Market-if-touched	Speed of execution
Market-on-close	Speed of execution
Market-on-open	Speed of execution
Market peg	Speed of execution
Market-to-limit	Risk limitation
Midpoint peg	Price improvement
Primary peg	Speed of execution
Reserve	Display
Stop, Stop-limit	Risk limitation
Sweep-to-fill	Speed of execution
Trailing stop, Trailing stop-limit	Risk limitation

Table 2.2 Stock EFG order book example 1

	19.80	19.90	20.00	20.10	20.20	20.30	Best offer	Best bid	Comment
(1) Working orders	4000	5000	4000	6000	8000	3000	20.10	20.00	No matches
(2) New visible offer 4000 shares at 20.00			4000						Trade executes
(3) Working orders after (2)	4000	5000		6000	8000	3000	20.10	19.90	Best bid changes
(4) New dark bid 8000 shares at 20.00	4000	5000	8000	6000	8000	3000	20.10	19.90	No matches
(5) New visible offer 4000 shares at 20.00	4000	5000	8000	6000	8000	3000	20.10	19.90	4000 shares execute
			4000						with improved price
(6) Working orders after (5)	4000	5000	4000	6000	8000	3000	20.10	19.90	No matches

visbile bid	visible offer
dark bid	dark offer

be what can be seen on a typical ELOB or exchange screen, with no notion of the depth of the dark orders; Table 2.4 replicates our first example, where steps 4, 5, and 6 reveal no indication of the 8000 share dark bid. In fact, much can be happening "behind the scenes" of which investors are unaware, and helps illustrate the power of being able to shield orders from sight.

Table 2.3 Stock EFG order book example 2

	19.80	19.90	20.00	20.10	20.20	20.30	Best offer	Best bid	Comment
(1) Working orders with discretion that is dark at 20.10	5000	7000		5000	5000	3000	20.20	19.90	No matches
(2) New visible offer 4000 shares at 19.90	5000	7000		5000	5000	3000	20.20	19.90	4000 shares execute against best visible bid
		4000							
(3) New visible offer 5000 shares at 20.00	5000	3000	5000	5000	5000	3000	20.00	19.90	5000 visible shares execute against discretion
(4) Working orders after (4)	5000	3000			5000	3000	20.20	19.90	No matches

visbile bid	visible offer
dark bid	dark offer

Table 2.4 Stock EFG order book example 1, without illustrating the dark trade

	19.80	19.90	20.00	20.10	20.20	20.30	Best offer	Best bid	Comment
(1) Working orders	4000	5000	4000	6000	8000	3000	20.10	20.00	No matches
(2) New visible offer 4000 shares at 20.00			4000						Trade executes
(3) Working orders after (2)	4000	5000		6000	8000	3000	20.10	19.90	Best bid changes
(4) New dark bid 8000 shares at 20.00 (Not On Screen)	4000	5000		6000	8000	3000	20.10	19.90	No matches
(5) New visible offer 4000 shares at 20.00	4000	5000	4000	6000	8000	3000	20.10	19.90	4000 shares execute with improved price
(6) Working orders after (5) (Not on Screen)	4000	5000		6000	8000	3000	20.10	19.90	No matches

Having reviewed major types of orders, it is critical to emphasize that order choice is not forced on an investor or trader by a broker or other financial intermediary. In a standard non-discretionary relationship such choices are driven by the end goals an investor/trader seeks, whether that is anonymity, price improvement, cost savings, immediacy, or some combination. At any point in time order routing to the dark may be optimal, in some other circumstances the lit option may be better –much depends on the state of liquidity, volatility and market conditions, and is thus never a static decision. To be sure, a broker or advisor can assist in clarifying the choices and can assist in the execution process (if that is the desire of the investor/trader), but the ultimate decision belongs to the investor/trader. This brings us to the sometimes "negative taint" associated with certain trading strategies and execution styles built atop the orders noted above, including dark trading, flash trading, algorithmic trading, and so on. We must remember that these options are available to all investors/traders in the pursuit of their end goals (sometimes for free, sometimes for a direct or indirect cost) – the fact that some choose not to use them does not suggest that markets are uncompetitive or that advantages accrue only to a certain class of traders/investors, as is sometimes touted.

Market structures

Various types of market structures exist to permit fair buying and selling of securities based on the order types we have described above; these apply to all manner of securities and assets, including stocks, bonds, commodities, foreign exchange, and derivatives. Markets can be classified in various ways, and in some cases these classifications can be combined. We may, for example, distinguish between

- Physical markets and distributed/electronic markets
- Continuous markets, call markets and brokered markets
- Quote-driven markets and order-driven markets
- Displayed markets and nondisplayed markets

Let us consider each one in more detail.

Physical and distributed/electronic markets

Markets can also be described by their physical characteristics, in particular whether they exist in physical form or whether they are a product of an electronic design. The actual operation of the two may be identical – that is, a physical market and an electronic market might both be structured for continuous two-way trading – but the interactions of participants are quite different.

A physical market, as the name suggests, is a marketplace with a central physical trading floor where floor brokers, floor traders, specialists, and other exchange personnel gather to conduct business, and where buying and selling is conducted via open outcry or negotiation. There are not, in fact, many major physical markets any more, as most have given way to the distributed/electronic model. That said, venues such as the NYSE and Chicago Mercantile Exchange continue to operate on this basis. Physical markets often match and price trades through floor auctions which, while well established and generally efficient, can also be challenging to manage – particularly if the markets are "trading fast" and the number of participants is large.[3] That said, physical trading creates speed and immediacy that is simply not available through an electronic marketplace (which necessarily has a degree of latency), and can thus create certain information advantages. In addition, the physical communication and interaction between buyers and sellers (typically floor brokers, floor traders, and/or specialists) can convey information about the markets which is lost to electronic traders.

Of course, it is wrong to assume that because a market is physical in nature and relies on human interaction that it does not incorporate technology and aspects of the electronic marketplace – quite the contrary. In fact, in order to remain efficient and competitive, physical markets rely on many of the same technologies as electronic markets, such as electronic order routing, electronic matching, real-time price feeds, electronic surveillance and data exchange, and so forth. In addition, most of these markets also operate separate electronic markets of their own as a supplement to their physical activities.

A distributed/electronic market is one that operates in the electronic sphere, through use of advanced technologies; the ability for participants to network into these markets from afar gives rise to the term "distributed." In fact, access from remote locations is a key feature of this form of market structure. Unlike physical markets, such markets do not rely on physical interaction between participants to establish prices or arrange purchases and sales – all dealing occurs through a variety of electronic mechanisms. An electronic market that follows a rule-based auction process to match trades often does so in a manner that causes it to look similar to a standard open-outcry floor auction – but with more uniformity and less room for error, and with possibilities for participation by a much larger number of buyers and sellers. Indeed, electronic platforms remove the human element from the trading process and appeal to those seeking complete objectivity in execution, as well as those wanting a rigorous electronic audit trail.

Of course, major exchanges that operate as electronic markets may still maintain a physical hub or center, as do bourses such as NASDAQ OMX, the LSE, and the Tokyo Stock Exchange, among many others. Such centers, however, are intended to house electronic operations and serve as a corporate nexus rather than to conduct actual trading operations. Electronic markets are not, of course, limited to "conventional" exchanges, such as stock exchanges or derivative exchanges. The entire class of ATSs and MTFs, which we describe in the next chapter, and which form a key part of the dark liquidity sector, represent an important part of the entire electronic market sector.

It is perhaps not surprising that in the twenty-first-century era of rapid technological advancement, the migration from physical to electronic marketplaces is accelerating and is effectively a matter of course. It is quite likely that the coming years will see the migration of all asset trading to electronic markets, causing the remaining physical markets to fade.

Continuous, call, and brokered markets

A continuous market, as the name suggests, is a market that trades on an ongoing basis during the trading session (e.g., 9am to 4pm for markets in stocks and listed derivatives) or throughout the day (e.g., 24/7 for markets in foreign exchange and certain electronically traded securities and derivatives). The continuous market is the most commonly encountered market structure in the financial sector. The quote- and order-driven mechanisms described below may be found in continuous markets, which bring the great benefit of immediacy.

The call market, in contrast, trades only when a "market" is specifically "called." This means that buy and sell orders are gathered at discrete points during the day and are matched or exchanged according to particular rules during each call session. The call market, which is generally order-driven rather than quote-driven, is rather less common than the continuous market, being reserved primarily for trading in government bonds and certain commodities as well as in equities on some dark platforms. The call auction market brings the advantages of price discovery, focused liquidity, and fairness, but does not offer immediate fulfillment. In fact, call auctions are often used for market openings, market closings (e.g., limit-on-close and market-on-close orders), resumption of trading following trading halts, and periodic crossings.

The brokered market is a third form of marketplace, though it is rather less than common than the two described above. A brokered market, as the name suggests, is one where agency brokers bring together interested buyers and sellers to arrange a trade. There is no dealer risk capital supporting or creating liquidity in such instances, simply an agency function that arranges execution on a negotiated basis; in fact, the market is said to "trade by appointment" rather than on a regularly scheduled basis. This marketplace generally supports the purchase and sale of very illiquid assets, as well as large blocks of securities. It is also de facto used to identify, and bring into the market, latent liquidity held by large institutional investors; in fact, such latent liquidity factors into dark pools.

While pure continuous, call, and brokered markets exist, the most complex exchanges and trading venues may rely on multiple mechanisms to take and provide liquidity and clear markets. For instance, while some exchanges might trade on the continuous model during the normal course of business, they may temporarily shift to a call market during a disruption that creates an order imbalance; once the imbalance is cleared, operation via the continuous mechanism resumes.

Quote-driven and order-driven markets

The quote-driven market is a market in which prices of securities are determined through quotes supplied by market-makers or dealers, which they alone are allowed to adjust in relation to relative supply and demand. In general, any party trading via a quote-driven market must execute through a market-market or dealer, and cannot execute directly with another trader, that is, the market-market or dealer must take one side of every trade (for that reason the market is often referred to as a dealer market). In fact, dealers can specifically choose who they want to deal with in this type of marketplace. Markets such as NASDAQ and the LSE are, mainly, quote-driven (though they have certain order-driven practices that are used on occasion).

The order-driven market is a market in which prices of securities are determined through the publication of offers to buy and sell particular quantities, which are conveyed via the orders described above. Buyers and sellers are permitted to execute with each other (and need not use a market-maker or dealer), but all trades must follow the order precedence rules established by the marketplace. NYSE Euronext is an example of an order-driven market (though it makes certain quote-driven demands of its specialists as a last resort); indeed, many global exchanges and ECNs are based on the order-driven concept.

Most order-driven markets are structured as auction markets, where buyers seek the lowest price and sellers seek the highest price; those who take liquidity from the market typically accept terms and pay a fee, while those that provide liquidity set the terms and earn a rebate (under so-called maker-taker policies). Though rebates vary according to market conditions, the competitive environment, the strategy of a particular venue, and so forth, rebates can range from 0.10 basis points (bps) for small orders to more than 0.75bps for orders of $40 million or more.

A market can use either the continuous or call auction mechanisms described above to match orders. Under the single price call auction, orders are arranged in batch by price after a market call or at the beginning of a trading session, at which point matches are made. Once matches are made, orders are then filled (totally or partly) or remain unfilled based on a single price. Under the continuous two-way auction, matches are made at different prices on a regular basis during the trading session, depending on how new orders interact with standing orders. Both types rely on rules-based order matching systems, which allow for automatic matching of orders based on a series of precedence rules. We will consider order-driven markets and order precedence rules, and their role in liquidity formation, later in the chapter.

Orders can enter quote- and order-driven markets in various ways: customers to brokers, brokers to dealers, brokers to markets, dealers to markets, and markets to markets. In some instances, customers can also enter a market directly, through direct market access. Orders are typically sent into venues through order routers, which are automated mechanisms for communicating order instructions, typically in a standard format (e.g., FIX Protocol sponsored by the FIX Trading Community). In addition to direct order routers, smart order routers, which embed orders into logic that optimizes the execution process, can also be used; we will discuss these topics in Chapter 6.

Displayed and nondisplayed markets

Another way of categorizing market structure builds on the display parameters noted earlier, providing a distinction between venues with orders that are visible or dark to the market at large.

A displayed market is one in which offers to trade are made visible to the public. Displayed quotes and orders are based on both dealer quotes on orders and exposed orders carried in limit order books. Of course, even within the broad class of displayed markets we may detect varying degrees of visibility. The most basic form of display is the so-called top of book, in which only the best bid and best offer in a given security are displayed. This "top of book" display typically arises when a specialist is setting quotes on a particular security. A deeper, and more comprehensive, form of display is the "market by price" construct, where bids and offers are shown at various depths – including those that are at the market (de facto top of book) and those that are behind the market. Very few markets are displayed 100% – most have at least some amount of nondisplayed activity alongside their visible activity.

A nondisplayed market is a market in which offers to trade are not visible to the public; such a structure is, of course, the dark market which is the subject of this book. We have briefly described in Chapter 1 the structures/components that comprise the nondisplayed market, and will review them in this section.

In the first instance, we may refer to undisclosed orders that are carried on the books of floor brokers or specialists, as well as reserve and hidden orders carried in limit order books. In addition, we may also consider non-displayed positions in the agency orders held by brokers in the upstairs market, dealer liquidity that is specifically not being exposed, orders on the blotters of buy-side and sell-side proprietary desks and latent orders resting with passive, buy-side investors. The sum of these orders, which comprise a nondisplayed market, can be spread across the market structures we have already described, including exchanges, electronic limit order books, crossing networks, and proprietary desks. The very fact that there are so many ways of transmitting orders that are not visible to the public reveals the complexities that arise in matching buyers with sellers; indeed, in the absence of a strong network of communications between brokers and dealers, advanced technologies, networking, pool partnerships, and algorithmic tools, we may well imagine that much of the buying and selling interest would go unmatched.

Figure 2.6 summarizes different types of market structures. Once again, it is important to stress that various subtypes can be combined together. We may thus speak of a displayed, physical, quote-driven market, a nondisplayed, electronic, brokered market, and so forth.

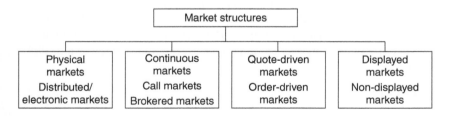

Figure 2.6 Market structures

Liquidity Supply and Demand

With some background on orders and market structure, let us now consider issues related to the supply of, and demand for, liquidity, and how market fragmentation – including the very fragmentation we see in the nondisplayed markets – impacts pricing and trading opportunities.

Measuring liquidity in a marketplace is a complicated proposition, made even more complex by growing pockets of activity in nondisplayed forums, where record-keeping and data reporting are not always mandatory or uniform, and where certain venues may have some interest in presenting statistics in one direction or another. Indeed, measuring the size of the nondisplayed market is complicated, for many of the reasons that draw investors to the market in the first instance – lack of transparency. Published figures by individual venues, and those compiled by independent data research firms, may be based on different metrics, and verifying their accuracy ex-post can be difficult. We will review the topic in greater detail in Chapter 7, but for now, note that some venues post liquidity and count it as volume, even if there is no fill; others are stricter, counting only trades which actually cross. Still others count as volume orders that pass through the venue en route to another venue. Consider, for instance, that any or all of the following metrics may be reported by individual venues as a reflection of their activity:

- Orders "touched" or "handled"
    Transactions routed and eligible for matching
    Transactions routed and not eligible for matching

- Orders matched

Each of these measures produces a different result. In addition, and as noted, trades executed in dark pools do not always have to print back to the market, adding a layer of opacity to the process.

Fortunately, transparency in the displayed markets is considerably better, and allows us to gain a general sense of supply and demand dynamics, and how these factor into the specific behaviors of buyers and sellers. Some of this can also be extended to the dark markets, without perhaps taking too great of a "leap of faith."

Theory and practice measure market (and asset) liquidity through four different parameters:

- Immediacy
- Breadth
- Depth
- Resiliency

The four are at once separate but related, all sharing a common reference to supply and demand. Let us consider each in more detail, and then discuss how their relative magnitude might affect trading behavior.

Immediacy is the degree to which a trade can be executed in the current moment. Depending on market conditions – that is, the supply of, and demand for, the security – immediacy may command a small or a large premium. For instance, if an investor wants to arrange an immediate sale of 10,000 shares of Stock ABC, it may do so by submitting a market order – the most immediate form of instruction. If the stock is in strong demand, with order books heavily weighted with aggressive bids, the cost of immediacy is likely to be negligible. Conversely, if those order books carry only modest buying interest, the cost of immediacy may rise. Of course, an investor can adjust the degree of immediacy it requires through submission of different types of orders. For instance, if the investor would like to sell out the ABC shares soon, but not necessarily right now, then immediacy is lower and the order type may change from a market order to a moderately aggressive limit order. In general, the more liquid a security (i.e., the more actively traded), the more balanced the bids and offers, the lower the cost of immediacy, and vice versa. There are, of course, exceptions to this rule.

Breadth is the cost of completing a trade, and is another term for the bid-offer spread on a security. In general, the less liquidity a stock features, the greater its breadth, or bid/offer, and vice versa. In addition, the more misbalanced the position in the security with regard to selling pressure, the greater the breadth. Indeed, we may consider a situation where Stock ABC is considered to be very liquid as it exhibits significant trading volume. If, however, the book is heavily misbalanced in the direction of sell orders, breadth necessarily increases. If the investor seeks to sell the ABC position when it is misbalanced, breadth will be wide and a greater cost of exit will accrue. Conversely, if demand is strong, breadth will be much narrower, indicating a much lower cost of exit.

Depth is the amount of a trade that can be done at a particular price, and is a true reflection of buying and selling interest in a security. The greater the depth a stock has, the greater the ability for investors to clear their books at a given price; the shallower the depth, the lower the ability to clear the books. Depth is crucial for those dealing in blocks, and is central in determining what type of concession must be given, or will be demanded, for crossing a block. If, for instance, an investor is selling 10,000 shares of Stock ABC and depth is very significant, then it may be able to execute all, or a significant portion, of the block at the quoted price. If ABC is thin rather than deep, the investor will be unable to fill much of the trade without accepting increasingly unfavorable prices.

Finally, we may speak of resiliency, which is the degree to which the price of a security reverts to its previous level following a trade. The more resilient the security the quicker the price will return to the pre-trade price. Thus, if the investor sells 10,000 shares of Stock ABC at an average price of $20/share, the market is said to be resilient if the price moves back to $20/share soon after the selling pressure abates (which may be a matter of seconds or minutes). If Stock ABC is not resilient, it may languish at lower prices, as the selling pressure overwhelms any lingering buying interest. In general, the more liquid the stock, the more resilient the stock price, though this again depends on whether supply or demand is heavily weighted in a particular direction.

Generalizing, we may therefore say that a stock which is deep is resilient, features immediacy, and has tightness in its breadth. A stock that is shallow is not resilient, may feature little immediacy, and is likely to reflect significant breadth. These four parameters help define the specific trading and investing strategies that investors, dealers, and other market participants will take at any point in time, and will indeed lead to the use of particular order types and venues in order to crystallize such strategies. In fact, we can envision an entire spectrum of liquidity suppliers and liquidity demanders – suppliers that are active or passive, and demanders that seek immediacy and those that can afford to be patient. Importantly, any party that posts, or supplies, liquidity can earn a rebate, while any party that takes, or demands, liquidity has to pay a fee. This helps ensure there are proper incentives and "penalties" in place.

Certain groups of traders and investors regularly offer liquidity. Proprietary desks, market-makers, dealers, and certain institutional investors (such as high frequency trading funds) post liquidity, de facto filling market orders and marketable limit orders and earning rebates. For instance, market-makers are in the business of providing instant liquidity, and do so by adjusting the breadth and immediacy parameters to reflect demand forces (and other market and internal[4] variables). This group essentially offers liquidity to take advantage of liquidity-demanding traders and investors who are obliged to trade – that is, those that face a high degree of immediacy. Other traders may also demand liquidity on a near-term, but not immediate, basis. These traders/investors might submit limit orders that are slightly away from the market, rather than market orders or very tight limit orders.

We can also point to various classes of passive liquidity suppliers. Periodic liquidity suppliers are those that intend to trade or invest at some point in time, but can wait; they are passive in the sense that they are not willing to trade at any price, but will supply liquidity if the return prospects are favorable enough. Certain types of hedge funds and value-driven investment funds, for instance, which have specific investment mandates but wide discretion on execution horizon, might fall in this category. A very passive liquidity supplier is an investor that has no plan to trade, or will not trade, unless immediate traders or investors make it worthwhile. For instance, pension funds, insurance companies, and other

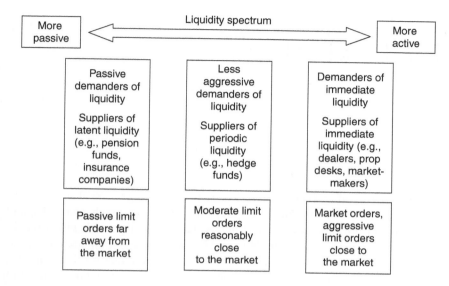

Figure 2.7 Liquidity spectrum

institutional investors with a long-term horizon might be regarded as passive investors, capable of supplying their latent liquidity to the market when it suits them. Passive suppliers of liquidity may trade by submitting limit orders that are priced well back of the market; if they are triggered, then they will enjoy handsome profits or well-priced entry points, and if they are not triggered, they will have lost nothing. So, the sum of immediate and passive demand against active supply and varying degrees of passive supply interact to determine prices and flows in individual securities.

Figure 2.7 summarizes a spectrum of liquidity supply/demand and relative active/passive stance.

Based on the comments above, it should be clear that market liquidity, built atop orders and markets, is crucial to the success of financial markets. The way in which that liquidity is accessed (i.e., dark or light) and the specific venues that are involved in providing that liquidity are also integral to the discussion, and form the topic of our next chapter.

3 | Dark Pool Structure

The trend toward off-exchange dealing has been accelerating in recent years, thanks to the catalysts we have described in the previous chapters. In this chapter we explore in more detail the general characteristics of dark pools, the mechanisms within established exchanges that create dark liquidity, and the venues that are partly or solely dedicated to fostering dark liquidity. Before embarking on this discussion, let us recall the key mechanisms for pooling or accessing dark liquidity noted in Chapter 1, as these will form the core of our discussion below:

- Exchange reserve/hidden orders and specialist/floor broker books
- Alternative trading systems/multilateral trading facilities, including electronic limit order books and crossing networks
- Broker/dealer proprietary desks
- Agency brokers

We will also consider these efforts in terms of hybrid business structures and briefly review the importance of understanding the profile or character of a dark pool. The main point to bear in mind is that dark pools are quite heterogeneous; each structure and venue operates in a slightly different manner, using different forms of technology and following different kinds of business models in order to service a specific segment (or segments) of the client base. Though common strategies may exist at an overall level, each dark platform is ultimately a unique creation.

General Characteristics of the Dark Business Structure and Model

The provision of dark liquidity has emerged as an important business opportunity for a range of exchanges and dedicated platforms. The characteristics and structures of dark pools, while varied, can be defined by each of the following parameters:

- Business/revenue model
- Ownership structure

- Technological infrastructure
- Target clients
- Order types
- Pricing/matching mechanisms
- Liquidity relationships

Exchanges and dedicated platforms must particularly examine the needs of potential clients to properly capitalize on the business opportunity. More specifically, the definition of a specific business model must address whether potential clients want or expect

- Full service versus discounted service
- High touch versus low touch
- Full order management versus execution only
- Specific execution rate levels
- Rebates
- Analytics and algorithms
- Post-trade support

As we will note below, each platform provides clients with differentiated levels of service to best match their requirements. For instance, some hedge fund clients may want the most sophisticated set of services so that they can take more active and aggressive control of order executions. High frequency traders may want algorithmic access and attractive maker/taker rebates. Certain passive pension funds may be satisfied with a more basic suite of offerings. The business model must therefore be designed to cater to these differences. In fact, the organizational structures described below may be geared to service specific segments of the client base; though some aspects of the business have become quite commoditized (e.g., an order management system tied to a crossing network with algorithms and DMA), other features remain specialized. Ultimately, of course, the key deliverable under any dark business model is access to liquidity with a minimum of information leakage and price impact, and with potential for price improvement. If these essential elements are lacking, there is little point in trying to attract client flows.

Exchange Orders and Specialist Books

Exchanges were the pioneers of visible trading and continue to hold the largest market shares in terms of tradable volume, as we noted in Chapter 1. Indeed, even as alternative platforms have developed around them, and have taken a growing amount of their market share, the main global stock exchanges continue to dominate displayed trading. The same is not necessarily true with dark trading. In many cases leading exchanges have found themselves on the defensive, having lost ground to upstarts. To challenge these platforms and regain some amount of lost dark share, key exchanges have spent the past few years enhancing their exchange reserve orders/ hidden orders and specialist book capabilities, investing more heavily in exchange technologies, developing ATSs of their own, and entering into partnerships with other electronic players. The latter points will be discussed later in the chapter, but first we focus on exchange reserve/hidden orders and specialist/floor broker books as the cornerstones of the exchange dark liquidity microstructure.

Exchange orders

Most exchange orders are visible to the market, providing full transparency regarding trading opportunities. However, many of the world's largest exchanges participate in the dark sector through one or both of reserve and hidden orders, which we have briefly described in the previous chapter.

As indicated, an exchange reserve order, or iceberg, is any order that resides within an exchange but is not fully exposed to the market – only a portion of the order is visible at any point in time, and represents the "tip of the iceberg." As each portion of the reserve order is executed in the visible markets, the next portion comes out of the dark and into the visible queue, taking its place in terms of price/time priority – in effect becoming the new "tip of the iceberg." This process continues until the entire order is either filled or cancelled. Thus, while a small piece of the order is visible, the majority is dark, meaning that it is unlikely to be negatively impacted by adverse market prices. That said, the process of executing the reserve order can take time, since each portion needs to reenter the queue in its appropriate price/time ranking. From an order precedence perspective, the nondisplayed portion of a reserve order ranks behind displayed orders, but ahead of hidden orders. Many exchanges have reserve order facilities, meaning that they participate directly in the formation and execution of dark liquidity.

A hidden order, in contrast, is an exchange order that is available for crossing, but is never exposed in the visible price queue. If the hidden order has the best price it can be crossed either with other hidden orders or against visible orders, and printed to the tape. Naturally, hidden orders must take their own place in the order precedence queue, typically behind visible orders and the nondisplayed portion of reserve orders. The concept of the hidden order within an exchange is not particularly new, but has certainly grown in prominence and importance because of the catalysts we have described in the previous chapters.[1] Whilst many global exchanges offer hidden order types, not all provide for reserve/iceberg functionality; Table 3.1 summarizes major global exchanges that support the use of reserve orders and the requirements for displaying the "tip of the iceberg."

Specialist and floor broker books

Specialist books are another potential source of nondisplayed liquidity within the exchange structure. Specialists (and equivalent functions that go by different

Table 3.1 Major global exchanges with hidden/reserve orders

National Exchange	Iceberg Restrictions
Australia	Must display 5,000+ shares
Austria	Order must be 1,000 shares+, and must display 10%
Belgium	Must display 10+ shares
Brazil	Must display 1,000+ shares
Canada	Must display a board lot
Denmark	Must display a round lot
Finland	Must display a round lot
Germany (XETRA only)	Order must be 1,000+ shares, and must display 10%
Ireland	Order must be 1,000+ shares, and must display 10%
Italy	Must display Euro10,000+
Mexico	Order must be 2,000+ shares, and must display 5%
Netherlands	Must display 10+ shares
Norway	Must display NOK10,000+
Poland	Must display 100+ shares
Portugal	Must display 10+ shares
Spain	Must display 250+ shares
Sweden	Must display a round lot
UK	Must display 40% of normal market size
US	Must display a round lot

Note: In instances where a national exchange does not offer direct reserve order capabilities, various brokers offer algorithms that can synthetically create an exchange iceberg.

names) are members of an exchange that are obliged to quote two-way markets in specific securities, and maintain an orderly market in those securities under a series of defined rules. Each specialist thus runs a "book" that contains orders of a particular stock (e.g., the GE book, the Sony book, the Exxon Mobil book, and so forth). Specialists are not found in every marketplace; in fact, they exist only in certain order-driven markets, such as NYSE Euronext, Philadelphia Stock Exchange, Deutsche Boerse, NYSE Euronext/ Paris Bourse, and Chicago Board Options Exchange, among others.

In order to maintain their status, specialists must adhere to both affirmative and negative obligations. From an affirmative perspective, the specialist must offer liquidity in assigned stocks at all times, including taking the other side of a trade when no other offsetting order is to be found (though this obligation may be temporarily suspended in certain instances, such as in a rapidly plunging market or when spreads are unreasonably wide); the specialist must also maintain a smooth market and reasonable spreads, and do whatever is possible to avoid erratic price jumps and volatile or excessively wide spreads. From a negative obligation perspective the specialist must respect various trading restrictions, so as not to benefit from privileged information. In fact, being in possession of information on order flows allows a specialist to profit directly by trading in front of the book – something which is strictly forbidden. Specialists are permitted to trade on a dual basis – for their own books (maintaining an inventory of securities through which to fill orders as necessary), and in a de facto brokerage role on behalf of clients.

The standard functions of a specialist include showing best bids and offers (thereby becoming a market-maker), acting as agent by placing electronically routed orders on behalf of clients, managing the order books containing client limit orders, and serving as principal by taking one side of a client trade against owned inventory. Specialists can broker orders for other brokers (through exchange order routers)[2] and can receive orders through direct contact with other dealers; floor brokers may also route agency orders to specialists so that the orders can be worked. Specialists may also be responsible for conducting auctions in the single price auction market framework, and for monitoring all activity within the limit order books to which they are assigned. By gathering and managing the order flow passing through the limit order book, a specialist can essentially determine which orders remain dark and which are made visible. For instance, if the specialist in Stock ABC has a client limit order to buy 10,000 shares, it alone knows how, where, and when to execute the trade – it is effectively dark, since the specialist is not publishing a market by price book to the market at large. It can execute against an offsetting customer order, it can execute against dealer inventory, or it can keep the order in the book – as long as the client is not prejudiced from an execution perspective. This, then, is an important source of dark liquidity.

A specialist is bound by order precedence rules and cannot trade ahead of a public order at the same price, and is generally discouraged (though usually not prohibited) from trading owned inventory against limit orders on the books – when a specialist decides to fill an open limit order against the book, liquidity is effectively removed from public investors. Still, the specialist is in a strong position to take advantage of order flow knowledge to dictate dark/visible matches and influence prices. Indeed, the specialist essentially sets market quotes, which an exchange reflects to the public, and has some discretion in the process. For instance, in top of book markets, specialists must expose only the most aggressively priced offers to trade (and in some markets also at least as good as the best bids and offers in their limit order books). But they can generally quote better prices or bigger sizes related to their own market-making requirements. If a specialist wants to increase the probability of buying (selling) in a stock, it can quote aggressive bids (offers) or improve prices for marketable sells (buys). Similarly, if it wants to decrease the probability of buying (selling), it can quote the best bid (offer) on the book.

Floor brokers are another source of nondisplayed liquidity, operating in a manner very similar to that of specialists. In particular, floor brokers holding discretionary (or market-not-held) orders have significant flexibility in when, and how, they expose and execute their orders. Recalling our discussion from Chapter 2, we know that discretionary orders are always dark. Floor brokers often reveal their orders after they have identified traders who want to trade, and not before; in fact, such orders can be crossed from within a book.

Alternative Trading Systems/ Multilateral Trading Facilities

As noted in Chapter 1, the broad category of alternative trading systems/multilateral trading facilities includes electronic communications networks/electronic limit order books and crossing networks. These platforms are important players in the dark pool space; in order to best reflect the sometimes confusing nomenclature, and to consider their differences and similarities, let us begin with some basic regulatory definitions.

An alternative trading system (ATS) is any approved nonexchange trading venue that is registered with the U.S. SEC, and is defined under Rule 300(a) of Regulation ATS of 1998 as:

> Any organization, association, person, group of persons, or system that constitutes, maintains, or provides a market place or facilities for bringing together purchasers and sellers of securities or for otherwise performing with respect to securities the functions commonly performed by a stock exchange within the meaning of Rule 3b-16 of this chapter; and that does not set rules governing the conduct of subscribers other than the conduct of such subscribers' trading on such organization, association, person, group of persons, or system; or discipline subscribers other than by exclusion from trading.

Under this broad definition we may find a variety of different venues, including electronic communications networks, electronic limit order books, crossing networks, matching systems, and call markets, the most important of which we consider in further detail below.

An electronic communications network (ECN) is a form of ATS that gathers and matches orders and executes trades with public quotes. Under SEC Rule 600(b)(23) of Regulation NMS an ECN is defined as:

> Electronic trading systems that automatically match buy and sell orders at specified prices. ECNs register with the SEC as broker-dealers and are subject to Regulation ATS. Subscribers, which are typically institutional investors, broker-dealers, and market makers can place trades directly with an ECN. Individual investors must currently have an account with a broker-dealer subscriber before their orders can be routed to an ECN for execution. When seeking to buy or sell securities, ECN subscribers typically use limit orders. ECNs post orders on their systems for other subscribers to view. The ECN will then automatically match orders for execution. An ECN may choose to facilitate compliance by a market-maker with its obligations under the Commission's Quote Rule by transmitting the ECN's best bid/offer to a national securities exchange or registered securities association for public display.

In fact, an ECN resembles an exchange, but operates like an electronic broker, disseminating widely any orders entered by a trader or market-marker and permitting those orders to be acted on; an ECN must be registered as a broker/ dealer or as a self-regulated securities exchange. Importantly, ECNs exclude any systems that cross multiple orders at one or more specified times at a single price set by the system and those that do not allow orders to be directly crossed by participants outside of such times, as well as any system operated by a market-maker that executes customer orders primarily against the market-maker's proprietary book (e.g., an internal engine). Within the general class of ECNs we find the electronic limit order book (ELOB) which operates as an off-exchange book of limit orders which may be visible, dark, or both. Despite the name, some ELOBs also accept market orders.

A crossing network is another form of ATS that matches buy and sell orders electronically without routing the order to an exchange or displayed market; executions are generally done to the midpoint of a market price. The SEC has defined a crossing network under 1997 rules as

> Systems that allow participants to enter unpriced orders which are then executed with matching interest at a single price, typically derived from the primary public market for each crossed security.[3]

As we will note in Chapter 4, price derivation, rather than price discovery, is an essential element of the crossing network structure, and distinguishes it from its ELOB cousin.

Though we have presented these definitions in light of specific U.S. regulations, we can consider the same concepts in terms of other global markets. For instance, MTFs, which are permissible in a European context under MiFID, are structures that effectively parallel the ATSs we have just described, offering visible liquidity, dark liquidity, or a combination of the two, and acting as price discoverers or derivers. An MTF[4] must be registered with the relevant national regulator before operation can commence.

We may note under the EC Directive 2004/39/EC that a

> "Multilateral trading facility (MTF)" means a multilateral system, operated by an investment firm or a market operator, which brings together multiple third-party buying and selling interests in financial instruments – in the system and in accordance with non-discretionary rules – in a way that results in a contract in accordance with the provisions of Title II.[5]

The UK's Financial Services Authority expands further, noting:

> Multilateral Trading Facility is, in broad terms, a system that brings together multiple parties (e.g. retail investors or other investment firms) that are interested in buying and selling financial instruments and enables them to do so. These systems can be crossing networks or matching engines that are operated by an investment firm or a market operator. Instruments may include shares, bonds and derivatives. This is done within the MTF operator's system.[6]

The same applies in Japan, where the private trading system (PTS) serves as the domestic equivalent of the ATS or MTF. Thus, we should not be too concerned about whether we term a platform an ATS crossing network or an MTF price reference system, or an ATS ELOB or an MTF ELOB or even a PTS – the operation and goals are largely identical, just that each is governed by its own national regulations.

Figure 3.1 summarizes general types of ATSs/MTFs that factor into the dark trading sector.

With these definitions in place, let us focus our discussion on ELOBs and crossing networks.

Electronic limit order books

An ELOB is an ECN that operates as an electronic "off-exchange exchange," posting visible orders and in some cases also managing portfolios of hidden orders; some ELOBs accept only limit orders, others accept market and limit orders. Unlike traditional exchanges that feature either specialists or dealers, ELOBs have no "middle man" – they simply aggregate bids and offers flowing through their networks, posting varying degrees of price and volume information. Certain ELOBs also enter into arrangements with brokers to have them direct their order flow into the venue in exchange for "liquidity fees."

ELOBs are relatively recent entrants to the new financial markets, and the success and growth they experienced around the turn of the millennium was based on advances in technology and changes in the order handling rules mentioned in Chapter 1. By 2000, the U.S. market featured more than a dozen ELOBs – including significant platforms such as Island, Archipelago, Brut, and Redibook. These platforms built successful business models (either as independent or as consortium-owned entities) and gained reasonable market shares, but a degree of consolidation ultimately followed.

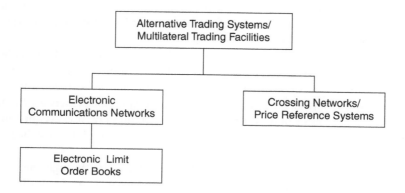

Figure 3.1   Types of alternative trading systems/multilateral trading facilities

Most of the leading platforms were acquired by exchanges, which saw the strategic wisdom of buying ventures with proven electronic capabilities and growing market share in the execution space. For instance, NYSE bought Archipelago in 2006 (as part of the exchange's transformation to a public company and prior to its acquisition of Euronext), while NASDAQ purchased INET in 2005, which was itself a combination of Island and Instinet (and, ultimately, Brut)[7] – and which became NASDAQ's Single Book (formerly SuperMontage). The introduction of MiFID and its attendant support of MTFs, including those that de facto operate as ELOBs, has also given boost to the European market, where platforms such as Baikal, Burgundy, and Turquoise, among others, made an early mark. As in the U.S., similar consolidation trends ultimately followed. For instance, the LSE took a 60% stake in Turquoise in 2009, merging it with its Baikal platform. Similarly, the Nordic-focused Burgundy was acquired by the Oslo Stock Exchange in 2011.

Buyers and sellers using an ELOB post their prices and depth (volume) in a particular stock anonymously. While each trade submitted into an ELOB contains a range of information, such as security ticker, buy/sell flag, trade price, trade date, order instruction, broker ID, and so forth, the only items which are displayed include the ticker, bid or offer price, and quantity. The ELOB gathers the information and posts it in strict price-time priority; as bids and offers are queued, price assumes priority, followed by time, and executions are conducted on a continuous basis – the orders are thus actionable. When an ELOB receives a new market order it determines whether the order can be executed immediately by crossing it with a standing order in the book; if it cannot do so, it will route the order to a primary exchange. As a result, market orders will be filled at levels which are at least as good as those on an exchange. When the ELOB receives a new limit order, it will first determine its marketability; if the order is marketable, it will be treated as a market order and be executed or sent to the best market, and if it is not marketable, it will be placed in the ELOB's order book. Similarly, if an exchange routes a marketable order to the ELOB, the ELOB will attempt to fill the order against its book. As a result of this process the exchange makes sure the limit orders to the ELOB are exposed. In order to eliminate the risk of double execution because of slow systems, order routing systems typically give precedence to the ELOB.

Let us consider a simple example. If an ELOB receives two market bids in Stock ABC at $30, the one submitted first gets matching priority against any offered interest in the book. The highest bid and the lowest offer in ABC form to create the book's inside spread. As each incoming order in ABC stock enters the ELOB, it is crossed if it meets or improves the best price; if it does not, it is assigned to the visible queue by price-time where it remains in the queue until it is matched, or is cancelled by the investor.[8]

Of course, many ELOBs support nondisplayed liquidity, through the reserve and hidden order mechanisms noted earlier. For instance, an institution may submit an offer for 1000 shares of ABC at $30, as well as a reserve order for a further 10,000 shares, also at $30. The ELOB adds up all nondisplayed reserve orders in ABC and either crosses the trades away from the visible market, or makes the flow available for interaction with other dark pools. Extending our example above, we may consider the following: if an institution submits a reserve bid into the ELOB for 10,000 shares of ABC at $30.15 when the posted bid and offer are $30.10 and $30.20, a subsequent sell order at $30.15 or below will generate a partial or complete cross against the reserve bid (depending on the size of the sell order); the execution is not apparent to the market. Of course, not every ELOB supports reserve or hidden orders; those that do not must be seen strictly as visible operators, with no impact on dark liquidity.

The ELOB model has proven successful because it can simultaneously deal in the light and dark markets – orders can be input directly by traders and become actionable, the delivery mechanism is generally client-friendly and latency is minimal. Most platforms charge fixed fees for access and then a per share fee for execution, and overall execution cost remains reasonable. In addition, ELOBs participate in the price discovery process, and are thus a central link in establishing clearing prices for securities. Knowing this, it comes as no surprise that they are an integral part of the trading landscape. That said, it is also true that many ELOBs are focused primarily on smaller trades rather than large blocks (certainly as far as their visible operations are concerned), suggesting that the influential block business is being crossed through other mechanisms.

Crossing networks

As we have noted, a crossing network (or price reference system) is a venue that aggregates and matches orders purely on an agency basis; in fact, some of the main platforms have their roots in the agency brokerage business. While on the surface a crossing network sounds similar to an ELOB, several fundamental differences exist. First, a crossing network displays no orders: there is no "trading screen" as with an ELOB, the platform simply serves as a repository of liquidity and matches bids and offers anonymously, "behind the scenes," generally in relation to some base price (such as the NBBO or EBBO). It can thus be viewed as a form of processor that tries to match both sides of a trade, with a focus on confidentiality. Second, certain crossing networks allow a degree of price negotiation to occur between buyers and sellers, something which is not structurally possible through an ELOB. While most trans- actions are executed with reference to NBBO or EBBO, price improvement may be possible. Third, crossing networks may cross trades either continuously or selectively during the trading day; ELOBs generally match orders on a continuous basis during the trading day and after market close. Finally, crossing networks may serve all trading sizes, or they may concentrate only on large transactions, whereas ELOBs are open to all trade sizes. Like ELOBs, crossing networks can benefit from order flows from brokers, and broker crosses can be arranged via order trading systems.

Crossing networks are still relatively new in the marketplace, so it comes as no surprise that fill rates are somewhat low as compared with ELOBs and exchanges. However, their growth shares are accelerating, and these venues stand to create the most significant in-roads in the coming years. Pioneering platforms such as POSIT, Instinet, and Liquidnet, along with a host of new platforms developed in the early/mid part of the millennium, have challenged the status quo of the marketplace dramatically and have become popular, especially with institutional investors. For instance, according to one market estimate, more than 90% of large institutional money managers have used, or currently use, a crossing network for some portion of their activities. This high participation rate is due to their positive experiences in identifying appropriate liquidity pools and achieving matches. Approximately 60% of small money managers report similar use. To be sure, crossing networks feature both advantages and disadvantages: advantages include improved confidentiality and lower costs/competitive pricing, while disadvantages include market fragmentation leading to lower fill rates. Let us consider these points in more detail.

Since crossing networks function solely in the dark, they provide real benefits to those seeking confidentiality. Investors can route orders to a crossing network confidentially, thereby reducing any chance of market impact; this is especially important for those managing large blocks or large program trades. Thus, an investor might anonymously submit a limit order to buy 10,000 shares of Stock TUV at $45.50. Upon receipt of the order, the crossing network will search, on a continuous or call basis, its open limit orders in Stock TUV and attempt to cross the trade in relation to a base reference price; if it can do so it will fill, if it cannot, it will either rest, reroute, or cancel the order, depending on the buyer's instructions. Importantly, the public remains unaware of the potential interest in TUV, meaning there is little possibility for market impact.[9] Only after the trade is crossed will the relevant parties receive a confirmation message (which again contains no disclosure of the parties involved); ex-post reporting into a trading reporting facility may also follow, depending on jurisdiction.

Apart from confidentiality, a crossing network also provides clients with lower execution costs. In fact, the additional competition these venues have added to the market has promoted competition and, thus, sharper pricing, to the benefit of traders and investors. Of course, this additional competition leads to fragmentation, which can impact the formation of liquidity – there is a fine line between having too few and too many players competing for a finite pool of trading assets. If a given crossing network has only a fraction of the available liquidity in a given security, then its chances of being able to offer investors a fill on an order decline. As more crossing networks enter the sector to operate alongside ELOBs and exchanges, fill rates can decline even further. In the extreme, an excessive number of participants may atomize the market so much that no critical mass of liquidity exists, causing prices to be skewed and fill rates to plunge. Since crossing networks are price derivers rather than price discoverers, they ultimately rely on efficiencies in the primary markets from which they draw their base reference prices.

The success of any single crossing network is based on its ability to attract liquidity. As indicated in Chapter 1, liquidity is the lifeblood of any venue – clients will be willing to route orders into a crossing network only if they believe there is some reasonable chance of a match. This becomes a particularly challenging issue for new platforms, platforms that have not yet had an opportunity to build a steady order flow, or those that are not associated with some strong "parent" or other partner.

Various types of crossing networks have been created in recent years, and it is helpful to consider them in terms of structure, function, and client focus.

From a structural perspective, crossing networks can be organized as follows:

- Independent crossing networks
- Broker/dealer crossing networks
- Exchange crossing networks
- Consortium crossing networks
- Aggregator crossing networks

Let us briefly review these structural variations.

The subclass of independent crossing networks includes those that are either broadly held by public investors or which are entirely private; independence from exchanges and other financial institutions is sometimes viewed as a competitive advantage, as the chances of any conflict of interest are nonexistent. Such independent crossing networks have, in some cases, been true pioneers in developing and advancing the business model and the associated technologies. Whether all such platforms remain independent in the future as industry consolidation continues remains to be seen. Examples of crossing networks in this category include ITG POSIT, Pipeline, and Liquidnet.

The next subclass, broker/dealer crossing networks, includes those that are owned and operated by brokers/dealers (e.g., investment banks, universal banks, and other international commercial banks). These broker/dealer crossing networks typically commingle external flows with internal flows captured by the sponsoring institutions through their proprietary desks and client flows. Examples of crossing networks in this category include Goldman Sachs' Sigma X, UBS's PIN, Morgan Stanley's MS Pool, and Credit Suisse's CrossFinder.

The third subclass, exchange-related crossing networks, includes those that are wholly or majority owned by major stock exchanges, often as a way of bringing more liquidity into the exchanges. Such exchange crossing networks operate in parallel with traditional exchange activities (including visible flow, exchange reserve orders, hidden orders, and/or specialist/floor broker orders), and form part of the hybrid business model solution described later in this chapter.[10] These platforms have generally proven successful, in part because leading exchanges have applied significant resources and technologies to the effort. Exchange crossing networks typically attempt to match incoming orders against those resting in the pool or those that reside within the sponsoring exchange itself; if no matches are possible, orders may then be rerouted to other pool partners. Through this architecture, exchanges receive order flow from, and send to, their own pools (and pools with which they have arrangements). Examples of crossing networks in this category include NYSE's Matchpoint, ISE's MidPoint Match, and NASDAQ's Open/Close, Intraday and Post Trade Crosses.

The subclass of consortium crossing networks includes those that are owned by a number of partners, such as banks, broker/dealers, independent crossing networks, and exchanges, and which are managed by independent management teams. Again, these crossing networks may form part of a multichannel business solution for those already operating their own proprietary crossing networks, or they can provide those without a presence in the space a "footprint" in a relatively inexpensive manner. In fact, consortium pools are very cost competitive, and have used this advantage to capture meaningful market shares. Since consortium platforms feature numerous institutions as partners, they are very receptive to supporting sell-side flows, but often do not receive order flow until it has been routed to internal desks or other pools owned by individual partners. Examples of crossing networks in this category include BIDS Trading and LeveL ATS.

The subclass of aggregator crossing networks, which may be independent or owned by a consortium, serves to link in with the broadest range of existing dark pools, directing flows to platforms where established arrangements exist (see Pools in Practice for more information). Certain block crossing systems operate in this manner, using their trade execution platforms to connect to various venues in order to capture the broadest possible amount of order flow. Examples of crossing networks in this class include Pragma's OnePipe, which unites more than 30 dark pools through its unique architecture.

*   *   *

Pools in Practice: Dark aggregation

Dark aggregators are an important mechanism in the marketplace, structured either as crossing networks (as noted above) or created through algorithmic programming. Regardless of structure, aggregators are designed to simultaneously or sequentially search out dark liquidity across multiple dark pools in order to support large trade execution or to conduct a quick search to identify pockets of liquidity (after which a trader may target or re-route orders to the most promising pools). While block crossing systems can be best for handling large size orders and single dark pools can be most effective when execution is the top priority, aggregators may be the best solution when finding liquidity across a fragmented trading landscape is the overarching goal.

While aggregators are meant to increase efficiencies, they can also be misused. For example, if an institutional investor with an aggressive "axe" (i.e., position to be sold) is seeking the best pool of liquidity it can use an aggregator to simultaneously scan the marketplace by "shotgunning" (i.e., sending in IOCs into multiple venues); however, these short duration bursts may not have enough time to uncover true liquidity (reflecting the tradeoff between protecting against predatory pinging and falling victim to "ships passing in the night"), meaning the process may yield suboptimal results. Some degree of patience and persistence is typically required to get the best possible outcome.

The best aggregators must be able to properly take account of the increasing types of orders (e.g., minimum execution size/minimum acceptable quantity, IOC, FOK, conditional, and so forth) and the myriad execution strategies that investors employ (e.g., passive, aggressive, full spread); indeed, high performance aggregators can quickly learn where the best pockets of dark liquidity reside, and use that information to refine search efforts as related to different strategies. For instance, we know passive strategies create savings by not paying the full spread, but are then likely to be subject to a lower fill rate; aggressive strategies demand immediacy but may result in a worse pricing and potential information leakage. This parameterization needs to be understood by the aggregator. Aggregators must also understand the nature and characteristics of different pools, distinguishing between broker-dealer pools running retail books and those with an institutional flow, agency pools, exchange pools, electronic market makers, and so forth.

Implementation shortfall is often used to measure the success of a dark aggregator. The metric, comprised of both execution cost and opportunity cost, is seen as a reasonable performance benchmark. In order to lower execution costs, an aggregator is typically designed to cross trades only at the best price, and to minimize opportunity costs it tries to cross as quickly as possible. While these are not necessarily mutually exclusive conditions, balancing the two is tricky – and is what separates good from bad aggregators. In the end, the aggregator should be able to trade against quality liquidity at fair prices. As more "quality constraints" are injected (e.g., gaming, pinging, fishing protections), fill rates decline and opportunity costs rise.

* * *

We can also consider crossing networks by examining how they function and how they may choose to specialize. From a functional perspective we can describe the following discrete models:

- Negotiated crossing networks
- Continuous crossing networks
- Call market crossing networks
- Block crossing networks

Let us consider these in detail.

The negotiated crossing network subclass is a unique model that permits a degree of price negotiation between participants. Through IOIs and electronic messaging, buyers and sellers can anonymously agree to cross a particular amount of shares at a price that they establish. Pure negotiated crossing networks are relatively uncommon, though the negotiation feature is available in certain platforms. Liquidnet and BIDS Trading, for instance, have negotiation capabilities.

The continuous crossing network subclass includes platforms that accept confidential bids and offers and cross them on a continuous basis. In fact, this approach follows the continuous auction process described in Chapter 2, and brings with it the usual advantages and disadvantages: the possibility of a quick fill or instantaneous rerouting to another destination, but also limited liquidity formation at any single point. Many of the sector's largest crossing networks are based on the continuous model.

The subclass of call crossing networks accepts confidential bids and offers into the pool and holds them until a call auction is declared, at which point the matching engine performs its matching routines to cross as many orders as possible. Though the number of calls performed each day can vary by platform, in practice it ranges from once a day to several times per hour. Several of the most popular platforms use this model, which brings with it the advantage of a pocket of liquidity at each call but the disadvantage of a delayed cross and execution opportunity.

The last of the major subclasses is the block crossing network, a form of platform that is designed to cater to institutional sized blocks, leaving retail flow and sliced institutional orders to other networks. This unique model has the advantage of capturing true blocks (attempting to disintermediate exchanges and pure agency brokers in the process), but the disadvantage of deflecting nonblock institutional flows and retail flows, which might otherwise add to overall contra-liquidity.

It is worth noting that under each one of these functional models an "advertisement" subtype can also be applied, in which the platform sends out alerts to trading books holding or wanting eligible shares when a particular order is available for crossing. Once the transmission is received, the relevant parties must take action if they are interested (i.e., enter an order for the quantity to be bought or sold). This type of platform is therefore not fully automated, and requires human response to an indication of interest. The nature of the alert being transmitted must be well defined in order to avoid information leakage. The way in which an alert is transmitted is also crucial – it may be symmetric, where potential buyers and sellers receive the alert simultaneously, or asymmetric, where one party receives an alert after the pool contains a committed order on the other side. Most pools using the advertisement model structure the alert to convey a minimum tradable amount, such as a fixed quantity based on the market capitalization of the stock, a percentage of the order size in a receiver's book, and so forth. BIDS and BlockAlert are examples of platforms with advertisement capabilities.

The crossing networks described above can cater to distinct client groups within the marketplace, a process known as restricted access. Possible models include

- Buy-side only
- Sell-side only
- Buy-side and sell-side

Some platforms prefer to deal only with the buy-side, keeping potential "competitors" out of their networks, while others prefer a completely open forum that captures flows from all segments of the client base in order to boost the chances of a cross. There is, as yet, no clear signal that one business model is superior to any other. In fact, it appears possible that various models can coexist.

The buy-side represents all institutional investors that serve as clients to large financial institutions, including hedge funds, mutual funds, pension funds, investment portfolios of insurance companies, sovereign wealth funds, municipal and government investment vehicles, and so forth. Some buy-side firms have a medium-to long-term investment horizon in the equity markets and tend to be passive or latent providers or takers of liquidity, while some, such as hedge funds, are more opportunistic and aggressive, serving as short-term liquidity providers and takers. From an order flow perspective, buy-side flow can come from DMA, algorithmic trading (direct and via DMA), high frequency trading, program trading, and block trading. The subclass of buy-side crossing networks caters only to buy-side investors, prohibiting participation by any sell-side institutions and making them something of a secure "closed shop." Liquidnet, for example, has successfully implemented this particular business model (and has also created a special offering, Liquidnet H20, to capture retail flows). Note that even within the buy-side only restrictions, some pools do not permit participation by hedge funds, under the assumption that they are simply seeking to take advantage of "less sophisticated" or passive investors that may frequent the pool.

As noted, the sell-side includes all financial institutions that are involved in servicing buy-side clients, and encompasses banks, broker/dealers, and securities firms. The sell-side platforms that cater to this segment of the market effectively bar buy-side clients from submitting orders. In fact, such platforms are quite uncommon; the ping venue noted below is a slight extension of this model, as it includes flows from sell-side institutions and highly sophisticated funds.

The combined buy-side/sell-side subclass is the most common form of crossing network, supporting all manner of institutions, investment strategies, and time horizons.[11] The business model of the combined buy/sell platform allows the sponsors/owners to capture the broadest range of flows, which may at any time be concentrated in different sectors. The sponsors must, of course, open their doors to other sell-side competitors, but this is seen as a worthwhile tradeoff in exchange for creating additional flow for crossing purposes. Platforms such as POSIT, for example, capture liquidity from the broker/dealer community and from buy-side investment managers.

Other "variations on the theme" also exist. For instance, the sector has seen the development of so-called ping venues, which are crossing platforms sponsored by hedge funds or electronic market-makers that operate "black box" trading strategies. The ping venue accepts only IOC orders from clients (who are primarily from the sell-side), and these orders interact directly with the sponsor's own liquidity; the sell-side participants themselves operate dark pool aggregators or smart order routers and "ping" such destinations as a matter of course. The models underpinning the venue determine whether any single IOC entering the venue should be accepted or rejected (permitting some degree of discretion and creating information asymmetries); the key driver for both parties is cost savings derived from not having to route to venues dealing at market spreads.

Though various business models exist, at least some portion of the buy-side seems to prefer independent crossing networks that do not feature proprietary flows coming from the sponsor or its partners. Others appear less concerned about such proprietary flows and even welcome contra-trades as an opportunity to cross their own orders. At this stage of the evolutionary cycle there seems to be enough diverse appetite to support multiple models. One of the keys to long-term success in this sector is to create an individual character or identity which attracts a specific group of traders/investors. If this can be successfully accomplished, the very commoditized nature of the service becomes a secondary matter.

Crossing networks should not, of course, be viewed as standalone entities. Many of them have crafted relationships with other venues over the years, so that they can provide their clients with access to additional pools of liquidity. Thus, a crossing network may link into other crossing networks, or may tap into visible or hidden orders held by exchanges or ELOBs. The intricate relationships that can arise make it all the more important that tools such as smart order routers and algorithms are available to market participants.

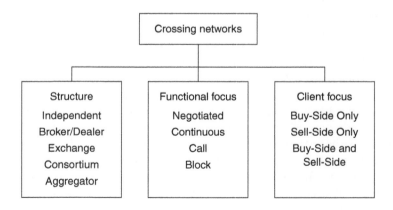

Figure 3.2 Key types of crossing networks

Figure 3.2 summarizes the key types of crossing networks by structure, functional focus, and client focus. Let us note again that specific types of crossing networks can be combined, so that we may speak of an independent, block crossing platform that caters to the buy-side and sell-side, or a consortium-owned, call platform that services the sell-side only, and so forth. In fact, flexibility in the creation of the business model is one of the key strengths of the crossing network.

Broker/Dealer Desks – Systematic Internalizers

Broker/dealer desks (or "systematic internalizers" as they are known under MiFID), operated by the world's largest banks and securities firms, are significant players in the nondisplayed liquidity arena, and have been instrumental in developing and expanding the upstairs market in recent decades. While the early days of the upstairs market featured voice-driven orders and execution, and somewhat manual processes, it set the stage for more significant operations in the dark sphere. By leveraging on these experiences broker/dealers began developing, in the millennium, more robust institutional mechanisms for capturing very valuable internal flows – from either client orders passing through the firm or proprietary trading activities, or both – in a process termed "internalization." Some of the biggest players in this sector created internal crossing systems to gather and match such flows, and some of the "early movers" were able to ultimately commercialize their systems, turning them into the public crossing networks noted above – essentially offering their liquidity pools to the buy-side. For instance, Goldman Sachs' Sigma X, Credit Suisse's CrossFinder, UBS' PIN, Morgan Stanley's MS Pool, Fidelity's CrossStream, and Citibank's Citimatch, among others, began as purely internal crossing efforts.

In fact, many large broker/dealer desks are now actively involved in crossing institutional and retail client flow and proprietary positions. The sum total of this activity creates cost savings on internal crosses (e.g., if crossed outside the internal flows, incremental costs will accrue) and proprietary trading revenue through application of the dealer spread (e.g., buying at the bid and selling at the offer) and can lead to better execution prices (and may include queue jumping to provide immediate fills). Ultimately, a broker/dealer should be able to perform fair broker blind crossing of institutional flow and retail flow without prejudicing any particular client or client segment. Of course, this activity reduces transparency, as all crosses occur within a firm's books and orders need not be reflected in other venues – though in most jurisdictions executed trades must be reported to a central hub ex-post (as we will discuss in Chapter 7). In addition, under MiFID a firm that executes against internal liquidity is treated as a form of "mini exchange" for regulatory purposes, meaning it must adhere to all of the pre- and post-trade parameters defined via the regulatory framework.[12]

Broker/dealer desks, particularly those that are not part of a firm with a large retail network, typically have extensive arrangements with third-party brokers related to the routing of customer order flow, a process known as preferencing. Those that have the benefit of a franchise have a natural base of order flow. For instance, large banks and fund companies, such as Bank of America Merrill Lynch, UBS, Fidelity, and Morgan Stanley, among others, feature large retail networks that generate a very large amount of "captive" order flow which can be routed internally for crossing. Those that lack such retail order flow franchises, such as Goldman Sachs, JP Morgan, Deutsche Bank, and others, may rely more heavily on third-party broker preferencing relationships. In exchange for directing orders to a dealer (which can then internalize by filling), a broker receives certain rewards from the dealer (i.e., "payments for order flow"). In addition to payment schemes, some dealers will guarantee execution at the NBBO or EBBO, even if the order size is greater than the displayed size, as a way of attracting flows.

Internal proprietary desks can add significantly to market liquidity and their contribution to the dark space cannot be underestimated. Naturally, aspects of this function can involve the commitment of risk capital in support of a trading operation (distinguishing it from the agency model described below) which suggests that a curtailment of risk capital, such as during a financial crisis or through the imposition of restrictive regulations (e.g., in the U.S., the Volcker Rule under the Dodd-Frank Act), may have an impact on available liquidity. In some cases, desks may extend beyond pure internal flows by entering into strategic relationships with other pool operators, causing them to look more like public crossing networks; Figure 3.3 summarizes this model. Furthermore, certain broker/dealers (and other institutional investors) can choose to cross securities among themselves, as nonmembers of an exchange, in the so-called third market. However, before this can occur, a member firm of an exchange must fill all limit orders on a specialist's book at the same price or better.[13]

Note that in addition to internal crossings, some of the largest international broker/dealers have established their own dedicated crossing networks, as indicated

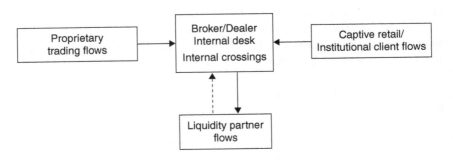

Figure 3.3 Broker/dealer desk model

earlier. Many also make use of algorithms in their proprietary operations, and make algorithms available to their clients; the algorithms have the potential of linking to other dark pools and generating additional dark liquidity. In fact, such algorithms have been central to the growth of dark liquidity, a point we will discuss at greater length in Chapter 5.

Agency Brokerage

Agency brokerage firms have emerged as an important structural conduit in linking buyers and sellers in the dark (and light) sectors. Such agency brokers are quite distinct from their broker/dealer counterparts, in that they commit no capital of their own, but act as traditional "middle men" by matching buyers and sellers of displayed and nondisplayed flow across a large number of different pools. Examples of players in this segment of the market include Lime Brokerage, Neonet, and ITG (which also operates as a technology company and runs the POSIT crossing network, as we have noted), among many others.

Agency brokers can also work orders for their clients, crossing them on their own books as agent. Note that orders that cross within a broker's own books are exposed only to the broker's other clients, and perhaps not to trades that can produce a better or faster fill. Brokers may also send orders to ECNs or crossing networks which they believe may house the type of liquidity that can result in a cross; such order flow is typically compensated through the payment of "liquidity fees." Alternatively, brokers may enter into preferencing arrangements with dealers, as described above. Importantly, brokers that accept payment for order flow or liquidity fees and also conduct agency crosses of their own could suffer from conflicts of interest and must ensure rigor in applying best execution practices. Best execution can, of course, depend on a client's specific aims – in some cases it relates specifically to speed (generally achieved through market orders) and in other cases to price (limit orders). In the former case, a broker must ensure that its execution is at least as quick as it would be in the primary exchange market; in the latter, benchmarking to a reference price such as the NBBO or EBBO, or equivalent, is likely needed, though this applies primarily to smaller orders and those that are accommodated within the displayed size, rather than very large trades.

Like broker/dealers, agency brokers often make available to their clients a range of algorithms which can help link into a variety of pools and generate additional flow. In fact, many brokers provide explicitly defined or customized algorithms that meet the specific requirements of clients. It is worth noting that agency brokers also attempt to tap into pools of so-called latent liquidity, or equity portfolios that exist with certain buy-side investors, such as asset managers and insurance companies. Such institutions often have very large positions in the equity markets but may not be making these portfolios available for displayed or nondisplayed execution. If brokers can access these pools of liquidity, they add to the overall pool of liquidity and potential crosses in the marketplace. This element of the business still requires the "human touch" – algorithms cannot be used to tap into latent liquidity.

Direct Market Access

Direct market access (DMA) is a process that allows buy-side investors to access liquidity without directly going through an intermediary (whether broker or dealer); in other words, orders flow directly from the trader/investor into a visible or dark market, without being "touched" by a third party (though such orders still flow though the infrastructure of the broker or dealer). While participating buy-side investors may have once routed their executions to an agency broker or broker/dealer for onward execution in a given light or dark pool, DMA eliminates a step in the chain. Naturally, DMA is not used by all buy-side investors – the main users are those with a certain degree of market sophistication and a relatively high degree of portfolio activity, as well as those that buy and sell large blocks. DMA first appeared in the late 1990s as ECNs became a part of the marketplace, and grew more prevalent in the early part of the millennium as the number of new hedge funds expanded and as major sell-side firms acquired specialists[14] capable of offering DMA to clients; it has expanded steadily since then, primarily in the U.S. and European equity markets. One study estimates that DMA market share in the U.S. is just above 20%, while in Europe it is approximately 15%; further growth is expected in the coming years.[15]

DMA linked with a smart order router (discussed in Chapter 6) and algorithms (Chapter 5) gives a buy-side client the ability to execute directly into an exchange or dark pool, lowering transaction costs, reducing latency, and eliminating errors from "worked" orders. If a bid or offer is in a dark or visible book and an investor using DMA enters an order at the same price or better, the order is automatically matched. The DMA process still requires infrastructure supplied by a sell-side sponsoring institution, but places control of order management and execution directly in the hands of investors (see Pools in Practice). While DMA is not a dark pool mechanism – that is, it does not create or house dark liquidity – it is another mechanism that allows tapping into dark (and light) pools.

* * *

Pools in Practice: Different degrees of direct market access

Direct market access has become synonymous with professional trading and execution, used by sophisticated investors who want to minimize, or eliminate, the traditional role of the broker-dealer. That said, direct access in its broadest sense still relies on a broker relationship, as we shall see. There are, in fact, varying degrees of direct access.

The simplest and most common form is standard DMA in which the client uses the broker's trading systems directly to effect execution, confirms flow back through the broker's books and records for the account of that client. So, while the broker is not involved in the actual execution of any trades (as in a standard relationship), the client still requires a relationship with the broker to execute via DMA. The second degree of access is known as sponsored access. In this case the client connects directly to an exchange or other marketplace using the broker's membership; unlike DMA, however, there is no use of the broker's accounting mechanisms. Notice again that sponsored access still requires a relationship with a broker. The final form of direct access is referred to as naked access and represents the greatest level of client independence. In this case the client's own systems are co-located at the exchange through the broker's membership, and trades are cleared through the broker's clearing account – almost as if the client were a "virtual broker" itself.

The advent of sophisticated technologies and the growing awareness of clients regarding the direct execution process have helped bolster interest in the direct access mechanism over the past few years. Not surprisingly, direct access in any of the three forms supports dealing in the lit and dark markets. Accordingly, we can view this type of execution architecture as a key element of the dark sector.

* * *

Hybrid Business Models

Exchanges, ELOBs, and crossing networks can be regarded as conduits that match customer flow against customer flow, whereas ping venues and the broker/dealer proprietary desks described above are those that match proprietary flow against customer flow. But other combinations can also be created. In the past years the boundaries have expanded significantly, as institutions have taken discrete elements of the dark pool concept and melded them together to create hybrid business models. It is thus no longer necessary for an institution wishing to act as a sponsor of dark liquidity to do so by pursuing a single channel: multiple channels can be combined, which is a significant advantage for those uncertain of what the future of the nondisplayed trading market will look like.

Consider, for instance, that certain global stock exchanges are able to cater to the nondisplayed liquidity sector through multiple mechanisms:

- The exchange's "floor" (whether physical or virtual) may feature floor brokers and/or specialists that cross trades within their books before posting out to the market;
- The exchange may have the facility to accommodate hidden orders and/ or reserve orders;

- The exchange may own, totally or partly, an ELOB, which can house hidden orders and/or reserve orders;
- The exchange may own, totally or partly, a crossing network;[16] alternatively, it may be a shareholder in a consortium crossing network.

We can see from this simple example that the exchange can pursue its traditional visible liquidity business while at the same time capturing its share of dark liquidity; importantly, this dark liquidity can simultaneously interact with the exchange's visible liquidity. Rather than place all of its "chips" on a single solution, it combines multiple solutions as a way of gaining a greater share of crosses, and preserves structural flexibility should one of the channels evolve or change at some future point.

Other hybrid models can also be considered. For example, large investment banks and international banks can participate in dark pools from multiple angles:

- The bank may own a crossing network that captures nondisplayed liquidity and interacts with other dark pools.
- The bank may be an investor in a consortium-based crossing network.
- The bank may capture internal crosses from client flow passing through its books and from its own proprietary trading capital.
- The bank may enter into dark pool agreements with other dark platforms and agency brokers to allow their nondisplayed liquidity to interact with other nondisplayed liquidity.
- The bank may develop algorithms for itself and its clients that tap into multiple sources of nondisplayed liquidity.

We can imagine many other variations on the theme, such as a crossing network negotiating multiple pool partnerships that direct flow to the venue, or a crossing network that attaches to broker algorithms that watch for a match and then send the orders to the venue for a cross. The point of these simple examples is to demonstrate that hybrid business models exist and can be used to help promote access to market share. The multiple efforts can also help unite otherwise fragmented pools of liquidity.

A Snapshot of the Dark Landscape

The dark landscape changes on a continuous basis, and will certainly do so in the future. Nevertheless, it is instructive to take a snapshot of the types of platforms that are in operation in the second t decade of the millennium to get a flavor for the variety of options that are available to institutional investors and other intermarket players. This snapshot – which moves us from the theoretical to the practical – is not exhaustive, as there are literally hundreds of other venues operating in the marketplace. We have attempt through this brief list to take a sample of different kinds of platforms to highlight similarities and differences in the marketplace. Note also that our examples must be seen as a point-in-time snapshot that will necessarily evolve over time, as consolidations, acquisitions, and other corporate changes take further hold.

Baikal: The pan-European dark MTF established and operated independently by the London Stock Exchange to cross dark orders through its midpoint match service (via random, periodic, crosses) and a continuous match service was merged into the Turquoise platform (below) after the LSE bought a controlling interest in Turquoise in 2010. The combined platform offers access to dark liquidity through a liquidity aggregator that routes to 20 venues in 14 countries, as well as to visible and hidden liquidity on the LSE itself; it also supports block trading and includes anti-gaming protection.

Bank of NY Mellon: The Bank of NY Mellon's platform provides for multi-asset class execution, block and program trading, DMA, dark pool access (its own and that of others), algorithms and analytics, and integrates with major order management systems. The bank also holds an interest in ConvergEx (see below) which operates the VortEx ATS, a dark pool that finds and aggregates liquidity from other dark pools, and ConvergEx Cross, which is a block crossing network. VortEx combines agency order flow with external dark liquidity in order to boost the chances of matching trades, and only interacts with liquidity providers that are prepared to trade. ConvergEx Cross, in contrast, permits control of orders by direct execution or negotiation. BNY has attempted since 2011 to divest its stake in ConvergEx in line with planned changes in its own operating model.

BATS: BATS was created as a U.S. ECN in early 2006 and converted to a registered national securities exchange in 2008, providing light and dark trading in NYSE, NASDAQ, and regional stocks. BATS also established BATS Europe in 2009, an FSA-regulated MTF dealing in pan-European stocks; it converted to Registered Investment Exchange in 2013. Orders in Europe may be placed in a dark book or in an integrated book that features light and dark trades, and executions are at the midpoint of the relevant base reference. BATS also offers dark trading of options through a separate options exchange subsidiary. To further expand its market share, the exchange acquired the Direct Edge ATS in 2014 (see below).

BIDS Trading: The BIDS Trading platform, launched in 2007, is structured as a continuous block crossing network that is owned by a consortium of 12 financial institutions. It features open access to sell-side firms and any buy-side clients sponsored by the sell-side, and accepts trades from order management systems, algorithmic engines, and trading interfaces. BIDS does not publish size, price, or clients, and even ex-post clients remain unaware of their counterparties. Selection can be made to auto-match within the NBBO as a base reference price or through price negotiation. Various order types can be submitted, and minimum block size must be followed. BIDS also operated the NY Block Exchange (NYBX) venue with NYSE as its joint venture partner from 2009 to 2012, where dark orders entered into

NYBX would search NYSE's order book to cross against light or hidden orders. That venture was ultimately closed down due to insufficient critical mass.

BlocSec: BlocSec, owned by French/Asian broker CLSA, was founded in 2008 as the first Asia-based ECN, giving investors access to dark blocks in large cap Asian stocks. BlocSec originally started matching and execution with Japanese and Singaporean stocks, and added equities from Australia and Hong Kong in a second stage. The ECN operates via a continuous, high speed order matching and execution platform that is designed to limit information leakage and minimize transaction costs.

Burgundy: Burgundy is an equity and bond MTF that was originally developed and owned by a number of Scandinavian banks and securities firms. The platform, which launched in mid-2009, specializes in nondisplayed trading in Swedish, Norwegian, Danish, and Finnish stocks and bonds. The Oslo Stock Exchange took over ownership and operation of Burgundy in 2011, and the MTF remains a key pillar in the Exchange's business model to the present time.

Bloomberg Tradebook: Tradebook is an agency ECN owned by Bloomberg that supports trading in equities, currencies, and other assets on a global basis. The venture's architecture provides routing to 15 US and 16 international dark pools as well as a broad range of proprietary single stock, pair/spread and program trading algorithms, including one specially designed to provide more real-time control of execution in small/mid cap dark stocks. It also employs smart order routing technology that allows investors to select from execution in one or more of the lit, grey and dark markets.

Chi-X: Chi-X, a venture owned by Nomura's Instinet brokerage unit and a number of other financial institutions acting as consortium partners, operates platforms in Canada, Japan, and Australia that cross in the dark and light. Following the success of the initial platforms, Chi-X entered into a venture with the Brazilian Stock Exchange known as Chi-Brazil, to trade in local equities. Note that another portion of the original platform, the MTF Chi-X Europe (which provides access to dark liquidity in 14 European markets via Chi-Δ, an anonymous central limit order book) was sold to BATS Global in 2011.

ConvergEx: This venture represents an interesting adaptation of the execution business, and helps illustrate the close linkage between trading technology and trade execution. ConvergEx began in 2006 as an IT company specializing in the design and implementation of trading execution systems, selling an interest in its venture to BNY Mellon (above). In 2009 it converted itself into a dark pool operator, buying NYFIX (itself owner of the Millennium ATS), adding to its own VortEx and ConvergEx Cross dark pools in the process. The three pools specialize in different segments of the market, e.g., one on block trading, one on buy-side execution and the third on sell-side execution. As a result of this unique structure and focus, ConvergEx has become one of the largest providers of agency dark liquidity – all while continuing its execution technology developments.

Credit Suisse Crossfinder: The Swiss bank's dark pool has been consistently ranked as one of the two largest dark pools for the past few years, a feat achieved through early mover status (the venue was one of the first to go live), sophisticated execution technologies (including low latency routing and comprehensive algorithms), and a broad range of marketplace access (including 14 EMEA markets, 4 Asian markets plus the U.S. markets as of 2014).

Deutsche Boerse: The primary German stock exchange operates Europe's largest conventional visible platform by market value, and has ventured into the dark space through Xetra MidPoint, a platform for crossing blocks on a nondisplayed basis. Unlike other European exchanges, Deutsche Boerse has opted not to create a separately capitalized MTF or participate as a shareholder in a consortium, although it entered into a partnership with Liquidnet in 2013 to allow crosses between Xetra MidPoint and Liquidnet books.

Direct Edge: The U.S. platform, an ECN which converted into an exchange in late 2009, was originally owned by a consortium including Knight, Goldman Sachs, International Stock Exchange, JP Morgan, and Citadel. The consortium sold Direct Edge to BATS in 2013, and the acquisition was completed in 2014 after receipt of regulatory approvals. Direct Edge deals in NYSE and NASDAQ stocks in the visible and dark markets and operates the Enhanced Liquidity Provider Program to link clients to multiple pools of light and dark liquidity. The venue also distinguishes between client bases through its EDGX and EDGA offerings, each tailored to a specific type of order flow. Though Direct Edge is part of the BATS group, it continues to operate under its original branding.

Fidelity: The large U.S. mutual fund company participates in the dark space through its Fidelity Capital Markets unit, which aggregates internally the natural order flow from the Fidelity client base, and its CrossStream crossing engine, which provides clients with access to nondisplayed liquidity, supporting market, limit, and complex order types. Fidelity also operates DarkSweep, a dark liquidity aggregator that draws liquidity from approximately 20 venues into a single entry point; all of the orders are hidden and execution is only against the NBBO. Since DarkSweep is an algorithm, users can customize the aggregation destinations as desired. Investors can also make use of BLOX, a block trading facility that interacts with Fidelity flows on an anonymous basis.

Goldman Sachs: The U.S. investment bank operates Sigma X, one of the largest of the broker/dealer crossing networks. Clients can post block orders which become nondisplayed top of book limit orders that interact with flow and other natural crosses. Sigma X performs point-in-time crosses, benchmark crosses,[17] portfolio crosses, and block crosses. The point-in-time crosses are based on the summation of orders at select points during the day, after which crosses and executions occur.[18] Sigma X clients have access to Goldman's algorithms/analytics and smart order router, and receive real-time and end-of-day reporting. Customers posting to Sigma X allow their orders to interact with algorithmic flows, DMA pass-through orders, and posted orders from crossing networks and electronic market-makers. The pool features minimum execution size and anonymity. Note that in addition to Sigma X for the U.S. market, the bank now also operates the Sigma X MTF in Europe and Sigma X Japan.

International Securities Exchange: The International Securities Exchange (ISE), founded in 2000 as an electronic options exchange, became involved in dark equity execution in 2006 via its Midpoint Match platform. In 2007 Eurex, the derivatives subsidiary of Deutsche Boerse, bought the ISE, while in 2008 a subsidiary, ISE Stock Exchange, entered into a venture with Direct Edge to further expand its presence. ISE now functions in part as an aggregator of dark pools, where all aggregated order flow interacts with order flow from members on an anonymous basis, and without preferencing. As noted in Chapter 2, the ISE's Midpoint Match order, which seeks to match at the mid of the best bid offer, is now an integrated order type used by various other platforms for clients who are seeking price improvement. Midpoint Match performs continuous crosses and is integrated with the displayed market. The platform requires a minimum order size and supports solicitation of interest, where a member with an executable interest displays the ticker of the order on a 500 share minimum; such orders have a 10 second execution priority over other orders.

Instinet: Instinet, the global equity execution venture owned by Japanese securities firm Nomura, was established in the U.S. in 1969 before being acquired by Nomura in 2007. The platform offers a range of equity execution services built atop its access to lit and dark liquidity in more than 60 markets. Its U.S. platform features the CBX, BLX, and VWAP cross pools designed to provide specific execution services through continuous order book, institutional dark block aggregation, and VWAP algorithm mechanisms, respectively. The company is also active in Europe through the BlockMatch dark MTF and the European VWAP algorithm, while in Asia it executes light and dark trades through pools dedicated to Japan, Korea, and Hong Kong.

ITG: ITG, as noted in Chapter 1, is one of the pioneers of electronic trading, having established itself as an agency broker and technology firm early in the cycle. ITG is active in the dark space through various venues. POSIT Match is the firm's crossing platform, which performs anonymous scheduled matches during the trading day, and is used primarily by portfolio managers focused on index rebalancing. POSIT Now, in contrast, provides for continuous, intraday crosses that occur every 15 seconds; the platform is dominated by open limit orders rather than pass-through orders, and it also sweeps to POSIT Match. The firm runs Match Now with Triact Canada to offer dark crossing in Canadian equities, and also operates Block Alert, a block crossing system that the firm created through a joint venture with Merrill Lynch (and which it subsequently purchased outright). Block Alert seeks blocks from participating clients before they enter the market, and alerts traders and potential clients when an opportunity arises. ITG operates the ITG Dark Algorithm, which aggregates liquidity from different ATSs.

JP Morgan: The large U.S. bank is active in the dark sector through various initiatives. First, it operates JPM Lighthouse, a dark pool based on algorithm to algorithm crossing technology that identifies internal crossing opportunities (while also keeping orders in the displayed and nondisplayed markets). The bank also runs Neovest, a broker platform that can tap into neutral dark pools. In 2009, following the acquisition of Bear Stearns and that bank's custody/brokerage business, JP Morgan launched a new dark ATS known as JPM-X which, unlike Lighthouse, is an external pool. In addition to these platforms, JP Morgan provides clients with access to a suite of algorithms that can access negotiated pools, scheduled and continuous networks, and the bank's own internal liquidity. It also provides access to an algorithm management system that allows traders to create customized flows through broker algorithms. Finally, the bank is a consortium partner in SmartPool, described below.

LeveL: LeveL is a consortium ATS registered as a broker dealer that is owned and operated by eBx, itself a venture of Fidelity, Credit Suisse, Citibank, and Bank of America Merrill Lynch. It accepts orders and IOIs and matches on a continuous basis during the trading day; orders are matched against IOIs resting in the platform and are either filled or cancelled, but are not rerouted. Clients can select from amongst two "levels" for their crosses: Level 1, which is essentially an internal pool and Level 2, which provides access to the liquidity of LeveL's counterparties.

Liquidnet: Liquidnet is a pioneering buy-side-only crossing network that does not permit sell-side access, DMA, or algorithmic flow. In fact, Liquidnet has carved out an interesting niche that exchanges, for instance, cannot replicate. Liquidnet services buy-side institutional flows through its main platform, and also captures retail flows through its H_2O liquidity aggregator; though H_2O uses sell-side tools, it does not interact with sell-side flow. Since Liquidnet operates on the buy-side only, is operates a "blotter scraping" mechanism where it is able to scan the blotters of participants and create messaging when a match is found; this leads to negotiation between the two parties prior to execution, at a level related to the base reference price. While this mechanism has proven to be quite effective for both Liquidnet and its clients, it is also true that at least some participating broker/dealers operate companion blotters that are not visible to blotter scraping programs such as Liquidnet's (e.g., where they might place block positions for crosses against other flows); this practice can limit Liquidnet's ability to access the broadest possible liquidity.

London Stock Exchange: While the LSE operates visible exchanges in the UK and Italy (via Borsa Italiana) it also permits hidden orders via its SETS platform.[19] In its other dark activities (as noted above), LSE formed the Baikal MTF (with Lehman Brothers, prior to its demise), which it agreed to merge with Turquoise in late 2009. The LSE is now majority owner of the Turquoise/Baikal platform.

Morgan Stanley: The U.S. investment bank is operator of MS Pool, a dark pool that crosses trades against internal and external flows. Initially focused on U.S.

stocks, MS Pool now supports dark trading in Europe, Japan, Hong Kong, and Australia. MS Pool does not support IOIs and, to control gaming, bans IOCs and requires orders to remain in the pool for a minimum "resting" period. Clients of MS Pool also have access to the bank's algorithm suite. Note that to encourage more institutional blocks in its pool, Morgan Stanley shifted in 2012 from a traditional price-time priority to a price-size priority, meaning that larger orders can jump the queue for the same price.

NASDAQ OMX: The global exchange operates in the dark space through multiple mechanisms, including a hidden order book on the U.S. NASDAQ exchange, and the Opening and Closing Cross, Halt Cross, and Intraday and Post-Close Cross crossing networks. All nondisplayed liquidity passing through NASDAQ can interact with its visible customer orders. In 2009 the exchange created the NASDAQ OMX Europe (NEURO) MTF to handle European stocks. Originally designed to match orders internally, and then route unexecuted orders to other nondisplayed MTFs in Europe, the platform was ultimately closed in 2010 due to lack of critical mass.

NYFIX Millennium: NYFIX Millennium's dark pool was the first continuous nondisplayed matching system in the U.S., originally established as a neutral pool open to all classes of flows from the buy-side and sell-side, including blocks and algorithm flows. NYFIX also launched the Euro Millennium platform in 2008 to deal in pan-European stocks, and also entered into a partnership with virt-x in late 2007 to supply nondisplayed liquidity in Swiss blue chip stocks. NYFIX was purchased by Warburg Pincus in 2006 and sold to NYSE Euronext in late 2009, which announced plans to keep the firm's technology base, close down the Euro pool and sell the Millennium pool to ConvergEx.

NYSE Euronext/Arca: The global exchange operates multiple dark mechanisms, including reserve orders and working orders with its specialists and floor brokers, a hidden order book, and crossing networks in both the U.S. and Europe; it is also a partner in BIDS and, as noted above, operated the NY Block Exchange joint venture with BIDS until its closure in 2012. NYSE's Dark Reserve and Block Reserve services aggregate dark and block liquidity on the floor of the exchange. NYSE Arca, the exchange's electronic trading platform, supports visible and dark liquidity and includes in its routing algorithm trading interest from participating venues; dark orders not matched on Arca are routed to participating dark pool partners. NYSE Matchpoint is the exchange's U.S. crossing network, which crosses orders aggregated from the flow of 30+ pools at specific points during the trading day. In addition, the exchange established SmartPool, a European dark block MTF, with consortium partners HSBC, BNP Paribas, and JP Morgan. SmartPool commenced operations in 2009, and provides dark cross on more than 1000 stocks in 15 markets. As noted, NYSE also has execution technology from its NYFIX acquisition.

Pulse Trading: Pulse Trading operates Block Cross, a U.S. crossing network that integrates with buy-side order management systems and features auto execution, where users set minimum and maximum shares they are willing to trade at the midpoint when a contra-trade is found. Block Cross also allows a trader to send out an IOI to flag a live block, but the IOI is visible only to high probability contra-trades from the buy-side. The platform is used primarily by program traders, algorithmic traders, and sell-side block desks. In November 2011 Boston-based State Street Bank purchased Pulse in order to provide dark trading opportunities to its securities and custody clients.

Turquoise: Turquoise was conceived in late 2006 and formally launched in 2008 as an MTF owned by seven financial institutions, with clearing and settlement services provide by EuroCCP, a subsidiary of DTCC. Turquoise originally offered a full range of crossing services, including anonymous block auctions, and operated its own routing protocol. Turquoise put itself up for sale in late 2009, with the LSE stepping in to take a majority stake in 2010. As noted above, the LSE's Baikal platform was ultimately folded into Turquoise and the combined platform now offers a fully integrated dark pool service built atop the LSE's technology stack.

UBS: The Swiss bank operates the PIN (Price Improvement Network) crossing network, which was originally developed to cross internal flows, but has since been extended to the bank's client base. PIN pools orders from retail and institutional agency flows and block trades. It also operates UBS MTF, a dark facility for European equities, as well as the UBS Cross dark platform, which is available to a broader range of clients (initially targeting Asian equities, but with plans for global reach).

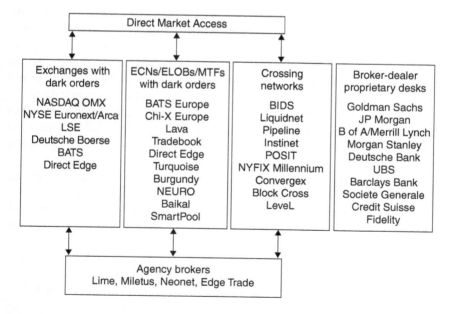

Figure 3.4   Examples of dark pool venues and mechanisms

The bank also offers UBS Direct Execution which provides clients with adaptive algorithms, and UBS Tap and TapNow, which take liquidity from PIN, other dark pools and exchanges (including their visible liquidity).

Figure 3.4 illustrates the structures featured in Chapter 1 with actual venues and mechanisms. Note once again that these examples are simply representative, and not exhaustive.

Sector Competition

In this chapter we have considered some of the significant changes that have occurred in the dark liquidity space in a relatively short span of time. These changes have been quite remarkable, and portend a continued migration away from the established world of pure visible liquidity, a topic we will discuss in Part III. The technological flexibility that is now part of the marketplace, along with benefits related to confidentiality and cost savings have been, and will continue to be, powerful forces in fostering sector growth. Importantly, the same framework is likely to create in-roads in other asset classes. While it has already begun in bonds, foreign exchange, and certain commodities, it has the potential of expanding into other areas, including other fixed income securities and certain classes of derivatives.

Naturally, the proliferation of venues through which to execute transactions is not necessarily all beneficial. Indeed, a policy of "the more, the merrier" may work contrary to the best interests of the market, as we have briefly noted in the previous chapter – while expansion in the dark market share can certainly continue, expansion in the number of dark venues has almost certainly reached a limit. In fact, it is quite possible that the "trial and error" phase of business models and the period of rapid proliferation of discrete venues are ending – future evolution will thus be based on refinement of a business model and acquisition of critical mass.

Each one of the business models described above gives rise to complex relationships between venues. It is easy to imagine, for example, that exchanges can pursue dark trading through any or all of the vehicles noted above, but they still rely on brokers to push volume through their venues. Brokers, for their part, may be willing to support the exchanges, while at the same time operating or participating in crossing networks of their own, in direct competition. Meanwhile, a large bank may run its own crossing platform and an internal desk, but may be a partner with an exchange in another dark venture – becoming a competitor and a partner at the same time.

Not surprisingly, the new competitive landscape has become very aggressive. Established exchanges and banks that did not fully perceive the scope of the opportunity and the strength of the disorganized band of "upstarts" that helped transform aspects of the sector in the early part of the millennium have changed strategy. The fact that the pioneering ATSs were small, fractionalized, and often thinly capitalized made it relatively easy to ignore their efforts or the market that was developing around them. But exchanges and banks are formidable competitors and have since placed significant resources into the development of platforms and relationships that can help them gain back market shares and improve execution rates. Independent firms, some of them backed by private equity or venture capital, are attempting to preserve niches of their own – seeking to avoid head-on price-war competition with the large players, but wanting to create a viable business model for their clients and stakeholders. The critical point to remember is that as the "upstream" dark mechanism grows, the chance of an order actually flowing into an exchange declines – meaning exchanges and others interacting with exchanges must be prepared to capture trades closer to the source.

All of this competition raises the fundamental issue of how individual platforms, whether independent or part of a major financial institution or exchange, can differentiate themselves. While much of the result is commoditized – namely, a crossed trade – the approach to gathering flow in order to fulfill the commoditized function is based on the focus and approach of each venue. As noted above, some venues have targeted very specifically the clients sectors they want to service. In addition, individual pools often choose to emphasize or market various additional "distinguishing characteristics." For instance, some venues

- Promote their ability to capture retail flows[20]
- Promote their execution rates and speed of execution
- Promote their use of partnerships and linkages
- Promote their geographic reach
- Support or ban indications of interest
- Support or ban pinging and IOC orders
- Support or ban algorithmic access

Each of these can help create an idiosyncratic brand, image, or character, which can appeal to a particular element of the client base. Whether this will be sufficient to allow them to overcome the stiff competition and the inevitable consolidation remains to be seen.

Dark Pool Profile

We may gather from the discussion above that dark liquidity exists in various venues and mechanisms and can be accessed by buyers and sellers in different ways. We may also consider that each one of these venues/mechanisms is driven by a specific business model rationale – which means there is an expectation of generating revenues by providing a specific set of services to one or more segments of the client base. Accordingly, each dark pool may be said to have its own character or profile. This is an important consideration for clients (or potential clients), as they have profiles of their own, and should ideally direct their business to the pool that most closely matches their own. By participating in a pool that is frequented by traders/investors with a different set of goals, negative selection may arise, leading to bad execution or lost opportunities.

Comingling investors/traders with very different profiles in a single pool can lead to varying quality of execution, a concept known as pool toxicity (see Pools in Practice for additional information). Consider for instance, a long-only investor that trades large blocks on a periodic basis against a benchmark. Such an investor is very likely to use a crossing network and may sit out entirely when markets are in turmoil or appear excessively volatile. Accordingly, it would not fare very well in a pool that is known to cater to high frequency long/short traders, or one that supports statistical arbitrage traders. In fact, dealing in such a pool could lead to bad fills for the long-only investor. A passive buy-side investor is also likely to fare better by staying away from so-called shark pools, or sell-side pools which are frequented by sell-side players and very aggressive buy-side traders. Such pools actively send out IOIs, cannot necessarily protect against negative selection, have significant proprietary flows and captive flows, and may fail to match the real-midpoint. A shark pool may be perfectly fine for other sell-side firms or aggressive traders, but certain classes of traders/investors routing orders to a shark pool may not fare very well. In order to prevent such exposure, an investor/trader using either a broker or an order management system is well advised to include appropriate instructions or routing logic to ensure toxic pools are avoided. Some platforms have taken the structural step of defining subpools so that clients may know where to best route their orders and avoid pool toxicity. Consider the example of Direct Edge, which distinguishes between its EDGA clients (proactive black boxes, retail market orders, statistical arbitrage orders, and active agency algorithm orders) and its EDGX clients (passive block boxes, retail limit orders, agency orders, and agency algorithm orders). Such clarity can reduce conflicts.

*　*　*

Pools in Practice: Dipping into a toxic pool

Toxicity is a critical issue for would-be users of any dark pool. Toxicity, in this context, can be defined as the quality of execution in a venue, and is generally measured by comparing the price of order execution to those orders executed immediately before and immediately after. A toxic pool is defined as one that regularly features slightly worse prices while a neutral pool is one that features slightly better prices. In general, low toxicity pools feature passive orders such as might be submitted by long-term institutional investors, while high toxicity pools host very aggressive orders that often come from high frequency traders and short-term horizon hedge funds. Of course, determining the level of toxicity or neutrality takes time – order execution has to be reviewed over many months, as any given month can feature better or worse execution levels.

The characteristics of a pool are, of course, defined by those who run the platform, and those who frequent it – together they give it a style which influences the amount and pricing "aggressiveness" of orders that enter for execution. We might draw a helpful analogy from our local pubs: one pub might encourage and thus attract a lot of loud, boisterous customers that consume enormous amounts of cheap liquor till last call, while a second one might prefer and draw a more genteel, sober clientele that sips quietly until a more reasonable hour. Mixing the two might create an unpleasant experience. Dark pool operators can similarly control the toxicity of their pools. If they wish to run an operation that welcomes all manner of order flow, they can request parties posting low rate flow to either improve on their orders or cease submissions. Alternatively, if they are quite happy to run aggressive platforms, they can freely welcome very aggressive flows – knowing that they will be catering to a specific subset of the marketplace. Ultimately a given pool's clientele will be aggressive, professional, large block, high frequency types, or patient, small order, passive, resting types, or perhaps some other combination.

Traders or investors routing orders should be aware of the nature of the pool before they dip in. It is also worth noting that just because an investor routes to a pool determined to be toxic, it doesn't mean that the investor is getting "gamed" or otherwise taken advantage of – simply that the investor's orders may cross at a slightly less favorable (i.e. more aggressive) price. In fact, if an investor doesn't want to opt out of a pool that is deemed to be toxic (perhaps because the pool offers the kind of liquidity the investor is seeking), it may still be possible to cross against flows within that pool that may be defined as "less toxic." This is typically done with a SOR that can either direct an investor's order to a neutral pool, or to the non-toxic order flow within an otherwise toxic pool. This kind of specialized routing typically requires the investor to work with a broker that is aware of different pools, their characteristics and the nature of the order flows.

* * *

Non-Equity Platforms

We indicated in Chapter 1 that most activity in the dark sector has appeared in the equity markets, hence the focus of our discussion. But electronic trading has also moved into other non-equity asset classes, and much of the dealing occurs on a dark basis; in fact, any trading that occurs over-the-counter rather than through a formalized exchange or venue might already be considered dark. For instance, various ECNs and crossing networks[21] support trading in a range of fixed income securities, including government bonds, municipal bonds, Eurobonds, and "vanilla" interest rate swaps. The mechanisms are quite similar to those described above, where traders submit bids or offers on specific securities or derivative contracts and are matched with opposing flows. Platforms such as e-Speed, BrokerTec, Muni-Center, ICAP, Market Access, and EuroMTS provide fixed income coverage of the U.S. and European markets.

Similar advances have occurred in the foreign exchange markets, where the migration from voice dealing and broking to electronic trading has been extremely dramatic. Major electronic platforms such as Reuters and EBS have been active in foreign exchange trading for more than a decade, commanding reasonable market shares at various points in time. By 1998, approximately 50% of currency trading had moved from voice to electronic, and by 2001 that figure had increased to 90%; the share expanded throughout the decade as new ventures were launched (e.g., Currenex, FXCM Pro, CME's own currency platform, and so forth), to the point where the market has become truly electronic, accessible on a 24/7 basis. This dealing is primarily over-the-counter, meaning it is already de facto dark.

*　*　*

Pools in Practice: Bond trading in the dark

While equities clearly dominate dark trading, a growing number of initiatives are putting OTC bond trading into the dark picture as well. Bond trading (whether government/agency or corporate) is still heavily driven by voice, with institutional trades being concluded through verbal negotiation, often built atop long-standing relationships; indeed, many of the large trades executed between institutional investors and their sell-side counterparts are done through the "clubby" network that has existed for years (not unlike the upstairs market in equities). Where such relationships don't exist, investors tend to steer their business to voice brokers, a process which is sufficiently anonymous to protect against market impact, but which adds to execution costs, as brokers charge sometimes significant fees.

The issue at hand is whether bonds can really be traded effectively via dark pools. After all, there are many more bond issues than equity issues in the marketplace, suggesting that liquidity doesn't mass around a single reference point and the resulting number of trades in any single issue will by definition be relatively low. Thus, while Company ABC will have only a single listed equity issue, it may have dozens, or even hundreds, of distinct bond issues. Multiply this by thousands of bond issuers, and add to this agencies, municipalities and federal government issues, and it is easy to see how coordinating trading and building enough liquidity to attract buyers and sellers can be a difficult task. In addition, in the absence of rules promulgated through Reg NMS or MiFID, there is no guarantee of best price execution in the bond market – it is truly caveat emptor.

These microstructure challenges are being compounded by a host of regulatory changes, which are already altering the landscape for bond risk-taking – some of which might well support further moves into the electronic space. For instance, the introduction of

Basel III (and Capital Requirements Directive IV), the Volcker Rule under the Dodd Frank Act, and MiFID II are all acting to penalize risk-taking (including risk-taking in bonds) through outright reduction in proprietary positioning or through higher capital charges. This means that financial institutions that might have previously held bond inventories to service client needs may reduce, or dispense with, this business. On one hand this will further imperil liquidity, while on the other hand will lead to at least some migration from the bond dealer model to the agency model. Both represent opportunities to expand electronic trading, including that portion which is represented by dark interest.

Despite the challenges, there are several dark initiatives in play. One such project comes from U.S. exchange NASDAQ OMX, which owns the eSpeed electronic bond trading platform. eSpeed currently operates as a form of institutional ELOB (minimum $1 million ticket size), featuring visible top of book prices on 2-to-30-year on-the-run US Treasury bonds. As part of its move into the dark sector, the platform will offer dark trading in on- and off-the-run bonds. The use of electronic matching will result in lower fees, while the absence of pre- and post-trade transparency will eliminate the potential for market impact. Other platforms in various stages of development evolution (and with specific expertise/focus) include NYSE BondMatch, Goldman Sachs GSession, MarketAxess, ITB Connect (as an ECN/dealer aggregator) and Liquidnet (in UK bond trading).

Ultimately these dark bond initiatives may succeed if a small number of venues can gather a critical amount of liquidity in benchmark/on-the-run issues. This suggests that the largest global bond investors will have to provide requisite support by channeling at least a portion of their requirements to a limited number of venues, while the largest sell-side houses (including those that might be migrating away from a risk-based dealer model) will have to regularly supply the platforms.

*　*　*

It should be clear that the structure of the dark sector is varied and evolving. In little more than a decade a large number of individual venues, following a handful of business models, have created a viable business proposition that is accounting for a greater amount of market share, a trend that is expected to continue in the coming years.

PART II

Micro Issues

4 | Topics in Pricing and Execution

Pricing and execution are essential ingredients of every financial product and market. In order to create a viable and enduring market, participants must derive some form of economic benefit, or interest will soon wane. Equally, for a transaction to be of use, it must actually be executed – it is pointless to submit orders that go unfilled or are rerouted so often that the speed advantages of the marketplace are lost. The same applies within the dark pool sector, where it is critical for clients to derive cost savings and venues to generate revenues, and for orders to be filled efficiently.

In this chapter, we will explore several essential topics related to the pricing process, focusing on pricing costs and benefits, price discovery, price derivation, and dark pool pricing impact. This will be followed by some of the execution issues that are specific to the dark sector, including execution rates, fungibility, fragmentation, information leakage, and adverse selection/information asymmetries. We will build on these practical concepts in the next chapter, when we discuss the nature of trading strategies that are routinely used to exploit market opportunities.

Dark Pools and Pricing

Discussion of pricing in dark pools is centered on costs and benefits and the key mechanisms of discovery and derivation. Of course, price discovery is central to activity in the visible markets, so we will use the opportunity to investigate how securities prices might be established for various lit orders. It is then relatively simple to extend the framework to dark trading, and to make specific adjustments to take account of trading that occurs via crossing networks as well as light or dark trading based on orders that are pegged to the NBBO or EBBO.

Pricing costs and benefits

The development of a business model in the trading and execution sector demands a rigorous understanding of costs and benefits affecting all stakeholders. Specifically, it is essential to understand the following:

- The benefits derived by the provider

- The costs borne by the provider
- The benefits derived by the client
- The costs borne by the client

Let us briefly examine these.

The benefits flowing to the provider of execution services (e.g., an MTF, ATS, exchange) relate to the specific business model employed: classic or rebate and, in some cases, a combination of the two (depending on the client base and flow).[1] Under the classic structure, a venue charges a small fee on every trade that is executed through its engine, regardless of whether the client is posting or taking liquidity. Certain ancillary fees might also be charged for access/connection and other services; these, however, are typically one-time or annual fees. Under the rebate structure, a venue that is building liquidity will pay rebates for those posting trades (as noted immediately below) but will generally charge more for those taking liquidity. For example, a venue might pay 0.20 bps per trade for adding liquidity (in the form of a rebate) and charge 0.30 bps per trade for removing liquidity (in the form of a fee), earning a net fee margin of 0.10 bps per trade. Interestingly, in some cases a venue will invert the pricing scheme for a period, in order to "buy" a critical mass of liquidity so that it can cross more trades. Thus, in our example, the venue might rebate 0.30bps for adding liquidity and charge 0.20bps for taking liquidity, creating a negative margin of 0.10bps on each trade. This model is not, of course, sustainable in the medium term, and must be seen only as a short-term mechanism for gaining market share.

The high volume/low margin paradigm underpins both the classic and rebate revenue models. Low margins are, of course, due to decimalization and competition. Sensitivity to volume is thus a critical input into the pricing models of providers, as an insufficient amount of crossing will ultimately create revenue shortfalls and an unsustainable business venture. Partnership arrangements that help boost volume can create additional revenues and protect against slow market cycles. Similarly, models that welcome algorithmic flow can increase flows, crosses and, ultimately, revenues. Naturally, each of these arrangements can affect pool toxicity, as noted in the previous chapter.

The costs borne by the provider are rather more difficult to analyze, as each provider tends to feature a cost structure with a significant fixed component and a smaller, though still important, variable component. The development of the platform that a provider uses to deliver execution services (e.g., servers, engines, application interfaces) is based, for the most part, on a significant technology investment (along with periodic upgrades), which is depreciated over time. Recouping this investment is a theoretical exercise of costing some fractional amount against every transaction executed, based on both projections and competitive realities. A provider's variable costs relate to the amount it must pay in rebates to attract liquidity, as noted above (to the extent it follows the rebate model). In addition, technical and support resources needed to handle increasing levels of volume are also a factor – as the number of clients and trades executed increases, variable costs rise by some proportion. Accordingly, every provider must determine the fixed/variable cost per share of execution and ensure that this remains below the revenues being generated.

The benefits accorded to the client come primarily in the form of cost savings from reduced market impact, as well as any rebates earned from posting liquidity (assuming the venue follows the rebate model). The elasticity of the market impact variable has a direct influence on the viability of the business model: a client must still be able to benefit from price improvements created through reduced market impact or else it will seek execution in some alternative venue, whether dark or light. Though buy-side clients are meant to receive best execution, they can be assured of this only by understanding in some detail whether one venue, mechanism, or solution is performing better than another. For instance, a given trading strategy may, under certain circumstances, face more price slippage through a liquidity aggregation algorithm than by tapping directly into a crossing network (particularly if time to fill is extended). Similarly, there may be instances where a periodic cross in a stock yields a better fill than one with a continuous cross, and so on. In addition, those using particular kinds of algorithms, such as volume weighted average price, need to understand how their fills performed compared with the market. To address this need, various vendors have developed transaction cost analysis (sometimes known as transaction cost research) modules that can help trace execution performance and true benefits (as well as costs, described below) obtained from executing through any single provider or solution. Portions of the process are based on time stamps and associated price points that arise during the lifecycle of a trade; these time stamps and price points can be decomposed to reveal patterns about the execution. The more sophisticated modules also consider market events that may appear during the course of execution, over which the venue or mechanism has no particular control.

From a cost perspective, the client must clearly bear friction costs in the form of fees for executing a trade through a classic model or taking liquidity from the liquidity supplier in the rebate model, plus commissions or spreads from executing trades through a broker or sales desk (this creates the revenue stream for providers, as described above). A client dealing through an ECN or crossing network may also pay a one-time or annual access fee. Of course, these costs have declined markedly in recent years with the introduction of competition from different venues. Those executing via DMA or an ECN or crossing network directly, rather than through a broker or sales desk, face even lower costs, which generally center only on fees for taking liquidity. In fact, there is evidence from various studies to suggest that executing via a dark pool reduces costs compared with other alternatives – a point which is true for both continuous and periodic crosses. A rigorous analysis must be undertaken by every institutional trader/investor, and the same transaction cost analysis services noted immediately above can be used for this purpose.

Putting these costs and benefits together for both providers and clients yields a theoretical pricing grid which permits execution to be offered and used in the dark liquidity space. In fact, studies of costs of dealing through various types of venues illustrate that crossing a trade on a confidential basis (periodic or continuous, or through a dark algorithm) creates real economic benefits for both providers and clients.[2] Furthermore, certain studies also show that direct execution via a call crossing network can be more favorable (and lead to fewer performance outliers) than a continuous cross venue, reinforcing the point that the massing of liquidity at a single point in time can yield the best economic benefits. Naturally, providers themselves need to see sufficient benefits in order to support their business models, which means a critical, and sustainable, mass of market share. One research study has indicated that the annual breakeven revenues needed to support an MTF ranges from €10 million to €20 million. Based on estimates of costs and revenues, this translates into a market share of approximately 5%, a feat which only a few MTFs have achieved, or are close to achieving, at the start of the second decade of the millennium (e.g., BATS Chi-X Europe).[3] Inability to gain sufficient market share to support the cost/revenue model should lead to further consolidation. It is, of course, important to note that primary exchanges, which have lost market share to the dark competitors, still command the lion's share of their "home markets" and therefore have much greater ability to set their pricing grids as they want. Their need to "buy" market share from upstarts is not particularly great, meaning their need to rebate liquidity posters is not essential; in some cases they may choose not to rebate at all.[4]

Price discovery

An exchange, in bringing together buyers and sellers, serves as a forum for price discovery, helping establish market clearing prices in securities. Transparency and fairness are essential elements of such a framework, as buyers and sellers must be confident they are being treated appropriately.[5] Other venues, such as ELOBs, can also fill a similar role.

Order books, which may be maintained by exchanges and ECNs/ELOBs, are the repositories for all open orders awaiting execution. Market orders can generally be filled instantly upon entering a market (unless the stock or security is particularly illiquid or the order book is heavily misbalanced), meaning that order books are generally comprised primarily of various kinds of limit orders, and perhaps some amount of market stop orders and market-if-touched orders. Knowledge of what resides in an order book is, of course, of great benefit to professional traders and institutional investors. By discerning the depth and pattern of bids and offers, an astute trader is in a better position to execute a buy or sell at a better price. Some order-driven markets feature only the best bid and best offer; as noted earlier, this is known as the "top of book." Others show multiple prices in an open limit order book (LOB) in a structure known as "market by price"; in fact, the depth of the market in a security is easily detectable in this structure. For instance, in Figure 4.1(a) and (b) we see an example of a deep market in Stock XYZ and a thin market in Stock ABC.

Order-driven markets use rules-based order matching systems to match buy and sell orders; some systems accept only limit orders, others accept limit orders as well as market orders (which can be viewed as very aggressively priced limit orders), along with stops and market-if-touched orders. In either case, the primary priority (or precedence) is price, where the best bid and the best offer dominate. Traders cannot execute at inferior prices in the public markets – that is, they cannot bid below the best bid or offer above the best offer and expect to be filled. Second priority is given to time. For any two orders with equal price, the one submitted first will receive the first matching priority. Of course, those who want to "jump higher" in the priority queue can do so by improving their price. Since the introduction of decimalization in many markets, the time factor is more easily overcome, as price improvement of 1 penny can change the ordering of the queue; prior to decimalization, price improvement of a single tick had a greater impact (e.g., in the U.S. it was 6.25 cents). As a result of this hierarchy the best prices are bid and offered at any point in time (e.g., NBBO, EBBO). Other priority rules, such as visibility and volume, may also exist though these will always rank behind price and time. A market may also feature public order precedence. This rule indicates that a member of an exchange, a specialist, or some other "privileged" party cannot trade ahead of a public order at the same price; this ensures that no inside party takes advantage of its position to front run or otherwise prejudice public orders.

As we have indicated, price discovery remains the domain of registered exchanges, which are responsible for pooling and matching orders with attendant pre- and post-trade transparency in order to establish prices. Pre-trade transparency, the visible aspect of the market, is essential to the process: investors on both sides of a stock (or any other security) can see a range of bids and offers and attendant market depth through the mechanisms supplied by exchanges. Of course, to make this a credible process pre-trade transparency depends on volume and market share. If there is insufficiency of either, then the robustness and, ultimately, dependability of the prices supplied via the exchange have to be questioned. This, of course, is a key issue as exchanges lose more of their visible liquidity to alternate venues and the dark markets. For instance, while migration from light to dark has been steadily increasing in the U.S., the lit markets still command about 60 to 70% of the market, depending on day, stock, and market – more than enough to create robust pricing references. The critical issue centers on the credibility of the lit price when exchanges have 50%, 40%, or 30% of the market volume, with dark markets commanding the balance. At that point we might argue that the price discovery mechanism supplied by exchanges is no longer credible. Whilst we are not yet at that point, the trends appear to be pointing in that direction – meaning that a new discovery mechanism will have to be considered.

* * *

Pools in Practice: Creating a synthetic NBBO

We have noted that in the U.S. market the public exchanges are responsible for establishing the National Best Bid-Offer, the protected inside spread on which virtually all trades are executed. In practice, the NBBO for a stock is created as a composite of top of book prices from all participating marketplaces, which send them to a consolidator known as a securities information processor (or SIP); the SIP computes the NBBO and then transmits it to vendors, who further disseminate to broker-dealers, traders, and others who are interested in paying for this direct feed. Whilst this sounds like a time-consuming process, computing and telecommunications power mean that the NBBO is computed and disseminated in a matter of milliseconds – effectively "real time" to the average trader or investor. For high frequency and low latency traders (which we consider in a separate section), this isn't quite fast enough. By at least one estimate the NBBO feeds from exchanges to consolidators are between 10 and 15 milliseconds slower than direct feeds. Capitalizing on the slight time lag can lead to potential profits.

Not surprisingly, this has led some ventures to develop the equivalent of a synthetic NBBO. Rather than taking the data from the vendor, these ventures take the raw top of book data directly from the marketplaces and perform the consolidation directly, computing a low latency synthetic NBBO in just over 1 microsecond – making it several milliseconds faster than data obtained via the SIP. For low latency trading firms interested in every time advantage to generate revenues, paying for access to the synthetic NBBO through the development of architecture that captures direct feeds or by contracting with one of the third party solution providers can be a justifiable investment. Ventures can thus successfully capitalize on the difference between the synthetic NBBO and the NBBO that is available in a given dark pool to make steady profits.

*   *   *

Let us consider how liquidity is formed and executed on an exchange or ELOB. We may think of this as a multistep process.

- Step 1: Orders entering the venue are ranked using established order precedence rules.
- Step 2: The matching engine determines which orders can be matched and traded.
- Step 3: The trades are priced using applicable trade pricing rules.

In step 1, the venue applies its order precedence rules to rank buy and sell orders in a hierarchy reflecting increasing precedence, and then matches those orders with the highest precedence first. Since price is the first priority, the top of the queue is populated with the highest bids and lowest offers. After this, the venue reverts to its secondary precedence rules, which may include time (i.e., first order submitted is superior to every subsequent order), display status (i.e., visible is superior to dark), and size (varies, with some venues favoring small lots over large lots, and vice versa).

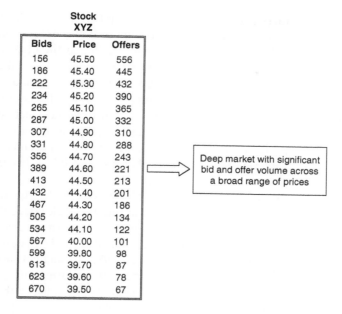

Figure 4.1(a) Limit order book: Stock XYZ

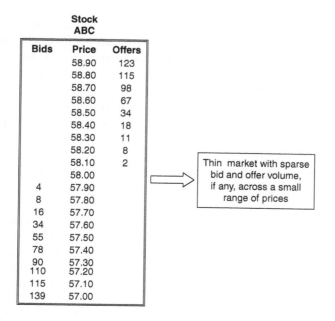

Figure 4.1(b) Limit order book: Stock ABC

In step 2, all the orders that have been ranked in step 1 are matched. The matching may occur through a market call at a specific point or it may occur continuously, depending again on the construct of the venue. Starting at the highest ranking order, the venue will match a buy and a sell. If these are of the same size, they will fill completely. For those of unequal size (which is a much more common occurrence), a venue will typically fill the smaller order completely against a larger order on the opposite side, and then fill the rest of the larger order with the next highest ranking order on the opposite side. This process continues through the order queue, until the ranking gets to the level where bid and offer are identical – the order will clear, but the one below that level will not, since the buyer's bid will be below the seller's offer.

Step 3 involves assigning prices to orders that can trade. Again, various mechanisms are available but two common ones include the single price auction with a uniform pricing rule, and the continuous two-sided auction with a discriminatory pricing rule;[6] we save for the next section a discussion of the derivative pricing rules applicable in certain nondisplayed liquidity venues like crossing networks. In the single price auction, all trades occur at the same market clearing price – in other words, the point where supply is equal to demand. At prices below the clearing price, excess demand will necessarily exist; at prices above the clearing price, excess supply will arise. As we might expect, when excess demand exists, all sellers have their orders filled, and when excess supply exists, all buyers have their orders filled. Figure 4.2 highlights these conditions.

Let us consider a simple example of the single price auction where nine different investors submit a combination of bids and offers in Stock ABC; eight of these orders are limit orders, while one is a market order (note that these could be either light or dark orders, or a combination of the two). Based on a single price auction with price precedence, we know that the market order will fill first against the relevant best bid/offer, after which the remainder of the limit orders will fill in terms of priority. Table 4.1 summarizes the state of the ABC order book prior to the market call and auction.

Based on the book's precedence, the order book will match in the sequence noted in Table 4.2, beginning with the market order submitted by Investor I, where 100 of the 400 shares to buy are filled at the best selling price of $29.80. The remaining 300 shares then match against a portion of Investor B's next best offer price at $30.00. From that point on the limit orders take over, and are filled using the same logic.

It is worth noting that no trades can occur following the partial fill for G, as the remaining buyers are unwilling to pay what the sellers demand. At the conclusion of the auction, the order book resembles the one noted in Table 4.3; the best bid in the book at this point is $30.00 and the best offer is at $30.10, so no further movement will occur until new orders enter the book.

In contrast to the single price characteristics described above, a continuous-order market uses discriminatory pricing via an order book to fill open orders. If a new

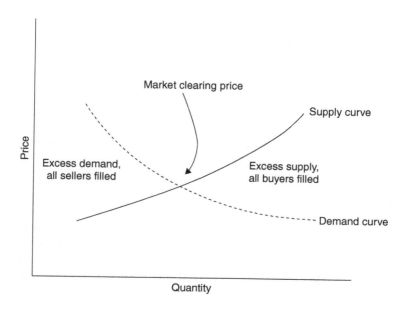

Figure 4.2 Supply, demand, and market clearing price

Table 4.1 Stock ABC order book, pre-call

Investor	Offer	Price	Bid	Investor
A	100	29.80	700	E
B	600	30.00		
		30.00	200	F
		30.00	300	G
C	200	30.10	200	H
D	500	30.20		
		Market	400	I

Table 4.2 Stock ABC order matching

Investor	Offer	Price	Matches	Investor	Bid	Price	Result
A	100	29.80		I	400	Market	A is filled, I is partly filled
B	300	30.00		I	300	Market	I is filled, B is partly filled
B	300	30.10		H	200	30.10	H is filled, B is partly filled
B	100	30.00		G	300	30.00	B is filled, G is partly filled

Table 4.3 Stock ABC order book, post-call

Investor	Offer	Price	Bid	Investor
		29.80	700	E
		30.00		
		30.00	200	F
		30.00	200	G
C	200	30.10		
D	500	30.20		

order enters the market, the matching engine tries to arrange an immediate match against its book: market orders and very aggressive limit orders are considered marketable and may be executed immediately, while nonmarketable orders are placed into the order book to wait for a match (unless the order is specified as IOC or FOK). The matching engine arranges a trade for marketable orders by matching a new order with the highest ranking order on the opposite side of the order book; if it is not totally filled, the balance is matched with the next highest ranking order, and so forth. Through discriminatory pricing, the limit price of an open order determines the price of each trade.[7]

Let us extend the example above to reflect the discriminatory pricing framework, making some assumptions about the sequence of orders entering the market in order to establish time priority (e.g., G submits first, then C, F, A, D, and so forth). These are summarized in Table 4.4.

The result of the continuous crossing is a series of fills and a book that ends with 700 bids at $29.80 and 300 offers at $30.20; no further trades can be matched.

Under both pricing schemes, the limit price of an order determines priority, and thus probability, of execution. But under discriminatory pricing the limit price determines the trade price, whereas with a uniform price the limit price does not usually determine the trade price – unless the orders are particularly large in relation to the book or market. In fact, large traders can always circumvent uniform price rules by slicing their orders up into smaller size, thus obtaining de facto discriminatory pricing. Ultimately, the single price auction produces the maximum gains from trading, but the continuous two-sided auction allows trading to occur at will, and permits trading of a larger flow of orders because it is not limited to trading at a single price. In either case it is relatively easy to see that the interaction of different types of orders at different prices leads to price discovery. We can also consider that although these examples are based on visible orders, the injection of dark orders into an exchange or ELOB will also contribute to price discovery. Indeed, the simple example above could easily be completely dark, such as a series of hidden or reserve orders. Only when dark orders are matched in a crossing network with reference to a base price does price discovery cease, as examined in the following section.

Table 4.4 Stock ABC, continuous-order market

Investor	Order	Type	Price	Result
G	Bid	300	30.00	No fill
C	Offer	200	30.10	No fill
F	Bid	200	30.00	No fill
A	Offer	100	29.80	Fill 100 with G at 30.00
D	Offer	500	30.30	No fill
I	Bid	400	Market	Fill 200 with C at 30.10
				Fill 200 with D at 30.20
H	Bid	200	30.10	No fill
B	Offer	600	30.00	Fill 200 with H at 30.00
				Fill 200 with G at 30.00
				Fill 200 with F at 30.00
E	Bid	700	29.80	No fill

Price derivation

While some dark liquidity can exist within exchanges/ELOBs and thus interact with light orders to establish prices, some dark liquidity is involved in a different pricing mechanism. Price discovery ensures that a security's bid or offer is "fair," and various regulations exist to ensure that this remains the case. However, whenever a trade is routed off an exchange, it becomes more difficult, ex-ante, to ensure that this occurs. The very lack of transparency that characterizes the sector and the delay in printing to the public data feeds adds to the challenges in pricing; in general, dark pools prefer not to print executed trades to public data feeds unless they are required to (and if the requirement is firm, they tend to delay as long as possible). Importantly, as more trading moves off exchange, the public price may reflect less accurately the true supply and demand dynamics of a security, calling into question the concept of a "fair price." In fact, this is a very critical issue – if the market evolves to the point where exchanges lose increasing amounts of market share to crossing networks, for example, then the displayed prices may not be sufficiently accurate to provide buyers and sellers with an accurate gauge of value. Similarly, if large order imbalances appear in a primary market, price instabilities can arise in the base reference, which can also impact executions on crossing networks.[8]

Nondisplayed liquidity matched through crossing networks does not contribute to price discovery; the same is true for other orders that are willingly executed against a base reference price – regardless of venue. A dark pool referencing a base price provides volume for execution (which is not shown to the public), but it does not participate in establishing prices or attempt to directly influence the market-quoted price. In the U.S., venues that offer dark liquidity generally execute against the midprice of the quoted market inside spread, or permit some amount of price negotiation between buyer and seller within the market's inside spread. In Europe, dark pools can retain their anonymity by basing their prices on a reliable reference

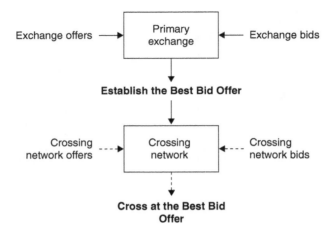

Figure 4.3 Crossing at best bid offer

(e.g., EBBO, which will have established such prices through the mechanisms described above); this exempts them from MiFID's pre-trade data publication rules. These approaches suggest a practice of price derivation, rather than price discovery, as summarized in Figure 4.3.

As noted in Chapter 3, certain crossing networks are structured as call markets, where investors place their buy and sell orders into the platform just before a call, after which the matching engine applies its order precedence rules. Matches that occur at the crossing price lead to a fill and a trade; those that do not remain in the crossing network's book are cancelled or rerouted. Other networks cross at the open, at the close, multiple times per day,[9] or continuously, but the principles they follow are the same, and they are always "users," of prices established elsewhere.

Let us consider the case of the crossing network as an order-driven market that matches trades based on prices that are determined on a primary exchange. Since the crossing network is not an auction mechanism but is a platform for gathering orders, it obtains crossing prices from the exchange involved in the price discovery process and creates crosses through derivative pricing rules. In short, there is no price discovery through the crossing network. As noted, crosses occur within the bid-offer, and therefore create no market impact. It is worth noting that since these venues do not develop the market clearing prices, there is usually an imbalance between supply and demand. As noted in Chapter 3, most platforms still fill only a portion of the volume that enters their books (e.g., less than 10%, though this depends on each venue) – meaning unfilled orders have to be cancelled, routed, or rested. Despite this relatively low execution rate, the preservation of anonymity, lower commissions, and reduced chance of market impact are, for some, equitable tradeoffs.

Though a crossing network can choose how to allocate buy and sell orders, a pro rata allocation methodology is rather common. Let us consider a simple example. Assume crossing network ABC receives sell orders in Stock TUV totaling 30,000 shares and buy orders totaling 150,000 and the platform derives a price of $10 from the midpoint of the base bid-offer established on an exchange. Since the buy orders outweigh the sell orders by 5:1, the sell orders will be completely filled while the buy orders will be allocated on a pro rata basis, where each buyer submitting an order will get a 20% allocation. The unallocated buy orders will then be held back for another matching cycle, rerouted to another venue to seek a further fill, or cancelled (depending on the specific instructions each investor has submitted). Importantly, the crossing network will not display any order imbalances after the call, helping ensure anonymity.

*   *   *

Pools in Practice: The robustness of the best bid-offer

Various European MTFs are structured as midpoint matching pools, using the midpoint of the primary exchange price as the external price reference (similar to U.S. practice, where a dark trading mechanism can use the mid of the NBBO). Under this construct, buyers and sellers submit limit orders with minimum execution size, either with IOC instructions or resting/day time limitations. The venue then matches the orders it can immediately with a price set using the external reference, i.e., EBBO. This yields advantages on the aggressive side, e.g., matching at the midpoint saves half the spread plus reduces market impact; the disadvantage is, of course, execution uncertainty. On the passive side advantages center on opacity – any resting orders can be discovered only through repeated pinging, and a given venue may have protections against such activities. The disadvantage, apart from execution uncertainty already noted, is that instead of getting full price improvement on the lit bid-offer, the passive side captures only half the spread.

A key issue under this mechanism is whether the mid of the EBBO is a fair representation of the current market price. More specifically, if the lit book is deep (e.g., tens of thousands of shares for top of book), then the spread is likely to be tight and the price stable – meaning it can be used as a dark price reference with a high degree of confidence. However, if the order book is thinly traded, or if prices are moving around very rapidly, the robustness of the price is rather more questionable; each incremental trade will lead to a quick widening of the spread (before it reverts). Research indicates that less liquid stocks do, indeed, tend to have less stable mid-prices. Under this scenario it is possible for algorithms to "game" the primary exchange price, locking in a small profit. By analyzing a stock's trading pattern ex-ante it is possible to detect instances where the EBBO may be a questionable representation of current market value. For instance, when overall volumes related to the BBO are low, the top of book looks thin and skewed, the next bid-offer prices are significantly worse than the previous ones and/or when the mid-price at any instant can trade outside the spread, then the primary exchange price must be seen as a weak pricing reference, open to at least some degree of arbitrage. If the primary exchange cannot offer a robust pricing reference, alternatives may exist. For example, it is possible that a large MTF that also operates a lit book will see enough volume to provide a reasonable pricing proxy to the primary exchange. Or, perhaps a series of MTFs with lit books can collectively serve as the source of price data that is averaged to become the base reference price. Regardless of the approach, it is important to remember that a fair reference price in a dark pool must be one where an aggressive order to any lit market cannot be executed at a better price.

*   *   *

Dark pool price impact

We know that execution prices in crossing networks come from a base price reference, which means that price derivation, rather than price discovery, is the central driver.[10] It also means that not all dark liquidity is the same from a pricing perspective. Interestingly, there is at least some belief by those operating in a dark pool that execution can have no price impact – certainly in comparison to trades executed in visible pools. In fact, this is not entirely correct. For instance, while those executing trades via a crossing network might not be able to directly influence prices, those using icebergs and hidden orders on exchanges or ECNs can – such orders interact with visible flows, which means that they can, indeed, affect prices. Let us consider a simple example where Stock XYZ is bid at $10.00 and offered at $10.10, with a hidden bid at $10.05. If a seller enters a market order of $10.00 it will be executed at $10.05 with the best bid remaining at $10.00. But if the hidden bid of $10.05 had not been there the best bid would have been at or below $10.00, indicating that the hidden bid has actually supported the market. In contrast, if the hidden bid in Stock XYZ at $10.05 had been in a crossing network rather than on an exchange, it would not have provided support and the best new bid would have been $10.00 or less. In this example, the use of the hidden order to park a large bid means the price will not fall for buy orders, demonstrating that some dark pool orders can affect price.

The fundamental mechanisms of price discovery and price derivation are central to the efficacy of trading in the light and dark markets. The two are at once interrelated and mutually reinforcing and clearly help define the nature of activity in the electronic trading sector.

*   *   *

Pools in Practice: Touch price crossing

Structural changes have appeared within the European sector that have given rise to new dark orders based on touch prices. While the first generation of MTFs allowed under MiFID matched trades at or within the mid of the EBBO (obtained from the lit market), more recently some MTFs (e.g., those run by Goldman, UBS, Instinet) have offered matches at the EBBO touch price (e.g., "at best"). This means aggressive orders cross at the touch price that would be obtained by sending the order to the lit market at that moment. For passive buys and sells this obviates the need to split the spread with the aggressive cross order; the benefits for the aggressive orders center on execution costs and potential price/size improvement.

Let's consider a simple example, where an aggressive buy can be matched against a resting sell at the lit offer (i.e., the "at best" touch price). The benefit for the passive sell in this case is capturing the whole spread as compensation for providing liquidity, which is clearly a compelling proposition. The benefit for the aggressive buy is somewhat less obvious – not trying to cross at the mid means leaving money on the table. Consider that if the mid-price has been attempted but liquidity isn't fully available to fill the order and there is no resting sell in the pool at mid, then an order can be sent to the lit market or to a pool with a bid-offer touch price. If the order is sent to the lit market a cross will occur at the displayed price, as per usual. If it is sent as a dark touch order it will cross at the same price (though the necessary liquidity may or may not exist at that precise moment). However, the touch order benefits from anonymity and lower execution cost. In addition, it may benefit from price/size improvement over the lit market, as the lit market will start "walking the book" as liquidity dries up. While touch price execution is used only for certain situations, it provides the marketplace with yet another dark execution choice.

*   *   *

Dark Pool Execution

Executing trades in a dark pool goes beyond simple pricing matters. Investors and traders considering their options in the dark space need also to consider a number of issues related to execution rates, fungibility, fragmentation, information leakage, and adverse selection/information asymmetries. Before considering these execution issues, let us recall that a trade can be executed only in the dark after it has been placed into a venue in some form. From the perspective of the trader, this can occur in one of several ways, some of which we will expand on in our discussion of order routing in Chapter 6:

- Direct routing to a crossing network
- Direct routing to an exchange or ELOB with an order delimited as reserved or hidden

- Automatic routing to a crossing network through a smart order router or algorithm
- Automatic routing to an exchange or ELOB with an order delimited as reserved or hidden through a smart order router or algorithm

Additional choices may apply in a European context, where LIS rules must be considered:

- Automatic routing to an MTF dark book if the notional value is less than the LIS, or else routing to an MTF's integrated light/dark book with an order delimited as hidden if the notional value is greater than the LIS

We can also view this from the perspective of the venue. Consider, for instance, that a crossing network or ELOB can receive an order via:

- Direct market access
- Broker routing
- Algorithmic routing
- Client routing through a FIX-enabled order management system
- Dark liquidity partner routing

Similar constructs would apply to other ATSs and MTFs, and even to the dark books of exchanges. Multiple routing avenues into a crossing network are summarized in Figure 4.4.

Once an order is within a dark venue or mechanism, it stands ready for execution.

Execution rates

Execution is at the heart of any dark pool and is perhaps the key determinant in the success or failure of any single business model. Execution rates, which can be defined as the number of shares entering into a venue that result in a match, are important, if sometimes opaque, benchmarks for measuring the success of a particular venue, and appear to be self-fulfilling: better execution rates attract more liquidity, lead-

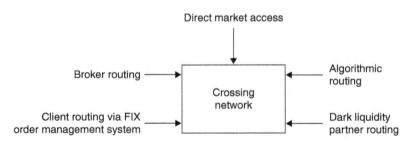

Figure 4.4 Order entry into a crossing network

ing to increased possibilities of matching and execution, which in turn expands market share and attracts more liquidity, and so forth. The reverse is, of course, also true – those unable to execute a minimum amount on a consistent basis will soon be removed from smart order routers and routing algorithms, leading to even less flow and lower execution rates, and so forth. Any venue that can legitimately boast an execution rate that is higher than that of its peers creates a compelling, and perhaps self-fulfilling, marketing pitch.

The pursuit of execution rates cannot be done at any cost, of course, as simply buying market share (through inverted pricing, for example) is not sustainable over the medium term. More viable, perhaps, is to craft an efficient and secure platform that minimizes gaming and limits information leakage. Developing partnership agreements with other pools can also help, though this cannot be done indiscriminately. In fact, a preferred method of boosting execution rates involves aligning orders by keeping them within the pool for a longer period so that there is a better likelihood of capturing the contra-trades as they pass through. Nevertheless, a longer "holding" period does not guarantee a fill, and can even create exposure to gaming, a topic that we will consider in Chapter 5.

The fact that execution rates may be low must be recognized ex-ante by clients or potential clients. Indeed, this should factor into any trading strategy so that there is clarity on what should be done if an order cannot be filled immediately, or after some acceptable resting period. It is incumbent upon traders and investors to also determine where the best fills can occur, so that appropriate routing can be determined before order entry; this brings us to the topic of reporting and transparency, which we will consider in Chapter 7.

Fungibility

One of the most important considerations in any discussion of dark pools relates to the fungibility of execution. It is quite evident in most asset classes, and certainly in the equity asset class, that execution is a standard, commoditized service. A client typically wants efficient and price-competitive fulfillment of an order. This has three implications: the provider of execution services at the lowest cost is likely to emerge as a successful player, the provider of a reliable pool of liquidity will gain some competitive edge, and the provider of differentiated ancillary services may find opportunities to capture additional client flow. Each one of these factors has the potential of increasing execution rates.

The first point suggests a move toward greater consolidation in the sector, among and within different segments of the market – ELOBs, crossing networks, and conventional exchanges. We know that ELOBs and crossing networks with greater volume (dark or light) have a greater competitive advantage as they can match and cross more trades. The consequence of consolidating such efforts supports the idea of economies of scale, moving into a thin margin, high-volume business model.

In fact, this consolidation process has commenced and is expected to continue, leading to further mergers and acquisitions, and the creation of greater economies of scale. In the second instance, more venues are creating additional partnership agreements or employing aggregation techniques to capture a greater share of liquidity, and to maintain some base level that permits steady execution. In the third instance, some platforms are able to provide premium services to their clients, adding to their revenue bases, and perhaps helping to subsidize pure execution services. Such premium services may relate to access to order interfaces, a broad range of algorithms, analytics, reporting, and so forth. Without advantages related to costs, base liquidity, and service differentiation, execution must be regarded as quite fungible.

Fragmentation

We may define fragmentation as the splitting or atomizing of a market into a number of separate submarkets. Each submarket possesses its own liquidity supply and demand forces which interact to fill orders to the greatest extent possible; if matches cannot be made, outstanding orders are cancelled or remain in situ, unless the submarket is in some way connected externally (e.g., through routing or pool partnership agreements). Fragmentation arises for a number of reasons, including client needs, competitive profit opportunities, and regulatory encouragement. In practice, it is now quite common for a security to trade in various submarkets simultaneously. Consider an example of a hypothetical security, such as large capitalization Stock XYZ. It might trade on a primary exchange (generally the original listing market), through one or more regional exchanges, through the third market, via the upstairs markets and internal broker/dealers desks, and via several ELOBs and crossing networks. It is not difficult to imagine, under this scenario, that liquidity forms in each of these venues. If communication and routing are not part of the process or operate inadequately, then each pool will trade according to its own supply and demand dynamics, leading to supply/demand imbalances and execution prices (either discovered or derived) and speeds that may be suboptimal. We noted in Chapter 1, for instance, the fragmentation that has occurred with stocks listed on primary exchanges. No longer are the NYSE, NASDAQ, LSE, Deutsche Boerse, and others the sole, or sometimes even majority, trading locale for their "home stocks" – activity has been dispersed, in some cases widely, across other venues.

A market might become fragmented in order to serve different client needs. Not every client requires or wants the same suite of services when it comes to market activities. For instance, the needs of a retail client are different from those of an institutional client, just as the needs of an active day trader are different from those of a passive, domestic long-term investor or an international block trader. Some clients want speed of execution/immediacy, some seek best price, some want large block anonymity, and so forth. Some venues can try to cater to all of these needs through a single business platform/model. In practice, however, this can prove difficult, and creates opportunities for individual ventures to provide a more focused client service – leading, invariably, to some degree of fragmentation.

Competitive profit opportunities also appear in the mix. If a bank, exchange, or private company believes that there is an opportunity to generate revenues by providing the kind of market execution service a sector of the client base desires, then of course this can be powerful motivation to introduce a "new platform." The advent of cheaper technologies has lowered the barriers to entry, so that it is entirely reasonable to suppose a sponsoring firm can enter the marketplace without having to commit an enormous amount of capital resources. Of course, whether such a platform can have enduring success is a separate matter, dependent in large part on its ability to gather and maintain a minimum amount of liquidity. Each separate profit-driven model, which may ultimately be populated by several venues, will necessarily generate fragmentation.

We can also point to regulatory measures as an important influence. In fact, regulations supporting the development of new trading venues have sanctioned the creation or expansion of new pockets of executable liquidity. Frameworks such as Regulations ATS and NMS, and MiFID, make allowances for the creation of alternative venues to trade securities. While they set forth the relevant "rules of the game" as part of the process, the very fact that they legitimize the establishment of alternative trading venues encourages banks, exchanges, venture capitalists, private firms, and others to do just that – leading to separate pools.

Measuring fragmentation is not straightforward, and depends on the availability and synchronicity of data and consistency of definitions; determining fragmentation among dark pools is even more complex given the sometimes total paucity of data and the need to make reasoned analytical estimates.

One interesting metric, developed by analytics/technology firm Fidessa for the global equity markets, is the Fidessa Fragmentation Index (FFI), which measures the degree to which trading is occurring in multiple locations (e.g., home exchange versus alternate lit and dark venues). The actual computation of the FFI is simply the inverse of the sum of the squares of market shares of each trading venue, and yields a coefficient that indicates how much fragmentation is occurring within stocks and across entire markets. Thus, an FFI coefficient equal to 1 means that all trading occurs within a single venue, typically the primary exchange; an FFI between 1 and 2 means increasing fragmentation, and an FFI greater than 2 means that trading no longer "belongs" to any single venue. An examination of FFI data at various points in 2013 and 2014 indicates that the most heavily fragmented markets (at or above 4.0) include the U.S. Dow Jones Industrials, S&P 500, and NASDAQ 100. Those with a very significant degree of fragmentation (at or above 2.0) include S&P Toronto TSX 60 and many of the large European indexes such as the UK FTSE 100, Oslo OBX, Belgian Bel 20, Dutch AEX, German DAX, and Swiss SMI. The least fragmented markets (close to 1.0) include Japan and Australia, where the two national exchanges still dominate the landscape.

On the positive side, fragmentation provides for competition. Trading venues are competing for order flow and this intermarket competition can, at least theoretically, lead to narrower spreads. In fact, the development of multiple venues for trading execution forces providers to supply the best possible service at the lowest costs – and, in a marketplace characterized by margin compression, the need to "keep the pencil sharp" on friction costs becomes paramount. Clients can benefit directly from this competitive fragmentation as far as friction costs are concerned. Another positive factor is that clients can deal more closely with pools that match their own characteristics, aims, and profiles. This, as noted in Chapter 3, can help ensure a positive experience and reduce the chances of adverse selection.

On the negative side, fragmentation has the potential of atomizing pools of tradable volume so much that execution becomes suboptimal – that is, trades miss the best possible fill in the market as a result of interaction with, or routing to, the wrong pool of dark liquidity. Indeed, it is possible given the number of light and dark venues where trading can theoretically take place that a trader/investor can miss entire pools of liquidity if not armed with the right tools.

Whether fragmentation actually leads to a reduction in liquidity is still the subject of analysis and debate. A single pool of liquidity can lead to better execution (e.g., a tighter inside spread) if it is very large. As the pool shrinks in size, the inside spread widens, leading to poorer execution. To some degree the issue is unresolved, and may ultimately depend on the architecture of the dark mechanisms: those that are very isolated and capture only a small picture of the available dark liquidity in the market (as a result of poor ties into other pools or other technological limitations) may indeed suffer from bad execution; those that are well connected, and equipped with the proper pool partnerships, algorithmic connections, and/or smart order routing, expand their horizons in a virtual sense allowing access to a broad, if conceptually fragmented, pool of liquidity.

In addition, we have to consider the nature of the venue that is filling bids and offers: those that are involved in price discovery (e.g., an exchange, ELOB) are different from those that are price derivers (e.g., a crossing network). Knowing this, we must then ask whether a crossing network that fills orders based on a price taken from an exchange is really atomizing liquidity – in some sense, it can be viewed as an extension of an exchange, filling orders at a price determined by the exchange/ELOB. However, in the most extreme case, if a crossing network draws so much liquidity away from the exchange creating the base reference price, then the base price will be rather questionable: price discovery in a thinly traded market is unreliable. Accordingly, the influence of the crossing network on prices may indeed be meaningful. That said, the argument is still theoretical, as no crossing network commands such a large share of off-exchange trading volume in major securities that it can have an indirect effect on pricing. The same is not the case, of course, for an ELOB, which is involved in the price discovery process, and for which the flow of liquidity is a determinant in the prices that it will post.[11]

It appears virtually certain that fragmentation and shrinking trade size will continue, at least until further sector consolidation takes place. Even in advance of any such consolidation, however, fragmentation can be "bridged" in a number of ways. For instance, traders and investors can adjust their orders (price, quantity, execution type) to reflect information gained from other traded markets and they can actively route or reroute their orders to those submarkets where they believe they will get best execution (however they define best execution). Submarkets can create arrangements or partnerships among themselves to share or pass liquidity that meets specific criteria. Algorithms and aggregators can be more broadly used by a larger number of investors to link disparate submarkets. And arbitrageurs can direct their own liquidity to submarkets where temporary profit opportunities arise, in order to bring them back in line. The combination of such forces may make it possible for fragmented markets to coexist, while still providing traders and investors with a sufficiency of liquidity.

Information leakage

A client submitting an order ideally wants to direct it to a single venue and have it crossed in its entirety, against contra-liquidity entering the pool; this eliminates any chance of information leakage. Block trades, as noted, are at the center of this issue. They are the subject of market scrutiny, as large blocks can move market prices. Although a block can, in some cases, be crossed in a dark block network, sufficient liquidity may not be available. This means that the order must be rested until contra-liquidity enters the venue, or a more dynamic process must be employed (such as breaking up the order into smaller pieces to find available liquidity). As already noted, any such fills will occur at "decreasingly beneficial" levels – the first fill is done at the best price, and each subsequent fill deteriorates from that point on as liquidity is exhausted. However, the expectation is that the average of the fills is still more favorable than the single large block fill with its market impact. Information leakage is more likely to occur in a setting where one or more participants stand to benefit at the expense of other participants; for example, day traders or quantitative funds may have ways of interpreting information embedded in a given pool populated by trades from passive funds. Understanding the profile of a given pool is essential before routing and execution, as noted in Chapter 3.

Consider, for instance, the potential paths of a block trade submitted into an antigaming crossing network:

- Immediate execution of the entire order size
- Partial execution, with any unfilled portion cancelled
- Partial execution, with any unfilled portion exposed to continuous flow as it enters the crossing network (i.e., resting)

Under this framework the unfilled portion is not routed to any other pool. Since the unfilled portion does not travel and cannot be "pinged," it is safe from information leakage. If this is true, then we would expect no attendant rise in execution costs.

The next issue to consider is the cost impact if the trade is routed to multiple pools via algorithms – where the likelihood of at least some information leakage increases. Under this scenario a trade can take one of several paths:

- Partial execution, with any unfilled portion routed to another pool
- Further partial execution, with any unfilled portion exposed to continuous flows as it enters the current pool
- Further partial execution, with any unfilled portion rerouted to yet another pool, and so forth, until completion

It is challenging under this scenario to directly gauge the cost effects of information leakage. We may derive some anecdotal evidence from increasing friction costs as the time to complete an order rises. In fact, some studies show that as execution time increases to several hours (as portions of the order are routed or rerouted until contra-liquidity is found), costs increase as well; this phenomenon appears to hold true across a variety of different venues/mechanisms (e.g., crossing networks, exchange icebergs, and so forth). In essence, friction costs appear to increase as the order is "shopped" by an algorithm to different pools. Whether this is specifically attributable to information leakage is difficult to ascertain, and can be proven definitively only by comparing the friction costs for an equal trade ported into a crossing network that resides there until execution is complete. However, there is a strong indication that this may be occurring.

Adverse selection/information asymmetries

Adverse selection is another impact factor, occurring when execution is conditioned on whether a price moves in the client's favor (e.g., a sell executed if a stock moves up, a buy executed if a stock moves down). Consider, for instance, that a buy order of 10,000 shares and a sell order of 100,000 shares in a dark pool will cause the buy to be executed entirely; the seller can then choose to take the remaining 90,000 shares out of the market and put it in the visible market, pushing the price down – effectively indicating that the buy trade is adversely selected. In fact, this is a real phenomenon that occurs in the traded markets.

Naturally, adverse selection can occur in a pool without any information leakage. When a pool has orders that are skewed, one party will be disadvantaged. However, adverse selection without information leakage is nonsystematic, meaning that at any time it can benefit either the buyer or the seller. However, when information leakage exists, it becomes systematic and can potentially favor one of the two parties (e.g., a proprietary desk receiving indications of interest for a pool may buy or sell based on knowledge of that information). Information asymmetries can, of course, arise as a result of the specific construct of a platform. For instance, when IOIs are sent into advertising/negotiation platforms, or when broker/dealers send IOIs to liquidity pool partners, the recipient of the IOI can choose to act, not act, or reroute, depending on what suits it best – clearly an information asymmetry, which will disadvantage the submitting party. Information asymmetries can also arise in the ping pools described in Chapter 3, as IOCs that enter are made available only to the sponsors, who can chose to accept or reject; an aggregator or router that "mistakenly" sends an IOC into a ping pool can, in fact, expose a client's hand.

* * *

Pools in Practice: Measuring dark market variables

Gauging the success of a dark market strategy and helping design trade routing for future execution requires measurement of some of the key variables that affect dealing, including immediacy, information leakage, and market impact. As we know, immediacy can be defined as the cost of executing a trade at any current moment (such as might be conveyed either through a market order or an IOC or FOK order) and is thus useful in determining whether an execution strategy makes sense in a given dark venue. One commonly used ex-post proxy for immediacy is the differential between the price before, and immediately after, the target trade is done: the wider the differential, the greater the cost of immediacy, and vice-versa. Whilst the measure is ex-post, a sufficient accumulation of data points from a particular venue can lead to analysis regarding its ability to host trades which offer immediacy, a fact which can be incorporated into a routing algorithm or SOR for future trades. Another measure can be found in fill rates. In general, the greater the fill rates in a venue, the greater the immediacy; conversely, we expect that the greater the need for immediacy, the greater the fill rates. An SOR can be designed to accommodate a strategy that balances between fill probability and execution cost: if immediacy is required then the SOR can route to venues that have high fill rates, under the assumption that the venue is attracting enough order flow to generate crosses. Alternatively, if cost of execution is more important than immediacy, the SOR can direct to venues that have lower fill rates; these venues may have a greater amount of passive resting orders.

Information leakage, which indicates the degree to which a large order entering into or resting within a dark venue is known by other parties, is a bit more difficult to discern, but many participants look at volatility of the stock in the aftermath of a large cross. Under this measure, the greater the volatility the greater the likelihood that some amount of information leakage has occurred. If this is a common occurrence within a dark venue, traders or investors that are crossing large blocks may choose to avoid the venue.

Finally we have market impact, which indicates the degree to which a cross (generally a large one) affects the price of a traded security. In this instance the easiest proxy is to look at the price of the security after execution: if it has moved up (for a buy) or down (for a sell) more than average, then the large cross has had an impact.

Measuring these variables is not a precise science, and is decidedly not a real-time exercise. But knowledge of how to gauge these effects can help a trader/investor create a general framework for backtesting, which can help future trading endeavors.

* * *

With some background on pricing and execution issues in hand, we turn our attention, in the next chapter, to the types of trading strategies that are commonly employed in the dark markets.

5 | Trading in Dark Pools

To continue with our micro themes, we turn our attention from pricing and execution to trading. The visible and dark markets must be seen as a compendium of individual, sometimes competing, trading strategies. This means that the performance of any one strategy affects all others – there is a mutual dependency and relationship. Performance of such strategies is also market-dependent: a quiet and thinly traded market may favor certain approaches, while a fast market with heavy volume may favor others. The most sophisticated players use this knowledge to adjust their trading strategies accordingly. They also consider very carefully where strategies can be executed to greatest effect – in the lit markets, the dark markets, or some combination of the two.

In this chapter we consider some of the key trading mechanisms and strategies that are commonly encountered in the dark pool sector. These include block trading, program trading, algorithmic trading (including benchmarking), high frequency trading, and gaming. Of course, not all of these strategies are exclusive or unique to the dark sector. Indeed, some can be executed in the lit markets while others call for interaction with visible liquidity provided through conventional exchanges. Nevertheless, the strategies we consider below constitute the backbone of trading activity in the dark sector. Before discussing specifics, let us review some general points on a trading framework.

The Trading Framework

Investors and dealers trade for different purposes, and over different time horizons, meaning their demand for, or supply of, liquidity can vary greatly. In Chapter 2 we described the nature of market liquidity that is built atop a range of order types and market structures. As we explore some of the commonly used trading techniques of the dark sector, it is worth expanding on some general aspects of trading strategies.

The process of trading typically follows a logical sequence that represents an entire cycle – this is true whether we speak of a single retail trade, a large block trade, a program trade with thousands of individual positions or a high frequency or index arbitrage strategy. The key elements of any trading framework include pre-trade, trade, and post-trade phases:

- Pre-trade

  - Analysis of the trading opportunity
  - Analysis of the opportunity in relation to the current trading portfolio
  - Identification of specific transaction strategies

- Trade

  - Order entry
  - Order routing
  - Order execution

- Post-trade

  - Reporting
  - Clearing and settlement

Let us consider the first three points in this section (i.e., the pre-trade phase), saving a discussion of the latter points for the next chapter.

The first step in any trading strategy involves the analysis of a potential opportunity. Traders use different techniques to detect opportunities, and these are most often related to their own style of trading or investing or the specific mandate they operate under. Fundamental analysis, technical analysis, benchmarking, and so-called black box models (related to index arbitrage, risk arbitrage, pairs trading, volatility dispersion, real-time tick analysis, and so forth) are all examples of techniques that are commonly employed by traders and investors. As we might imagine, these vary in complexity and sophistication, and are supported by electronic tools that can be sourced off-the-shelf or developed through proprietary research. Regardless of the technique, the output of this process is the identification of a specific security, or portfolio of securities, that should be bought or sold as a way of creating a return.

The second step involves examining how the potential trading opportunity will impact the current portfolio. Most traders do not simply establish a long or short position in a security in isolation, without understanding its impact on the existing portfolio. The effects of correlation and concentration are key drivers in the risk and return performance of any portfolio, and the addition of a single security, or entire subportfolio of securities (e.g., as in a program trade) can radically reshape the characteristics of the portfolio. Understanding these effects before the execution of a trade is critical, and is most often accomplished through proprietary analytics or those that are contained within the order entry application that a trader is likely to be using (a point we will consider in the next chapter).

In the third step, the trader moves to the practical step of defining a trading strategy to capitalize on the identified opportunity. This brings us closer to the concept of how, when, and where an order will find its way into the market:

- What venues should be sought out (or avoided)
- When the trade(s) should be executed
- What price points are acceptable
- What types of orders are best suited for the situation
- When the search for liquidity should cease

A trader must also define ex-ante a strategy that addresses any situation in which an order is not filled immediately:

- Whether to cancel, reroute, or rest
- Where to reroute orders that do not cancel or rest
- Whether to convert an unfilled order into a different form

Furthermore, a strategy needs to be established regarding

- Whether to search for liquidity actively or passively
- Whether to break up the order into smaller pieces or keep it as a block
- Whether to directly control the order or relinquish it to one or more brokers
- Whether to display the order or keep it dark, or use some combination of the two

A trader must consider whether immediacy is required, or whether motivations are opportunistic and can be exploited over time. Those who absolutely must trade must submit orders that are certain to cross, meaning market orders or aggressive limit orders – execution trumps price. If immediacy is not an issue, limit orders submitted at good value levels may be preferable – if they are eventually filled, then a profit will ensue, and if they are not, nothing is lost. In addition to the establishment of a position, a trader must apply the same type of analysis to the exit strategy. Each one of these points contributes to the development of an overall trading strategy.

Consider a simple example: a trader managing a pairs strategy (e.g., long and short positions in individual equities, with the intent of capturing the spread between the two) runs a proprietary screening model that generates two potential stock candidates. Once these have been identified, the model applies them to the existing portfolio to generate a hypothetical portfolio with new risk and return parameters. The investor then runs an algorithm contained within an order management system, which analyzes the two stocks in relation to the current markets, and develops a strategy to route the stocks; since the investor does not want to publicize the pairs trade, the algorithm only searches for liquidity in dark pools, using certain historical statistics to propose a "ping sequence" (or routing map, as we will discuss in the next chapter). Once the orders are submitted, the algorithm tracks progress through the execution stage (which in this case allows for rerouting from one dark pool to another). Though this is a simplified version of the real process a trader might undertake, it illustrates a methodical process that might be used.

When a trader is developing a trading strategy, considerable focus is placed on the current market spread and the best type of order to submit. As we have noted at various points, the spread (breadth) is the price that an investor must pay for immediacy: that is, buying at the offer and selling at the bid, representing the compensation to dealers and limit order traders. When the bid-offer spread is wide, the price of immediacy is expensive, and when it is narrow, it is relatively cheap. Ultimately, the size of the spread determines whether a dealer will provide liquidity and, if so, how much. We also know that the size of the spread is subject to supply and demand, meaning that in a competitive market, a dealer cannot set any spread level it wants – the dealer can only set a spread that covers some normal level of profitability. In fact, the spread itself can be dissected into two broad components: one portion to cover transaction costs and a second portion to provide a return on the risk capital used in support of the purchase or sale of securities.[1] The second portion also covers informational asymmetries, which arise when one party is better informed than the other.[2] Dealers have higher costs than public investors, which can lead to a higher transactional cost component; however, they are also privy to order flows, which can reduce the risk capital component (and which they can adjust more rapidly).

If spreads are wide, market orders are less attractive than limit orders and become more attractive as they narrow. If investors primarily use market orders, the small number of limit orders in the market can set prices far away from the market, since excessive market orders will ensure a trade. However, the spread will become so wide that market orders will no longer be submitted; limit orders will be used instead. As these limit orders enter the market, spreads will narrow as investors submit more aggressive limit prices. However, if most investors use limit orders rather than market orders, spreads will be narrow as the limit orders try to get fills from the market orders. This will make limit order investors switch to market orders and will, in turn, lead to wider spreads. According to this thesis, there must be some equilibrium point dictated by supply and demand of limit and market orders.

We know that displaying buying or selling interest carries a benefit and a cost. Advertising willingness to trade will draw in other trading interest, including latent liquidity, and increase the likelihood of execution – a clear benefit. The cost is, of course, market impact, or getting filled at prices that do not reflect the best price levels that might be obtained through a true dark strategy. Traders and investors must therefore consider the relative costs and benefits closely. In practice the largest players are likely to employ multiple strategies. They may tap the light and dark markets, simultaneously advertise and hide, use multiple dark venues, publish indications of interest rather than firm orders, use deceptive strategies to shake off any front runners, and use multiple brokers in some situations and take direct control of their orders in other cases.

Beyond these fundamental points, any trader developing a strategy needs to know where trades are likely to be executed. As noted in Chapter 3, understanding the profile of a dark pool is essential in minimizing the chance of bad executions. This means that the trader must examine the following:

- What types of buyers and sellers frequent the pool
- What degree of sell-side participation is likely to be encountered
- What execution rates a pool averages
- Which metrics best describe the pool's performance (e.g., fill rate, opportunity costs, implementation shortfalls, and so forth)
- Where orders are routed if they are not executed in the pool
- What other flows the orders are likely to interact with
- Whether internal flows go through the sponsor's pool
- Whether the pool is truly dark, or whether some possibility of leakage exists
- Whether IOCs are permitted as a way of "pinging" the pool for gaming purposes
- Whether minimum execution sizes are used as an antigaming measure, and so on

Each of the strategies described below may be best suited for execution against contra-liquidity in a pool that attracts a particular "style" of liquidity. Thus, an investor seeking to sell a large block and minimize market impact should not be looking for contra-liquidity in pool used by high frequency traders, which could lead to adverse selection. Answering the questions noted above will help to identify the best liquidity; once this is done, the relevant "go" and "no go" pools can be identified within routing/smart order routing algorithms. Naturally, a pool may evolve over time, so this should be considered as a regular process.

Block Trading

In Chapter 1 we introduced the concept of the block trade, and its importance in fuelling activity in the dark sector. While all trading flows are important for dark pools, block trades are especially suited for the mechanisms supplied by the dark sector – either in pure form, or as "raw material" that can be sliced into many small orders. Venues can offer one of two different models for block crossings: they can create a dedicated block crossing system where clients can go to find contra-liquidity through submission of orders or IOIs; this model favors the block order approach. Alternatively, they can develop a full service platform so that clients can access multiple liquidity sources through a single entry point; this model favors the sliced order approach.

Naturally, a trader can still choose to cross a block in the visible markets through a block dealer, which essentially provides depth of liquidity, as per our discussion in Chapter 2. The trader, through the dealer, may be able to take advantage of certain outsize rules to gain priority over time-driven orders, but will still have to print matched buys and sells to the tape to remain consistent with price priority rules.[3] Alternatively, the trader may execute a sunshine trade, exposing the block to the market as an invitation to deal; this, of course, conveys a free trading option to the market at large, and is quite likely to create some degree of market impact.

In practice, however, dark pools present a logical solution. Confidentiality and an attendant reduction in market impact are, of course, key reasons why block trades are so appropriate for the dark sector. However, even if a decision is taken to route the order to the dark sector, the trader must still communicate with a block broker or block dealer to identify the right tactical approach to execution. In fact, the communication between these parties can help ensure a smooth execution, out of the spotlight, at a price that eliminates or reduces market impact. Consider, then, that a trader with a block of shares to sell has multiple options:

- Submit an IOI into one or more dark pools with general parameters on what is being sought to determine whether potential interest exists for most, or all, of the block
- Submit a block order into a block crossing network specializing in block trades
- Submit the block order into multiple dark pools in the form of smaller slices
- Submit an IOI to a broker capable of uncovering latent liquidity within the investment management sector
- Trade through a block dealer with price concessions, away from the market (note that the dealer itself may then turn to one of the above-mentioned dark options to flatten its position)

All of these emerge as viable dark strategies. The fundamental economic issue a client must consider is whether the price concessions demanded in dealing through a block dealer or submitting through a block crossing network or into a pool of latent liquidity are bigger or smaller than the increasingly "worse" prices obtained by slicing the order into many smaller pieces. As noted in Chapter 2, each slice of an order is likely to fill at an increasingly inferior price as liquidity is absorbed from the market. Accordingly, the decision on whether to execute a block in a dark space or slice the block into many orders and route them to dark (and/or light) venues is likely to be based on some ex-ante analysis. Whichever mechanism is selected, the goal is to match buyer and seller away from the visible market in order to execute at a better price.

Program Trading

A program (or portfolio) trade can be defined as a single trade comprised of a portfolio of stocks, which is developed through a proprietary model and executed electronically. Rather than selecting individual stocks and executing individual orders, the program trade creates a portfolio of dozens, or even hundreds, of stocks and executes them in a batch form. The reverse can also occur: in some cases an investor holds a portfolio of stocks that it wants to liquidate in one step and can use a similar approach to exit – either directly or via blind broker bids.[4] Some exchanges have more precise definitions of what constitutes a program trade. For instance, the NYSE Euronext classifies a program trade as one with more than 15 stocks and $1 million market value. Regardless of the specific size or number of stocks, program trading is an extremely popular strategy that can be found in both the visible and dark markets. In fact, some exchanges (such as the NYSE Euronext) have noted a continued trend toward program trading and away from block trading[5] in recent years. For instance, in 2013 the NYSE's program trades averaged more than 25% of total exchange volume, with spikes to more than 40% in some months.

Since program trading contains significant elements of both analytics and technology, it lends itself to computerized analysis that can determine both optimal trading size and optimal trading location. For instance, a model might generate a basket of 100 stocks based on an investor's defined criteria. It must then check that most, or all, of the stocks are sufficiently liquid to trade in the optimal size; most program trades avoid a large number of target stocks that exceed a significant percentage of average daily volume. An algorithm might then be employed to identify the best way to execute the program trade – including parceling individual stocks among different venues (dark or light), slicing up orders within the program to minimize market impact (perhaps using a volume weighted average price method, as described below), creating a routing pattern should immediate fills not occur, and so forth. Ultimately, creating an entire list of orders and executing them en masse is a faster and more efficient way of gaining exposure, and lends itself to the advantages of the dark sector – particularly for large portfolios that demand anonymity.

*   *   *

Pools in Practice: Cash neutrality

Cash neutrality is an important factor for institutional investors that have to execute program or portfolio trades comprised of long and short positions (which may be a combination of long stock positions and short index futures, or long and short stock positions). Keeping cash neutrality implies balancing buys and sells, so that as trades are executed in one market, they are offset by opposing trades in another market (in a process known as "legging")." By doing so, the open directional market risk position on the unexecuted portion of the portfolio is minimized, reducing the likelihood of a loss.

In fact, maintaining cash neutrality in lit markets is a simple and well established practice, as it is easy to see where and how to optimally execute a long/short portfolio so that open risk is minimized. It is rather more difficult to do the same in the dark markets, for several reasons: dark pools don't provide an ex-ante indication of liquidity or a guarantee of execution (as the right orders may not be available for crossing at the time needed), and most dark pools don't accept portfolio order instructions (i.e., the joint buys and sells cannot be "dumped" into a venue en masse). Accordingly, to execute large cash neutral long/short portfolio trades in the dark several approaches can be considered. In the first instance, an algo can send small short and long pieces of a portfolio into a venue for dark execution; this is readily achievable, and part of the ordinary course of business in the dark sector. However, by sending long and short positions in piecemeal, the trader fails to take advantage of potential price improvement from any block liquidity which might be resident in a pool. Alternatively, an algo can send large long or short pieces to a dark pool for execution, whilst routing the offsetting short or long pieces to a lit market. While this process doesn't fully take advantage of potential dark block liquidity, it does so partially and still minimizes open market risk, which is the overriding goal in such a strategy.

Consider the following example: ITG has a dark algo that can be used to maintain cash neutrality across dark pools that have different characteristics. The algo consistently allocates long and short trades to a set number of approved dark venues (especially those that allow IOIs or cash constraints), using a probabilistic model to determine the likelihood of getting a fill on a real time basis; key inputs include average trade size and expected hit rate. The algo uses real time agents to allocate orders and update the remaining schedule. By following this methodological schedule and updating everything in real time, the algo can work through the legging process without creating a market risk position. Various other brokers offer similar algos, making the cash neutrality process manageable for those dealing in the dark.

* * *

Algorithms and Algorithmic Trading

Algorithms, like the orders described in Chapter 2, provide instructions on how, when, and where to execute a purchase or sale of securities. However, they are much more sophisticated, flexible, and dynamic, and can be viewed more appropriately as a set of trading rules/logic that initiate and direct trade execution. Algorithmic trading, by extension, can be defined as any form of trading that makes use of computerized processes to determine when, where, and how to execute financial transactions in the marketplace. Such trading, which dates back more than two decades, originated on proprietary desks of major banks and eventually expanded to the buy-side client base; agency brokers and third parties gradually joined in by creating their own algorithms. Greater acceptance and use appeared in the early years of the millennium as a result of the growing trends toward electronic trading, the introduction of decimalization (and resulting margin compression cited in Chapter 1), and the steady promulgation of the FIX Protocol from the FIX Trading Community (described in Chapter 6) as a common communication mechanism.[6] For instance, the forces of decimalization caused more institutional players to split their orders into smaller pieces via computerized methods to improve average execution prices; the "order splitting" algorithm, which we describe in more detail below, has become a standard of the sector – reducing average trade size by even more than might have been expected following the introduction of decimalization.

Algorithms and algorithmic trading, which have become increasingly powerful and sophisticated, are central to all types of institutional trading, allowing for anonymity, efficiency, control, and benchmarking. Hedge funds, investment funds, pension funds, and others employ them in daily trading activities to execute arbitrage and benchmarking strategies, tap into block liquidity, reduce risk, and take greater control of the execution process.[7] Market surveys suggest that between 25% and 30% of U.S. trading volume is handled through algorithms, and that 75% of institutional investors employ them in some way; within the subset of the most active institutional investors, 95% use algorithms regularly.[8] Algorithm use in the European markets is nearly as broad. Greater expansion of algorithmic trading into other assets classes is also anticipated (it is already a feature in the foreign exchange markets, where an estimated 25% of volume is handled by algorithms, and in listed derivatives, where just under 20% of volume flows through algorithms). Cross-asset algorithms are also making their way into the market.

The marketplace for algorithms involves strategies that range from supplying light and dark liquidity (e.g., high frequency traders and broker-dealers) to taking liquidity (e.g., institutional and retail investors), to placing/slicing large block trades. Whilst algo trading was once the exclusive domain of institutional traders, retail investors have begun participating much more actively through suites of algos offered by various broker-dealers. These "standard" algos typically relate to timing, price/quantity allocations, routing priorities, and order slicing, all with a view to reducing market impact and improving execution.

With algos becoming a mainstay of the financial landscape, it isn't surprising to note that they have had an important impact on securities trading, including the provision of liquidity. Certain research suggests that algo trading helps create liquidity in large capitalization stocks (as shown via spread tightening). That said, they remain controversial in some quarters, because they are viewed as "black boxes" that can exacerbate negative market movements or "take advantage" of less sophisticated clients. Indeed, algorithmic trading in Europe is coming under greater scrutiny through the efforts of MiFID II, as we shall discuss in Chapter 7.

As a result of algorithmic trading users are no longer limited to submitting market or limit orders into visible or dark liquidity, but can create very specific definitional parameters related to

- Location: where to execute the order.
- Routing: where to transfer the order if immediate execution is not possible.
- Quantity: how much of the order to execute.
- Price: what price to execute the order at.
- Time: when to execute the order.
- Benchmarking: which specific reference to measure performance against.
- Flexibility/Adaptability: whether to adopt a new strategy in light of changing market patterns and conditions.

The rules can be customized to the specific needs of users and their desired end goals. Some representative examples of algorithms include

- Finding the best price and liquidity among participating dark pools and executing immediately.
- Working an order passively for 1 hour, and if there is no fill, crossing the spread.
- Not posting any liquidity, simply waiting until liquidity appears and then executing at the midprice of the NBBO or EBBO.
- Reconstituting a previously split order that has been only partially filled into a single order and routing into a new venue for execution.
- Working an order into the close, and executing at least 50% at the mid-price of the NBBO or else canceling.
- Searching for specific trading patterns in a given stock during a defined period and executing buys/sells if a pattern is revealed.
- Benchmarking against a specific daily performance measure or market index.

We can easily imagine hundreds, even thousands, of other types of instructions that might be defined and coded. Algorithms can, of course, be applied to various types of trading strategies, including directional trading, trend trading, intermarket spreading, statistical arbitrage and market-making, among others. The trading rules allow specific tasks to be carried out – which can include the management and execution of orders according to particular priorities, the identification of alternate sources of dark liquidity, and so forth – with the goals of achieving the lowest execution costs, the lowest market impact, the fastest fills, the best management of market risks, and so forth.

Algorithms are not, of course, related solely to dark liquidity – a significant amount of algorithmic trading and execution occurs in the visible markets. While some of the most popular algorithms have focused on searching for hidden liquidity, others have expanded beyond this fundamental role to find the best combinations of liquidity/price – acting, essentially, as liquidity aggregators. In fact, algorithms can be viewed as an "equal opportunity" mechanism, executing trades in light or dark pools. That said, algorithms have been central to the growth and success of the dark sector. The advent and widespread adoption of algorithms has helped spur more buying and selling activity in the market at large. The design of a typical algorithm is such that it continuously searches for liquidity at the best possible price regardless of location, and is thus involved in a self-fulfilling cycle. Venues can thus build liquidity through their own efforts, but also by remaining open to algorithmic flows; many platforms follow this model.

Structure

Algorithms come in different forms in order to fulfill different tasks, and most are proprietary in nature. However, the operation of certain algorithms is by now well understood, and we can readily summarize key points of such general structures in this section. The design of any algorithm must, of course, factor in speed and accuracy. Indeed, speed is absolutely essential to success, as algorithms must operate in a fast moving, competitive market against other algorithms, high frequency trading flow, large program trades, and so forth. Since latency can destroy effectiveness, considerable effort is placed in both designing an efficient algorithm and then ensuring that it ports through a fast network or is otherwise proximate to the nexus of one or more matching engines. Accuracy is also fundamental: a set of trading rules that yields the wrong execution result is obviously of little use.

Let us consider, as an example, a fairly standard algorithm that slices up orders and routes each piece for execution using volume weighted average price (VWAP) – in other words, for a given user-defined percentage of participation of average daily volume and a start/end time, the algorithm will work the order. The algorithm uses order generation logic, order placement logic, and router logic that takes a parent order (essentially an overarching order), slices it up into various child orders (individual suborders that can be executed independently), and routes them to appropriate venues.[9]

Order generation logic includes mathematical instructions that determine how a parent order is to be parceled into separate child orders for individual execution across a time horizon. For instance, the order generation logic on a full day VWAP[10] algorithm divides the parent order in proportion to the historical volume achieved over the day to achieve a better average fill price. More formally, each trade in the VWAP is weighted by the size of the associated trade, and can be defined as

$$VWAP = \frac{\Sigma \left(\# \, of \, shares \, purchased * share \, price \right)}{Total \, shares \, purchased}$$

Note that a full day time weighted average price (TWAP) follows the same logic but works orders against linear volume during the trading day. As noted above, the time horizon is user-defined, e.g., full day, half day, 1 hour, and so forth.

Order placement logic includes mathematical instructions that indicate how each individual child order should be executed. For instance, the logic may specify that each child order should be executed as a market order or a limit order; if it is a limit order, it may indicate the price; if no execution is possible at the limit price, it may indicate when to switch to a market order; and so forth.

Router logic includes mathematical instructions that indicate where each individual child order should be placed. This may involve spreading the orders across as many venues as possible to capture available displayed and nondisplayed liquidity. In the case of orders tapping into nondisplayed liquidity, care must be taken not to leave any telltale "digital fingerprints" that might otherwise create market impact. Alternatively, the logic may concentrate orders in a single venue that is known to historically feature sufficient liquidity to accommodate the order at hand. Note that the ability for router logic to successfully detect liquidity and channel orders is an essential element of the process. It is important to emphasize that routing orders to venues with dark liquidity is a feature in the logic of many algorithms. In fact, it would be somewhat shortsighted to avoid dark pools when these may be the source of additional liquidity which can be obtained at the NBBO, EBBO, or some other benchmark, and which can be executed anonymously.

Continuing with the VWAP example, we can image how algorithm logic factors into the dark liquidity space. In the first instance, the order placing logic works the first child order, leaving the rest of the parent order as nondisplayed liquidity within the platform, until the first execution is completed – once this occurs the second child order is drawn from the remaining parent order, and so forth, until the execution is complete; throughout this process the algorithm must keep track of fills to ensure that it is remaining on a proper VWAP trading schedule. The VWAP will be considered successful if the price of a buy order is less than the VWAP, or the price of a sell order is higher than the VWAP; it will be considered unsuccessful if the reverse occurs. An additional consideration is to determine whether the residual dark liquidity from the parent order can take advantage of other dark liquidity ahead of any scheduled execution embedded in the logic. Ultimately this relates to the level of rigidity encoded in the time/size schedule; most VWAP (and TWAP) algorithms limit the degree to which order generation logic allows access to dark liquidity outside the prescribed schedule. For other types of algorithms, a greater degree of flexibility may exist, meaning that interaction with other dark liquidity is entirely possible. For instance, shortfall algorithms do not contain the same time/size schedule constraints, meaning the parent order can interact with any available liquidity at any point in time. Other algorithms slice up parent orders and sequentially route them, posting (but not displaying) the residual parent orders in various venues, which allows them to interact with other dark liquidity. The central point is that algorithm logic determines the degree to which different sources of liquidity can be accessed at different points in time.

As we might expect, algorithms require more definitional parameters than conventional limit or market order trading and supporting interfaces must be able to accommodate a wide array of algorithms. The order management system (or other similar platform) must be able to understand and interpret different types of algorithms; in fact, they must be designed with sufficient architectural flexibility to accommodate what is a continually evolving element of the traded markets. Ultimately, the structure of an algorithm depends on the goal it is intended to fulfill – some goals are easy to achieve, others much more complicated. Some key algorithm parameters that must be considered with regard to complexity include

- Price Sensitivity: The greater the price sensitivity of the underlying security, the more complex the algorithm structure, and vice versa.
- Horizon: The longer the time horizon of the trade, the more complex the process and the attendant algorithm structure, and vice versa.
- Predictability: The greater the predictability of the characteristics of the trade, the less complex the algorithm structure, and vice versa.
- Confidentiality/market opacity: The greater the need to retain confidentiality, the more complex the algorithm structure, and vice versa.
- Immediacy: The greater the need to complete an order instantly, the more complex the algorithm structure, and vice versa.
- Need to finish: The greater the need to finish or fill an order by a specified time, the more complex the algorithm structure, and vice versa.
- Tolerance: The greater the client's tolerance to risk, the less complex the algorithm structure, and vice versa.
- Passivity/aggressiveness: The greater the client's willingness to be passive, the less complex the algorithm structure, and vice versa.

*   *   *

Pools in Practice: Real life algo orders...

We've noted that traders/investors and their brokers have access to many different order types, sometimes sent in directly and other times forming part of an algorithmic strategy, which provides for more precise control. Before looking at some real life examples, let's highlight two of the parameters from the previous section to see how a trading strategy can be calibrated against confidentiality (or market opacity) and price passivity/aggressiveness. In this case, confidentiality (market opacity) is simply set as a selection between lit, grey, and dark, while passivity/aggressiveness is reflected through the bid-offer spread level of the order, varying between passive, neutral, and aggressive. This provides several options which can be incorporated into any algo:

- Lit: route to lit markets only
- Grey: route to either lit and dark markets, or to the reserve order blotter in lit markets
- Dark: route to dark markets only

- *Neutral: pay or accept the mid-point of the spread*
- *Passive: pay or accept the passive side of the spread*
- *Aggressive: pay or accept the full spread*

For example, we can say that an order that needs to be executed immediately is likely to be sent to lit and dark markets with an aggressive spread instruction, a discreet order that is focused on good execution would be sent as dark and passive, and so forth. Of course, compound orders (such as first doing x and then doing y, if a condition in x is/isn't met) make things a bit more complicated, and help illustrate the power of the algo. Let's see how this works in practice.

In our first example, assume that an investor wants to buy 10,000 shares of QRS as quickly as possible, up to a specific limit price. Since immediacy is the overarching goal, the investor can "spray" IOC or FOK orders to a whole series of lit and dark venues with a specific limit price: the 10,000 share order will start to get filled as crosses are made in one or more venues. Of course, the algo will cease the spray once fill confirmations have been received back from the venues in an amount totaling the 10,000 shares. Alternatively, the investor could use an ISO sweep, collecting partial fills as it "walks the book" at a given venue without rerouting. In either case, the order will be fully priced (the cost of immediacy) and will get a total fill (the benefit of immediacy), though it may be subject to at least some degree of information leakage.

In our second example, we now assume that the investor wants to fill the 10,000 share block as soon as possible, but doing so while minimizing market impact – in other words, wanting quick but not necessarily immediate execution, and not wanting to touch the lit quote. In this case the algo can be directed to execute in one or more designated dark pools, doing so by paying a full spread dark quote. The block will get executed in the dark but the investor will "pay up" for doing so.

In our third example we find the investor wanting to fill at least half of the 10,000 share order in the dark at the mid (e.g., a dark neutral strategy); once liquidity is exhausted the investor is willing to pay full spread (i.e., converting to an aggressive stance). In this case the priority is good execution with no market impact; only the rump of the order becomes aggressive. The investor may further specify that if the 50% threshold can't be reached, the unfilled portion of the order rests (but is not passive), awaiting further contra flow. In this case the algo will route the full order to a dark venue as a passive midpoint match; once it hits a fill rate of 50%, and assuming no further available liquidity, the order becomes an aggressive full spread dark trade that waits for the next wave of contra flow, where it will be quite certain to cross.

In our fourth example, we assume the investor is now interested in getting an average execution price over an afternoon's trading session (i.e., the last 4 hours of trading) whilst minimizing market impact on the 10,000 share block. In this case a dark TWAP algo routes the order to a dark pool and executes 2,500 shares each hour; since the investor is accepting a periodic market price, the entire order will fill. Of course, rather than using TWAP, the investor could instead use VWAP, where it would slice the order not by time, but against a predicted volume profile appearing during the same 4-hour time period. This approach is likely to be built atop an analysis of past volume trends during particular times of the day, calibrated for any unanticipated changes.

There are many other examples we could review (including the broad categories summarized in the next section), because the types and sequences of both orders and algos are almost limitless. However, these examples should reveal that the theory devolves to practice in a very real manner.

*   *   *

Classes

Many types of algorithms have been developed by major banks and securities firms (e.g., Credit Suisse, UBS, Citibank, Goldman Sachs, Bank of America Merrill Lynch, GETCO/Knight, Citadel), as well as financial advisory/technology firms (e.g., ITG) and brokers over the past few years. Providing a complete list of all such algorithms is, of course, impossible. We can, however, delineate the general types of algorithms that are used in the displayed and nondisplayed markets. In fact, some of these algorithm types are by now so common that certain investors use them as benchmarks.

- TWAP: An algorithm that works orders over time against a linear volume distribution.
- VWAP: An algorithm that works orders over time by spreading trades along historical volume distribution. The VWAP can be executed in various forms, such as full VWAP, nonblock VWAP, proxy VWAP, and so forth.[11]
- Flexible: An algorithm that adapts its generation, placement, or routing logic in response to the execution experience gained from previous child orders. Such algorithms are extremely sophisticated as they are able to adjust tactically to improve execution success.[12]
- Pattern recognition: An algorithm that searches for particular trading patterns in order to initiate trades.
- Predictive switching: An algorithm that alters parameter setting in real time based on changes in market conditions in order to establish entry and exit points.
- Liquidity mapping: A predictive algorithm that attempts to anticipate where liquidity will appear over some future time horizon.
- Best: An algorithm that seeks out the best available price for a security on any exchange or ELOB.
- Meta: An algorithm of other algorithms that helps determine which broker algorithms are best suited for the needs of a given client.[13]
- Participating: An algorithm that participates at a certain percentage of printed volume.

- Close: An algorithm that works order into the day's close, trying to obtain a price better than the closing price.
- Implementation shortfall: An algorithm that attempts to create an optimized trading plan that minimizes the difference between the decision price (or arrival price) and the final execution price (we consider an example in the section below).
- Smart order routing: An algorithm that detects liquidity from multiple sources and routes orders to those providing the best price and liquidity terms (we consider smart order routing in Chapter 6).
- Dark/sniffer: An algorithm that attempts to detect the presence of other dark liquidity pools or algorithms to determine how they may impact execution.

The most sophisticated algorithms are those which are able to adapt their logic in response to current events, such as breaking financial data or other market-sensitive news, and redirect their execution efforts accordingly. Such algorithms are built atop complex event processing (CEP), or event stream processing (ESP), logic which uses streaming data and real-time constraints to monitor, analyze, adapt, and execute "on the fly." The underlying set of event-based rules comprising such an algorithm, which are hosted inside an engine, is continuously updated in light of new information. Such CEP/ESP logic can also be applied to the SORs described above and discussed in more detail in the next chapter.

The active selection and ongoing review and use of algorithms is important, and must match the specific goals of the users (whether buy-side or sell-side) and current market conditions. For instance, a passive algorithm may be appropriate under certain market conditions, but may achieve few crosses in an active market. Although it is true that algorithms have improved efficiencies and may ultimately prove to be very profitable mechanisms, it is also true that they remove from the equation the intuition of traders and investors with regard to market conditions and opportunities; it is important not to lose sight of this fact.

Ultimately, of course, investors and traders must select from amongst a broad range and number of algorithms. Although various specific goals can influence the decision, the result must typically be one that yields, for the buy-side participant, reduced costs, faster execution, trading discretion, and/or improved performance.

*　*　*

Pools in Practice: Looking in the dark with algos

As we have noted, the number of algorithms in the marketplace is large and growing: some are fairly standard and conventional, while others are a great deal more sophisticated; some are centered on optimizing execution in the lit markets, others specifically target dark liquidity. While the design of value-added dark algos is very complicated (it is easy to spray orders to all dark venues, much harder to be analytically discerning in weeding out bad pools), identifying them isn't always hard – they're the ones with the sinister names, to wit Ambush (Bank of America), Nightowl (Morgan Stanley), Guerilla (Credit Suisse), Nighthawk (Instinet), Raider (ITG), Dagger (Citi), Swoop (UBS), Hydra (Barclays), Mercury Dark (Citadel), Sonar and Blockstrike (Goldman), Aqua and Arid (JP Morgan), and so on. Let's consider a handful of these.

First we have Bank of America Merrill Lynch's algo suite, which seeks liquidity from dark and light sources, both internally (against the proprietary/client order book) and externally; the algo has the ability to opt out of dark liquidity entirely, or by specific venue, should that be desired. It also runs a dark-only algo in Europe that routes order to the MLXN internal crossing network and then into major dark pools (e.g., BATS Chi-X Europe dark book, ITG, Turquoise, Xetra Midpoint). The algo, combined with smart routing, seeks best execution through specificity related to minimum/maximum cross amount, limit price, dynamic order slicing, and so forth. It also has the ability to post between venues based on analysis of historical data and real time statistics.

Next, consider the case of Morgan Stanley's Nightowl dark algo. The bank originally developed the algo in 2008 (and has refined it several times since then) as a way of finding dark liquidity in the U.S. markets; it now also supports the search for dark trades in other markets, including Brazil and Canada. The main point behind this process is to shield client orders from toxic pools, or those deemed to pose a greater-than-average risk of information leakage. Amongst other venues, Nightowl connects to the Trajectory Cross pool, which crosses orders on a discretionary basis within the spread (unlike the bank's own MS Pool, which crosses straight to the mid).

Deutsche Bank is active via Stealth, an algo strategy that ranks dark pools based on both real time and historical liquidity and protects against fishing, pinging, and other gaming. In fact, Stealth can be viewed as an overarching optimizing algo that uses SORs to access lit liquidity and SuperX+ for dark liquidity in the best possible combination. The algo also has a call on various supporting models, including one which executes trades relative to an index (making dynamic adjustments to order execution as the price of any single stock starts drifting away from some benchmark index), another that executes against short-term price movements by analyzing tick data and still another that focuses on stock price momentum to increase/decrease allocations, and so forth.

These are just three of many dark algos presently at work in the markets. Many others are available, often featuring similar core functionality (e.g., most allow order routing specification of dark only, dark and light, or dark with price improvement) but different options for searching, routing, and executing. Not surprisingly, clients using such algos usually want some assurances that they will work as advertised – providing good execution whilst protecting against information leakage. This is often possible only by gaining experience with a given algorithm.

* * *

Benchmarking

Algorithms can be used for benchmarking purposes, which makes them quite popular for investment managers that are measured against a specific metric. While benchmarking versus, for example, broad indexes or specific sectors has been a common practice within the investment sector for many years, the advent of algorithms has facilitated the process. By defining a specific target benchmark, an investor can employ an algorithm that is designed to replicate the parameters associated with that benchmark and then allow it to execute per specific logic. In addition to common market references, VWAP and TWAP are also forms of benchmarks, while the implementation shortfall is a benchmark against a price. In fact, the implementation shortfall, which is a very common benchmarking algorithm, measures the distance between the pre-trade decision price (or "idealized" price), and the actual price (or "realized" price), and is an effective way of gauging effectiveness over any defined implementation time-horizon (e.g., 1 hour, first intraday call auction, full trading day, multiple days). The implementation shortfall can be viewed as the sum of execution versus arrival cost plus the potential cost of executing the rest of an unfilled order based on the current price. For instance, if an investor submits an order to buy 10,000 shares of ABC and 3500 shares are filled at 3 basis points below the average price, the remaining 6500 shares may have an opportunity cost of –7 basis points, leading to an implementation shortfall of 5.6 basis points. Figure 5.1 illustrates a hypothetical implementation shortfall routine.

Figure 5.1 Implementation shortfall routine

The creation of a benchmark is typically done in the first step of the trading framework described earlier. The essential pre-trade analysis focuses on the benchmark goal, cost estimates, and acceptability of deviation from the benchmark (i.e., if the benchmark cannot be hit precisely, the level of dispersion that is still acceptable under a particular cost constraint).

We may surmise from the preceding section that algorithms are popular and well suited for dealing in dark pools, though they are certainly not ideal for every situation. We summarize the key advantages and disadvantages below.

Advantages:

- Creates lower costs than worked orders, increases efficiencies
- Allows real-time execution monitoring
- Allows access to multiple venues
- Creates flexibility through a large number of choices
- Ensures anonymity in the market
- Permits consistency and error minimization
- Creates a neutral benchmark indicator to track performance

Disadvantages:

- Leads to possibility of increased gaming or information leakage
- Creates fragmentation
- Delivers average price execution at best
- May miss on large blocks
- May be passive, difficult to react to rapidly changing markets
- Requires investment in analytical work/development

High Frequency Trading

High frequency trading (HFT) is a form of automated, tick-by-tick, high turnover trading that is based on real-time data analysis and fast execution times, and accounts for increasing amounts of exchange and off-exchange turnover; indeed, some estimates place high frequency trading at up to 50% of all daily market turnover on leading venues such as NYSE Euronext.[14] Note that this fast execution trading shares some important similarities with ultra low latency trading (which we describe in Pools in Practice). While high frequency trading occurs regularly in the visible markets, it can also occur in the dark markets or in both simultaneously (i.e., a trader might enter a position on the passive side of a lit book and exit at mid-tick in the dark book for a ½ tick profit). One of the keys to success, as we might expect, is rapid execution speed and resulting low latency – if execution cannot be guaranteed to occur within a particular window of time, typically measured in milliseconds (or in some cases even microseconds (one millionth of a second)), then it is of little use to the high frequency trading firms that operate in the market, such as GETCO, Renaissance, and Citadel. Since this type of trading requires access to, and analysis of, real-time tick data on individual stocks, the demands on technology platforms increase substantially. Consider, for instance, that a liquid stock generates between 2000 and 3000 tick changes per minute – all of this data factor into the models used by high frequency traders and when we consider that this type of data requirement is needed for full trading days and for a multiplicity of stocks, we can see how data handling, data storage, computing speed, and connectivity are paramount.

Typical HFT strategies are based on the provision of liquidity (either as de-facto market makers, posting and taking liquidity, or as rebate traders, receiving rebates from exchanges for posting liquidity), statistical arbitrage (taking advantage of perceived discrepancies between stock pairs, baskets, indexes), momentum trading (taking advantage of price discrepancies deemed to be the result of supply and demand imbalances), technical trading (using technical analysis to generate buy/sell programs), and filter trading (taking advantage of changes in price movement or volume), among others. Some dimensions of high frequency trading rely on, and benefit from, flash prices. As discussed earlier, flash trading allows HFT customers paying for a feed to receive a "flash" of an order for several milliseconds before it is exposed to the market at large. This window is sufficient for the most sophisticated traders to make relevant trading decisions. Whether such strategies continue in the future remains to be seen, as exchanges and other venues are increasingly abandoning the order type. HFT strategies can be executed in lit or dark markets, or both. Regardless of the location of liquidity, these HFT firms employ advanced technologies and algorithms in order to minimize trading latency.

As indicated, some high frequency traders consider themselves liquidity providers and even market-makers, but many have no positive obligations to quote prices and can disappear from the market as quickly as they appear. Indeed, they may provide liquidity when it suits them (earning rebates in the process through their "rebate harvesting" algorithms) but they may step back from liquidity provision when markets are volatile – and are therefore unlikely to be considered true market-makers.[15] In fact, they must really be viewed as pure proprietary outfits (not unlike the "SOES Bandits" of the 1970s and 1980s). Most high frequency traders flatten their positions as quickly as possible, so as not to carry risk overnight, and few employ leverage. In fact, the business model is predicated on contra-trading, or the practice of buying and selling shares within the same settlement period so that no payment need be made. Contra-trading, which is also common among day traders, occurs when a trader purchases shares during the day and closes out the position before the close of business (or vice versa); since both transactions settle on the same day (e.g., T + 3), the trader has no gross cash outflow.

Regardless of how high frequency trading might be characterized, it is clearly an important and growing dimension of the marketplace, accounting for more than half of all trading volume on certain exchanges.[16] In order to capture this flow, exchanges have in recent years overhauled their technological processing capabilities so that execution times can be shortened. For instance, in 2009, NYSE Euronext replaced the aging SuperDOT order processing system with new technology that cut execution time down to 5 milliseconds (from 105 milliseconds in 2008 and 350 milliseconds in 2007); further upgrades have occurred since that time. However, even that appears slow compared with NASDAQ OMX and BATS, which can offer faster times, and which have been able to attract high frequency traders armed with algorithms. Visible ECNs, which used to be the main vehicle for high frequency traders, have ceded some ground to dark pools, which have captured portions of the high frequency order flow.

*   *   *

Pools in Practice: Ultra-low latency trading

The advent of very sophisticated technologies and the incredible improvement in communications speed has given rise to a new style of trading that depends heavily on speed of transmission and execution – the world of "ultra low latency trading" (or ULLT for short). ULLT shares some characteristics with its popular cousin, high frequency trading – namely, a reliance on speed to attempt to capture very small price spreads in the dark or light markets. However, while HFT is based on very frequent trading and execution to generate its profits, ULLT need not necessarily be a high frequency strategy – though it can be. The most important thing in ULLT is fast speed, or low latency.

Let's consider some of the key elements of ULLT. In the first instance, an effective ULLT strategy is built atop an architecture that does everything possible to eliminate "wasted time" – stressing again that speed of order transmission and execution is measured in milliseconds. Not surprisingly, ULLT strategies cut out broker interaction entirely, relying on DMA or sponsored/naked access interfaces with the marketplace. A typical ULLT strategy can be decomposed into several phases. First, a trading analytics engine receives financial information from a data feed provider rather than through traditional financial newswires (which take their own feeds from the data feed provider – one step removed, which can cost several milliseconds of latency, see Figure 5.2). Second, the engine analyzes the data according to some proprietary process to create a trading decision. Third, the engine generates an order based on the trading decision and submits it to a dark or light market directly. Fourth, the market receiving the order sends back a message confirming execution or, if no execution is possible at that instant, an acknowledgement of the order transmission. In the broadest sense latency measures all four steps – under the supposition that the trader or venture with the fastest processing, analytics, and transmission gains a time advantage over competitors that can be measured in milliseconds and which can translate into profits. In a stricter sense, the ULLT latency focuses only on the third and fourth steps – from the moment the order hits the fiber (or microwaves) to the moment it is received and executed/acknowledged by the receiving marketplace. Thus, any latency in the front end is excluded from the speed computation (as are any passive executions which, by definition, are price rather than time sensitive). In today's world, an "acceptable" time frame for steps three and four is approximately 1 millisecond; in fact, major exchanges and ECNs have reduced their turnaround time from double to single digit milliseconds in recent years, and marketplaces such as BATS, DirectEdge, CBSX, and Liquidnet are leading the way in further reductions. As we might imagine, the time frame is bounded in a theoretical sense by the laws of physics (e.g., information travelling at the speed of light in a non-vacuum), but also in a practical sense by the efficacy of routers, switches, and protocols which transmit the order from trading engine to marketplace. In fact, in order to reduce some of the physical limitations, many trading ventures have chosen to co-locate their engines next to the servers of marketplace matching engines – saving precious milliseconds in the process (e.g., more than 100 trading ventures have located their own engines next to NASDAQ's severs). Consider that using fiber it takes 7 milliseconds to convey data from Chicago to New York, and 35 milliseconds from the West Coast to the East Coast – an eternity in ULLT. Or, let us think about this example: in 2012 NASDAQ OMX created the Nordic@Mid dark pool, which offers dark trading in liquid Nordic stocks (in competition with other dark pools, including Chi-Delta, Turquoise, UBS PIN, and BATS Europe), using price matching from NASDAQ OMX. The critical point is that Nordic@Mid's pricing engine is located at NASDAQ OMX, whilst all of the other competitors run their engines from London. This creates approximately 10 milliseconds of latency, meaning the ULLTs trading via Nordic@Mid can see prices an instant before the London refresh.

Interestingly, in the brave new world of ULLT (and HFT), impressive progress is being made with microwave, millimeter wave, and laser transmission (as potential alternatives to fiber optic networks): these comprise the so-called race to zero, which is the differential between order transmission and the speed of light. So critical is this area of trading that according to research group Tabb, major financial institutions invested $1.5 billion in 2013 for high speed technologies, double the amount of 2009. If fiber is on the slow end of the spectrum, microwave transmissions via dishes are an improvement. From there we move into millimeter wave transmissions which, though faster, require a greater array of dishes as the waves cannot travel the same distance as microwaves; consider that data between Chicago and New York can travel at 4.1 milliseconds, almost half the time it takes via fiber. Finally we arrive at laser transmissions, which are the newest and fastest technology. While lasers can offer further time improvements, they are expensive and subject to regulations. Still, investments have been made to link data centers between NYSE and NASDAQ (35 miles apart) with lasers, the first phase in a project intended to eventually link multiple exchange/venue data hubs in the U.S. Those participating as investors or users may ultimately get the time advantages that define this area of trading.

Regardless of method of transmission, measurement of latency is critically important. Average latency is the mean average time it takes for an order to go from point to point, and is thus an essential measure of a ULLT's success. Equally important, however, is the variance of the latency – known as latency jitter. If the trading architecture features large latency jitter, then its reliability in a profit-making framework is questionable. For instance, if the average latency of a venture's ULLT strategy is 2 milliseconds and that allows it to be profitable 75% of the time, but its jitter is 3 millseconds, which reduces its profitability in half, then clearly the strategy must be seen as unreliable. Throughput is another key measure, indicating how much data can be processed per unit of time (e.g., sent, received, processed). Not surprisingly, the greater the throughput, the lower the latency. By at least one estimate, a one millisecond advantage can lead to revenue increments of tens of millions of dollars per year (depending on the amount of capital deployed).

ULLT can, of course, be seen as both a light and a dark strategy, directing orders to the venue or marketplace that supports the overarching strategy. In some cases this will involve light trading, in other cases dark trading, and in still others, both. Typical ULLT (and HFT) strategies can center on automated market-making as well as a range of arbitrage programs (e.g., pairs, statistical arbitrage) and predictive trading. Extending the simple example of dark trading in Nordic stocks, we can easily imagine a ULLT arbitrage of a stock between Nordic@Mid and Turquoise, taking advantage of the 10 millisecond latency to enter (and/or exit) a position.

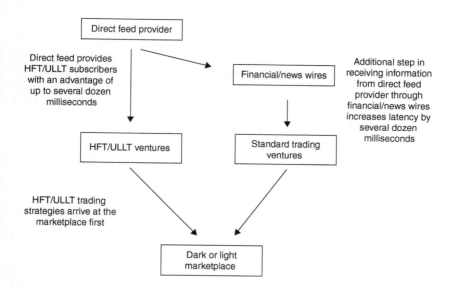

Figure 5.2   Data feeds in HFT/ULLT ventures

*   *   *

Gaming

The dark sector clearly adds benefits to participants. But it can also present certain dangers for traders or investors who are inexperienced or unaware of market protocols. In this section we consider some of the players and tools that roam dark pools in search of profit opportunities – including those that come at the expense of unsophisticated traders and investors.

A shark or a fisher is the name given to any individual or institution that searches for a distinctive strategy being used in the dark (or light) sphere, and uses that knowledge to front run or position itself to profit. This is done through algorithms that are specifically designed to identify particular trading patterns and behaviors, or to detect the presence of dark trades. Such practices are not illegal, but are not appreciated by neutral participants or passive traders/investors.

One common technique involves tracking order flows and trading activities and subsequently positioning to take advantage of assumed activity patterns. Consider, for instance, that broker algorithms tend to feature a certain "style" – some are known to always hit the bid, others will always execute at the mid of the NBBO, others will always gravitate sequentially through specific pools in a pre-defined order, and so forth. Indeed, research studies suggest that the performance of certain broker algorithms is highly predictable. A shark that is able to identify such patterns through its own algorithmic models can be on the other side of the trade, taking full advantage of the "digital fingerprint" left by a specific broker algorithm.

Gaming is another way for fishers to take advantage of activity in dark pools, and involves detecting the presence of large orders in a pool, and then positioning to profit from that knowledge. Again, gaming is not illegal, but is frowned upon by those operating pools, as a successful gaming operation can cost a venue's clients real money – to the point where clients may choose to avoid the pool. Accordingly, many venues impose certain antigaming controls, as we will discuss below.

The general gaming process begins with a fisher "pinging" one or more pools to determine where a large hidden order might be resting. Once this exploration phase yields a potential discovery, the fisher positions its book to take advantage of the hidden order, executes on a profitable basis, and then exits as the market reverses. All of this happens very quickly, sometimes in matter of seconds or minutes.

Let us consider a simple example. Assume that an investor has a large buy order of 10,000 shares of Stock GHI resting in a dark pool, awaiting contra-flow. A fisher, in search of game, has been sending ping orders to a variety of pools looking for potentially large dark orders. The ping order is sent automatically by the fisher's algorithm as a 100-share IOC sale of Stock GHI. As the ping order enters each venue in sequence, one of two things will happen: the pool will confirm an immediate buy match of 100 shares of GHI, filling the fisher's order, or it will confirm a cancel if it has no match – hence the use of the IOC order. If the IOC sale executes immediately, then the fisher may have reason to believe additional liquidity exists in GHI, perhaps in large size. It may then test the venue with a second ping order of a 500-share IOC sale of GHI, repeating the same process. If the second order is matched, then the fisher will now have good reason to believe that a much larger passive buy order in GHI is resting in the pool. Accordingly, it moves into the second phase of the game, which is to buy shares of GHI in the open market, in a quantity sufficient to push the quoted price of the stock up by a few cents (e.g., perhaps 5000 shares is adequate in this case). As the price of GHI rises, the fisher then submits a block sale order of 10,000 shares back in the dark pool, which crosses against the resting buy order at the temporarily inflated midquote. The fisher thus makes a profit through the game, while the passive investor gets crossed at an unfavorable price as a result of the game. We must remember that this sequence of events may literally take seconds or minutes to complete, and is therefore difficult to monitor or detect, except perhaps on an ex-post basis.

Based on the brief example above, it should come as no surprise that many investors and traders actively avoid pools that are subject to gaming or which lack antigaming controls. Such antigaming controls can take various forms. For instance, some venues feature minimum execution size which limits the ability for gamers to submit small ping orders to look for large blocks. This minimum execution size defeats the purpose of pinging a pool, as a reasonably large block of shares is needed to detect a large, passive order sitting in a pool. Some pools block IOC orders, which are a common way of pinging a site; of course, this means that "legitimate" IOC orders cannot pass into the pool, but that may be deemed an acceptable tradeoff for some venues. Other pools analyze trading patterns to determine whether there is potential gaming activity occurring. Although this is an ex-post exercise, it can provide sufficient evidence to allow a pool to bar entry to past "offenders." For instance, a venue may, through its analytic tools, analyze the price movements before and after a cross occurs; by averaging across many crosses, a "gaming signature" may emerge for each one. Small pings can also yield a pattern. Of course, all of this analysis must be interpreted in the context of other variables, such as limit orders that affect prices, as well as the fact that some open orders can be simultaneously worked in the open market.

The possibilities for trading and investing in the dark sector are clearly varied (and can sometimes be a bit dangerous). The strategies described above are not, apart from gaming, unique to the dark sector, and are readily pursued in the visible markets as well. But the important fact to emphasize is that traders or investors that ignore the application of such strategies in the dark market are doing themselves a considerable disservice. Regardless of the specific strategy being followed, it is obvious that a great deal of liquidity resides in the dark sector, and any program trade, block trade, arbitrage strategy, or algorithmic strategy that fails to capitalize on such pools of liquidity misses potential profit opportunities.

6 | Aspects of Technology and Architecture

The technology and architecture used in the dark sector is critical to the success of any single venue, and of the market at large. We have briefly noted in Chapter 1 the seminal role played by technology in helping advance off-exchange crosses from the manual/phone-driven processes of the late 1990s, to the automated processes that are so common today. Absent this technological progress, the market would still be in a relatively nascent state and feature much smaller pools of off-exchange liquidity (perhaps approximating those of the upstairs market of the 1980s and 1990s).

As individual venues develop or expand within the sector, we can point to certain standards that are common to virtually all of them, including

- Reliability
- Access
- Speed
- Security
- Redundancy
- Flexibility
- Scalability
- Network capacity
- Data capacity

Although a detailed discussion of these parameters is beyond our scope, the central point to emphasize is that unless a venue can deliver to its clients such standards, any attempt to build a business platform may ultimately be threatened. An order management system, a router, a matching/pricing engine, a communications protocol, and so forth, will be partly or completely useless should one or more of the fundamental aspects listed above be substandard.

Of course, the process is not only about technology, but also about making sure that the proper architecture and business linkages exist between venues and, by extension, pools. Let us use a simple analogy: if we imagine that each individual dark venue is a small puddle of water, its ability to sustain itself depends on rainfall. If this is a closed system, the puddle will eventually evaporate if rain is no longer falling. Far better, then, to make sure that an open system exists – that these puddles are somehow linked and connected, so that flow can trickle from one to the other as needed, depending on where the rain is falling. Similarly, if any dark single venue is completely isolated, its ability to generate/attract its own flow is key to its survival. If, however, it establishes liquidity partnerships with other platforms and/or permits client or algorithmic flows to enter and interact with its resident liquidity, it can attract more business, ensuring a better chance of execution. Indeed, when one source of order flow dries up, another can help replenish the pool. Accordingly, success in the sector is not based solely on the technological sophistication of the platform, but also on the business model and relationships that are developed as part of the overall business architecture. This does not suggest that those venues with the most relationships are the most successful – it means that a properly executed set of mutually beneficial liquidity relationships can help maximize client satisfaction and help ensure the success of the venue. Ultimately, if a client trade is not accessing the right pool, it will miss on available liquidity. It is therefore incumbent upon those designing and operating pools to ensure that the right business architecture exists.

In this chapter we will consider, in "nontechnical" terms, the essential dimensions of technology and architecture that touch both the user and provider of dark services. We begin with a continuation of the trading framework introduced in the previous chapter – focusing on the steps from trade entry through execution and clearing/settlement – in order to identify the different components of technology involved in the process. Then we focus on several key elements in the chain, including, from the users' perspective, order management systems/execution management systems and routing algorithms and engines, and, from the providers' perspective, the pricing/matching engine. We will also examine the common communications protocols that surround much of the process, focusing specifically on the FIX Protocol.

Naturally, this is a simplified version – the process is a great deal more complex and includes many other dimensions of technology and architecture that go into creating a seamless execution process. However, a review of these essential components helps us comprehend the backbone of trading and dark liquidity. We may also note that not all of these components are exclusive to dark trading – much of this exists in, and is applicable to, visible trading.

The Trade Lifecycle and Technology

To complete a transaction, a buy or sell order needs to migrate through various stages, which together comprise the "lifecycle" of a trade. Some stages, such as trade entry, are very short, lasting no more than a few milliseconds or seconds. Others, such as execution, can last for milliseconds, seconds, minutes, hours, or even days, depending on the specifics of a transaction. And still others, such as clearing and settlement, can take up to several days to conclude.

Not surprisingly, technology touches virtually all aspects of the trade lifecycle, regardless of the time required to complete a given stage. In fact, some of the most complex aspects of technology found in the trade life-cycle are used to reduce latency/waiting time and increase efficiencies and cost savings. Indeed, exchanges, banks, and individual venues invest significant capital to improve different aspects of technology, creating benefits for clients and themselves.

Let us build on aspects of our discussion from the previous chapter, where we described the various stages of the trading/investing framework.[1] To recap, these include

- Analysis of opportunity
- Analysis of the opportunity in relation to the current trading portfolio
- Identification of specific transaction strategies
- Order entry
- Order routing
- Order execution
- Reporting
- Clearing and settlement

We have discussed the first three points in the previous chapter. Let us now place the last five points in the context of a technology primer, noting the following:

- Order entry: technology is focused on voice transmission, order management systems, execution management systems, and application program interfaces
- Order routing: technology is focused on network connectivity, smart order routers, and routing algorithms
- Order execution: technology is focused on pricing/matching engines
- Reporting: technology is based on electronic messaging and standardized reporting transmissions
- Clearing and settlement: technology is based on clearing engines and book-entry systems

These dimensions are supported by market data feeds and communication and messaging (e.g., FIX Protocol). In some instances a trade may be handled through so-called straight through processing (STP), which provides a seamless link from order entry through execution to clearing/settlement, meaning human intervention in any single step of the trade lifecycle is effectively eliminated. STP is well supported through certain platforms, and is particularly applicable to financial instruments that trade and clear/settle on a standardized basis.

Order entry, which permits market access, is the first step in executing a strategy that has been developed by a trader during the first three stages of the trading framework. Order entry is, of course, a positive action that must be taken by the trader – no one can coerce or force such an action, meaning that if a decision is taken not to buy or sell securities, no order entry can, or will, occur. Order entry mechanisms are varied, and may include

- Voice via broker
- FIX messaging via broker
- ECN/ELBO entry via interface (e.g., order management system, application program interface)
- Crossing network entry via interface
- Broker algorithm via interface
- Proprietary algorithm via interface
- DMA/"no touch" via interface

All of these mechanisms are valid, but are presented in "evolutionary order" – whereas voice via broker can be used, it is less common in today's marketplace, while algorithms and DMA are increasingly common. In fact, large buy-side investors have been sending less order flow to brokers and sales desks for several years – because they can do so on their own more efficiently, at reduced cost, and can simultaneously minimize the potential for information leakage. The advent of easy-to-use and flexible technologies for order entry places greater options and costs savings at their disposal.

Of course, the order entry stage gives the trader the opportunity to define precisely what should be done with regard to the purchase or sale of securities. Referring back to our discussion in Chapter 2, we know that numerous types of orders can be selected, with parameters that define price, time, venue, and so forth. More complex and sophisticated order types can also be used, whether a conditional or benchmark order or some other hybrid instruction or algorithm.

As noted, order entry can take one of two forms: verbal/telephonic communication to a broker, or direct input into some type of order application – a trading interface, order/execution management system or other API. Certain clients rely on voice-only orders, which are typically taped in order to ensure accurate transcription of details, and which may also be followed by a confirming message from the broker to the client before, or immediately after, submission. Many other clients prefer to directly input their own orders electronically, supplying relevant details in the entry fields provided by the application. Clearly, the more complex the order details, the greater the flexibility needed within the application. This process works well for a few discrete orders that might be entered during the course of the trading day. Of course, the process must be automated when strategies call for a much larger number of orders to be entered, as in the case of high frequency trading, statistical arbitrage, index arbitrage, or other program trades. In such cases, batches of orders may be generated automatically by the trader's model, and submitted either directly into the market or via a router to one or more brokers or venues.

The second stage of the trade lifecycle involves order routing. Even though an order has been entered into an order management system or conveyed verbally to a broker, it must still find its way to a marketplace, so that it can be acted on. As we may well imagine, routing is heavily dependent on technology – the only practical way for tens of thousands of individual orders to enter into a marketplace at any one time is by placing them into an electronic pipe and pointing them to a destination. Simplistically, the pipe is a network that connects client/broker terminals with the servers that feed the engines of a particular market-maker, exchange, ECN, or crossing network. Not surprisingly, the "fatter" the pipe (meaning the faster the network connection and the more robust the server architecture) and the closer to the physical proximity of an exchange or venue,[2] the quicker the delivery, and the lower the execution latency, points we have mentioned in Chapter 5 in the context of HFT/ULLT. The pointing is done through router logic, essentially a set of instructions supplied by a client/broker indicating where an order should go (and not go). Some of the routing is very standardized and can be viewed as a simple set of instructions stating that the order should be moved from the order entry terminal and delivered to a particular destination, where it will be handled per the instructions defining the order (e.g., fill at market, fill at limit, cancel, rest, reroute, and so forth). But sometimes the routing is much more "intelligent" – meaning complex and demanding. Such routers, known as smart order routers (SOR) or routing algorithms, ensure that the order is treated in a very specific fashion if it is not filled at its first "port of call." This means the order can be moved sequentially through other random or defined dark or light venues in search of best fill opportunities.

The third stage of the trade lifecycle centers on the "main event" of execution. Traders submit orders so that they can be routed and then executed – and a specific result can be achieved. Execution is, in fact, completely technology-driven, based on pricing and matching routines that run in an automated fashion. Indeed, it is unrealistic to think that execution could progress without advanced technologies in an era of very large order volumes and fast response times. Accordingly, orders routing into a venue have to flow through pricing and matching engines which allow them to be matched and executed, or cancelled, rested, or rerouted, with a minimum amount of latency. The loss of even a few milliseconds in the process can prove detrimental to a trader's position. The logic embedded in pricing and matching that leads to execution must be designed to give clients best execution and adhere to any relevant order handling and execution regulations. Venues that serve as price derivers rather than price discoverers must link their engines to a data source that can provide the base reference price used to anchor pricing. Again, the bandwidth that a venue has in support of its execution process is critical, as are redundancy and backup.

After an order has been executed, details must be reported to relevant parties; this comprises the fourth stage of the trade lifecycle. Reporting typically serves various constituents, including traders executing orders, regulatory bodies, and the market at large. There are, of course, different levels of detail which must be reported, and different time horizons over which reporting must occur. In some cases it is virtually instantaneous, such as confirming an execution back to the client (directly through an order management system or similar application, or through electronic messaging to the trader and/or broker), while in other cases it may occur at the end of the trading day or at some later date, such as reporting to the public consolidated tape or to regulators. It follows logically from the point on executions above that reporting is largely driven by technology, particularly given the large number of trades passing through a venue at any point in time. We will consider reporting in more detail in Chapter 7.

The fifth and final stage in the trade lifecycle centers on the dual process of clearing and settlement. Once a trade has been executed and reported, it must pass through the clearing process, which is typically managed by an independent clearinghouse or the clearing function of the hosting venue. Clearing involves confirming and reconciling all of the relevant details of an executed trade, including counterparties, price, quantity, and so forth. If any of these details do not match (e.g., as in a "questioned trade" or a "don't know trade"), then the process is diverted to a resolution area where further investigation must be undertaken; only when the details have been properly reconciled is a trade considered cleared. As we might expect, this process is largely based on technology, as automated verification of relevant trade parameters can be performed very rapidly. Settlement is the final stage of the process, and centers on the delivery of cash for shares (and vice versa), between the two parties to the trade through the clearing and settlement agent. This phase is also extremely automated, and typically involves electronic debits and credits to the cash and securities accounts of buyers and sellers; the physical exchange of cash and securities is either prohibited or simply not supported. Thus, the sale of securities from one client to another involves electronically debiting the cash account of the buyer and crediting its securities account with a book-entry of the dematerialized shares, and crediting the cash account of the seller and debiting its securities account. Once this stage is completed, the trade lifecycle is concluded.

As noted in the previous chapter, trading strategies are often developed on the basis of real-time market data, which must be supported through the technology platform; this is especially critical for high frequency traders, but also applies to algorithmic trading, program trading, index arbitrage, and so forth. In addition, messaging and communications are central to the entire order process, so it is perhaps not surprising that a common "language" that helps define the key steps we have described can greatly speed the process; indeed, this is a key reason why common protocols such as FIX have proven to be integral to the construct.

We may gather from the brief discussion above that the simple act of buying or selling securities in the dark or lit markets is heavily dependent on technology. Indeed, this is the only rational way of supporting a business and marketplace that has expanded tremendously in terms of number of clients, volume of trading, and number of venues supporting trading and execution.

Figure 6.1 Trade lifecycle

Figure 6.1 summarizes aspects of the trade lifecycle described above. In the following sections we will create a more granular picture of some of the most essential dimensions of technology, including OMS/EMS, pricing/matching, and communications.

Order Management Systems and Execution Management Systems

Order management systems (OMS) and execution management systems (EMS) are software- or hardware-based platforms[3] designed to manage the order entry, routing, execution, and management of securities transactions, and serve as the centerpiece of advanced human/electronic market interaction. Although OMS and EMS platforms are not a prerequisite for those dealing in dark or visible markets (as an order can simply be submitted to a broker, who can then handle the balance of the process), technology makes it possible for virtually any investor or trader to reap the benefits of an OMS/EMS process. In addition, in a world where investors/traders are confronted with a range of sometimes complex possibilities regarding order types, execution venues, algorithms, and so forth, an OMS/EMS can simplify the entire process. Accordingly, we can view the OMS/EMS platform as virtually standard for any active sell-side or buy-side player.

The essential features of a typical OMS or EMS platform are by now quite commoditized, as versions of the platforms have existed for many years; enhanced versions with new features are, of course, regularly introduced by key third-party developers.[4] Early OMS platforms appeared in the 1990s and have evolved considerably since that time; EMS designs are relatively more recent, and resulted from a desire by clients to take greater control of the execution process. The two platforms focus on different tasks, though some platforms are blurring the lines and evolution into a fully consolidated platform seems likely. Though we simplify for purposes of our discussion, we can consider an OMS to be primarily an order manager and a post-trade administrative manager, useful for active, if straightforward, trading/investment management. An EMS, in contrast, is an execution application that is particularly well suited to complex trading, HFT/ULLT, black box trading, and arbitrage strategies.

Although all platforms offer the same core functionality, advanced platforms have unique features that are customized to the needs of specific users. Core features of most OMSs include

- Direct connectivity to brokers, broker/dealers, exchange floors, ECNs, and other ATSs, typically through a protocol such as FIX.
- Real-time order management via an on-screen blotter, including

  - Order entry for routing to specific destinations, directly or via smart order routers (as discussed below)[5]; permission from the venue to enable access to the order entry domain rather than, say, a passive market feed domain is generally required.
  - Change, cancel, update of orders or order routings.
  - Database update upon execution.

- Detailed monitoring and review of open orders, indications of interest, advertised trades, allocations, and completed orders.
- Access to a suite of standard or broker algorithms.
- Post-trade support and reporting, including performance reports, risk reports, and compliance reports.
- EMSs typically include direct connectivity, real-time order management capabilities, and algorithmic access, as well as
- Advanced execution functionality, including

  - Customizable execution routines.
  - Real-time execution monitoring in support of complex trading strategies.

Some platforms allow integration of OMS/EMS functionality with DMA capabilities, which essentially allows clients to use the infrastructure of the sell-side provider while retaining control of the trade management and execution process. As we might expect, OMS/EMS platforms are designed to handle a wide range of order types, including those defined in Chapter 2.

Open orders to a venue conveyed via OMS or EMS are generally cancelled automatically by the venue if no message is received within some predefined "heartbeat interval" (and where the trader using the OMS/EMS defines the length of the interval, typically a minimum of 5 seconds). The intent is to ensure that orders do not get "lost in the ether" as a result of a technical or communications malfunction, leaving both the trader and the venue uncertain as to its status. Many venues reject orders that are received outside of posted trading hours.

Regardless of the specific features of a given platform, buy-side and sell-side clients use the OMS/EMS structure to improve connectivity and execution response times, lower trading/execution costs, increase operational efficiencies, and manage and monitor multiple/complex access points.

The selection of a platform depends on the needs of the user. Common issues to consider include

- Whether to purchase or develop, which depends largely on whether an off-the-shelf product already exists that addresses substantially all of a user's requirements, or whether very specific features are needed and have to be customized. Generally, buy-side clients tend to fall in the "purchase" camp, while buy-side firms running complex strategies and sell-side firms may purchase and customize or develop. For those purchasing a platform from a third-party vendor, proper due diligence and evidence of future support are essential. A clear understanding of initial investment and ongoing costs is important in both instances.[6]
- Level of functionality, which can range from the most basic to the most comprehensive. Naturally, the essential starting point for any client is defining whether the trading/investing strategy demands order management or execution management. Basic functions include inputting and slicing orders, and allocating them to specific venues; more complex offerings allow for real-time monitoring and analysis, compliance checking, portfolio modeling, and so forth.
- Form and standards of technology, which can range from pure software to a combination of hardware and software, depending on the client's needs and the requirements of the platform. However, there are many critical issues surrounding this topic, including those related to databases, storage, internal and external network connectivity[7]/ speed/capacity,[8] real-time data/batch transfers, essential infrastructure upgrades, reliability and redundancy,[9] and attendant performance and costs. Though many of these issues are client-specific, minimum standards regarding latency and capacity are a given – an OMS/EMS should not be disadvantaged by speed issues and should not slow down when volumes spike.
- Internal interfaces, which relate to the degree to which the OMS/EMS needs to tie into other internal functions and processes, such as accounting, risk management, regulatory reporting and compliance, custody, and so forth. Clearly, the more intricate the web of internal ties, the more complex the package.

The result of the process should be the installation of a platform that can ensure accurate and timely execution of orders in any chosen market, at a reasonable investment cost.

Routing Engines/Smart Order Routers

We know from Chapter 2 that an order can be submitted to an exchange or an off-exchange venue, and hopefully be filled according to the price and time parameters accompanying the order; this applies particularly to limit orders, stops, and certain other classes of touch orders. If some, or all, of the order remains unfilled, three choices remain: the order can be cancelled, it can rest in the order book of the venue, or it can be rerouted to some other location.

Order routing is very common, particularly in the dark space where execution rates are still lower than in the visible markets. Accordingly, most technology platforms support order routing, providing a crucial link between pools and helping ensure that an order can be filled somewhere. In fact, routing is not particularly new, having existed within the visible markets for many years via routers such as SOES and SuperDisplay Book (the successor to SuperDOT), among others. Those creating OMS/EMS systems and other interfaces have leveraged on the same concepts to speed execution in the visible and dark markets. In addition, algorithms have been created to function as SORs, taking an order and directing it to different venues that might feature the appropriate degree of liquidity. In fact, certain ECNs and crossing networks feature such SORs in their product/service offerings; other SORs are available from the sell-side, including brokers.

An order entered into OMS/EMS can be directed to a single venue which, upon execution, will return a verification indicating execution price, quantity, and time, in accordance with the nature of the order submitted. More likely, however, is for an OMS/EMS to link into a SOR or routing algorithm that channels the order in a manner which takes advantage of pockets of liquidity – wherever they exist – according to specific instructions. An order can thus be sent into the visible and/or dark marketplaces for quick execution, and at the best available price. Within this construct it is possible for orders to remain in particular pools for periods of time, awaiting contraflow, or to jump in and out on the basis of an IOC instruction or some other trading rule.

Specific routing strategies can be developed using SORs and other routing algorithms, each crafted to client specifications. For instance, a router developed by a financial institution for its clients might take orders and route them to the following:

- Its dark liquidity partners for potential price improvement and/or lower fees; if portions remain unfilled after passing through the dark liquidity partners, the orders may then be routed to a preferred ELOB and from there to other ELOBs on a sequential basis
- An ELOB, then dark liquidity partners, and then protected markets
- Protected markets only, routing on a sequential basis
- An ELOB or dark liquidity partners simultaneously, but permitting execution on the ELOB first if it has the best price
- An ELOB or dark liquidity partners for several milliseconds as a flash trade, before rerouting to protected markets
- The ELOB offering the highest rebates for posting liquidity or the lowest fee for taking liquidity, before rerouting to all other ELOBs and protected markets
- The financial institution's internal book, then its pool partners and then an ELOB

Many other routing possibilities can be considered – the main point to stress is that routing strategies are quite flexible, and can be adapted to the specific requirements of clients as a way of gaining best price execution while minimizing price impact and information leakage. Figure 6.2 summarizes this routing exercise in a generic manner.

Based on this discussion we may consider that routing orders from an OMS/EMS is standard practice, though one which is still wrapped in proprietary details driven by the specific goals a sponsor or architect is seeking to achieve generally, or on behalf of a particular client specifically. That said, we can dissect the individual steps involved in the process to gain a sense of the logic used in a routing process. Let us do so by considering a simple example, where the goal is to route an order sequentially into a number of different dark pools to gain the best execution price in the shortest possible time frame, without resting in a pool to wait for contra-liquidity, until the order is filled or until all available volume in participating pools has been exhausted. Upon completion of one pass of the cycle through all available pools the routing becomes passive, where any unfilled portion is converted to a single limit order and sent to an exchange/ECN.

- Step 1: Denote all relevant definitional parameters, including
    - 1.0 Instrument identifier (e.g., ticker symbol, ISIN, CUSIP).
    - 1.1 Bid price or ask price.
    - 1.2 Number of units (e.g., shares).
    - 1.3 The routing "method."

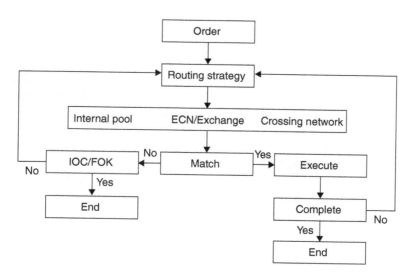

Figure 6.2   Routing process

- Step 2: Define the sequential logic of the routing "method"
    - 2.0 Define a "ping sequence" that indicates the sequence of multiple routing paths (e.g., which dark pools will be approached, and in what order).
        - 2.0.a The sequence may be based on historical touch or match statistics or other user-defined preferences; in this case the sequence is based initially on best price, and then on secondary parameters including historical liquidity patterns and historical execution speed.
        - 2.0.b Determine the ability of individual pools to handle FIX Protocol (as described below), and convert messaging to FIX whenever relevant during the routing sequence.
    - 2.1 Place the order within an automated order router that is capable of managing multiple routing paths.
        - 2.1.a Compare the bid price or ask price (1.1) with the price reflected in an exchange/ECN to determine whether it is marketable, that is, where the bid price (for a buy order) ≥ best offer on the exchange/ECN or the ask price (for a sell order) is ≤ best bid on the exchange/ECN. If the order is submitted as a market order, then it is always classified as marketable.
            - 2.1.a.1 If the order is not marketable, route directly to an exchange/ECN.
            - 2.1.a.2 If the order is marketable, compare the bid price or ask price with current quotes and unit/share availability on the exchange/ECN to determine whether it is immediately executable.
                - 2.1.a.2.a If yes, route to the exchange/ECN for execution and flag the order as complete.
                - 2.1.a.2.b If no, move to 2.2.
    - 2.2 Route the order to a dark pool in the "ping sequence" as an IOC order.[10]
    - 2.3 Reduce the outstanding number of units/shares by the amount filled in 2.2, receiving back from the current dark pool the results of the IOC.
    - 2.4 Check the number of remaining units/shares left in the order.
        - 2.4.a If the number = 0, then flag the order as complete.
        - 2.4.b If the number > 0, then align the router to point to the next dark pool in the "ping sequence."
    - 2.5 Revert to 2.2 with the next dark pool in the "ping sequence" and repeat the process, verifying that the order is still marketable; if it has become nonmarketable, revert to 2.1.a.1.
        - 2.5.a If, after routing through the entire "ping sequence," the remaining number of shares/units ≠ 0, convert the incomplete order into FIX Protocol and route to an exchange/ECN.

2.5.a.1 Determine how many shares are immediately executable.
    2.5.a.1.a If no current availability, submit as a limit order.
    2.5.a.1.b If availability exists, determine best available price for a specified number of units/shares that can be immediately filled, and reroute subportions as needed to multiple exchanges/ECNs as a series of market orders.

These comprise the main steps of the routing process.[11] Let us attach an actual trade example to the routing rules established above. In particular, assume that an institutional client wants to buy 10,000 shares of Stock ABC at $35/share and where Dark Pool X has certain preferential characteristics that are decisive once price priority has been taken into account. Table 6.1 summarizes the share blocks and associated offers that currently exist in the market.

Through the sample routing logic described above, the order will be sequenced and filled as per the results reflected in Table 6.2.

Based on market conditions at the time the order was submitted, the smart order router is able to fill 4250 of the 10,000 shares in various dark pools before converting the unfilled balance to a limit order executed on an exchange.

Table 6.1 Share blocks on various dark pools

Dark Pool X		Dark Pool A		Dark Pool B		Dark Pool C	
1000	$ 34.85	750	$ 34.85	200	$ 34.89	1200	$ 34.88
1000	$ 34.89	100	$ 34.92				

Table 6.2 Order fill against various dark pools

Route	Price ($)	Shares	Venue
1	34.85	1000	DP X
2	34.85	750	DP A
3	34.88	1200	DP C
4	34.89	1000	DP X
5	34.89	200	DP B
6	34.92	100	DP A
Total fills after routing		4250	
Convert unfilled to limit order			
7	35.00	5750	Exchange

Matching and Pricing Engine

The matching and pricing engine forms an integral component of any electronic venue that receives bids and offers and attempts to fill them. In fact, a matching and pricing engine can be considered to be the "brain" of any platform, performing the essential tasks of evaluating orders as they enter, rejecting those that do not meet specified criteria, and then aligning and comparing them with others already in the venue to determine whether a match can be made. Matching engines can be found in all of the dark and light mechanisms we have described in Chapter 3, including exchanges, ECNs/ ELOBs, and crossing networks. Broker/dealer desks which cross internal flows must also have some type of matching capability, to cross client flows with other client orders and/or proprietary positions. It is important to note, of course, that the specific function and business model of the platform will influence the type of matching engine it employs. For instance, an ELOB that runs an integrated light and dark limit order book and is involved in price discovery will necessarily have different specifications in its engine than a crossing network that derives prices externally and simply crosses dark trades. That said, certain features are common to all platforms.

A matching engine typically must meet minimum specifications so that it can be properly classified under regulations as an automated platform. These vary by jurisdiction, but relate primarily to ensuring a technologically appropriate environment (typically based on the standards listed in the first section of the chapter), a fair and transparent mechanism for collecting and matching orders, and adherence to pricing standards as set forth under various rules. The matching engine must also make clear which trading state is in effect at any point in time, such as auto-matching (matching is permitted and incoming orders are being matched continuously), auction (matching is permitted but new orders entering will be matched only during designated call auction periods), or halted (matching is not permitted and new orders will not be matched until the next matching cycle). In the balance of this section we will consider some of the key features that might be found in a typical matching engine, such as in an ELOB that accepts market orders, limit orders, and peg orders referencing a base price. The ELOB can participate in price discovery through its market and limit orders or it can fall back on price derivation for peg orders.

In the first instance, the platform must receive an order and place it in a matching book accessible by the matching engine; an engine is likely to be connected via a direct access server interface in order to improve connectivity and reduce latency. In most instances orders are submitted and received by way of common messaging, such as FIX we describe later in the chapter (though alternates can also be used, e.g., the CMS protocol). The matching engine first screens for acceptable order types to make sure they conform to specified criteria, rejecting via return message to the submitting party any that do not conform. In this example, the engine may accept only displayed and nondisplayed market, limit and peg orders, plus those with IOC or FOK designations, effectively rejecting all others before any attempt to match is even made (note that we can also imagine the example of an engine rejecting outright any IOC orders as part of the venue's antigaming measures). Similarly, it may screen for, and reject, orders with nonstandard characteristics, such as nonstandard settlement parameters or subpenny increments on securities priced above $1. Once the screening is complete, any order submitted and accepted is regarded as firm, implying that the party submitting the order is obliged to deliver monies or securities if the order is matched. This remains true until, or if, the order is cancelled by the submitting party.

Once accepted in the engine, the order is allocated by ticker into a separate subprocess dedicated to handling other orders with the same ticker. These subprocesses can be reallocated to support heavy order flow in a particular security in order to optimize the processing capabilities of the system. At this point the price contained in the order is compared with standing limit orders in the ELOB's sub-book for the security and a matching decision occurs:

- If the incoming order is deemed to be an improper trade-through it is routed to another market or, if classed as a "do-not-route" order, it is cancelled (with a message returned to the submitting party). If the order does not violate trade-through rules, it continues through the matching process.
- If the incoming order is a peg and can be executed within the base reference price (e.g., the NBBO or EBBO) against a standing limit order in the sub-book, the order is flagged for execution. Typically, an engine can match orders on a share for share basis and odd lots can be permitted to match outside the base reference price.
  - The engine matches according to rules of priority logic, such as the common "waterfall" described earlier in the book.
    - First priority: Visible liquidity: Displayed orders by price/time
    - Second priority: Dark liquidity: Nondisplayed portion of reserve orders by price/time
    - Third priority: Dark liquidity: Hidden orders by price/time
- If the incoming order can be executed only outside the base reference price, then a match is rejected and the order is placed within the sub-book and immediately quoted.
- If the incoming order either locks or crosses the base reference price, then the order is rejected, and a message is sent to the submitting party.

We must reemphasize that if the orders, whether light or dark, can influence price, the engine will make an allocation based on the bids and offers of the orders, similar to the example presented in Chapter 2. If the orders are pegged or in some way reference the base price, the engine need only draw in, via a market feed, the NBBO or EBBO derived on a primary exchange.

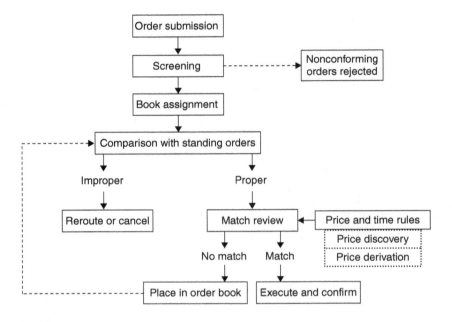

Figure 6.3 The matching flow

Though this view is rather simplified, it conveys the essential points of matching. The entire process is, of course, dynamic, updating continuously as new orders enter the platform, are matched, cancelled, rejected, or rerouted; electronic messaging is generated through each one of these actions. Not surprisingly, the matching and pricing engine demands a significant amount of computing capability in order to perform its matching tasks on an instantaneous basis. Figure 6.3 summarizes a typical matching flow.

The FIX Protocol

The Financial Information Exchange (FIX) Protocol supported and sponsored by the FIX Trading Community has developed as a de facto industry standard for messaging and communications within the trading sector. FIX was introduced in 1992 as an open and free specification which software and applications could reference, and has since grown to become an important "common denominator" in the electronic trading world. Indeed, it features prominently in the architecture of many OMSs/ EMSs, crossing networks, ECNs, ELOBs, and so forth, and certain estimates indicate 80% of all messaging in the trading sector relies on FIX. It is not, of course, the only protocol in existence, but it is widely used and has gained acceptance across a large segment of the market, particularly in light and dark equity trading.[12]

Given its prominence, it is useful to consider some general points regarding FIX and its role in supporting venues involved in dark trading; we will, of course, present this discussion in a nontechnical manner, referring interested readers to alternative resources for a detailed review of the technical aspects of the topic.[13] We will briefly consider connectivity, the engine, and messaging, all of which are used to support optimization of market data transfer and acceleration of electronic transaction routing and execution.

Connectivity

FIX network connectivity from an application or OMS/EMS to a venue (and vice versa) can occur via a leased line, a wide-area network (such as the Internet), a point-to-point virtual private network (VPN), or a hub-and-spoke setup; in practice, VPNs and hub and spokes tend to be most common, as they provide for proper transmission speeds and can minimize latency problems. A VPN features a single connection to a network, but individual logical connections to each venue or counterpart; a hub and spoke has a single physical and logical connection to the network, and all communication passes to venues through the hub, which may contain a FIX engine that receives a FIX message indicating how the message should be directed.

Engine

The FIX engine is a software module allowing an application, OMS/EMS, or venue to perform a variety of functions, including

- Managing network connections (as above)
- Creating and parsing in/out messages in a consistent manner (as described below)
- Storing and recovering essential data

The FIX engine is divided into different "layers," each of which is responsible for performing specific tasks; thus, a session layer takes responsibility for messaging, an application layer takes charge of business flows, and so forth. In essence, the engine serves as an interface to the external marketplace, operating via a network. The FIX engine must be equipped with minimum capabilities, and should ideally support all major forms of financial messaging (e.g., FIX, CMS, etc.), allow for data logging and monitoring, feature top performance and redundancy capacity, and incorporate appropriate levels of encryption and architectural flexibility.

Messaging

Messaging is, of course, at the heart of FIX, and the common communication language that emerges through standardization is essential for rapid transmission and interpretation of all manner of communiques. Many types of messages can be conveyed (and can vary by sector, e.g., buy-side versus sell-side), but the core types include many of the terms that are relevant to our discussion of dark trading in stocks and other securities. Specifically, standard message types exist for

- Indications of Interest
- Single Orders
- Day Orders
- Multi-Day Orders
- Order Modify Requests
- Order Cancel Requests
- Order Cancel Rejects
- "Questioned Trade" and "Don't Know Trade"
- Order Status Requests

This common method of communicating contributes to rapid execution, which is essential to electronic trading and the expansion of alternative trading platforms. We can easily imagine the delays and complications that might arise when a common language link is not employed; such delays, particularly in time-sensitive transactions, can work against best execution. However, we stress once again that FIX is not a mandatory, uniform protocol in electronic trading that is used by all parties – other alternatives exist, some of which operate on similar principles or which seek to achieve similar goals.

Let us consider an example of how common messaging can be used to convey an order from an OMS/EMS into a venue for matching, pricing, and execution. We will consider this example in normal terms rather than in FIX technical terms to demonstrate the logic of the construction. Converting to FIX is then simply a matter of translation, much as we would translate a sentence or paragraph from English to another language.

The construction of a standard order template can vary somewhat by venue but in most cases includes the parameters we discuss below; indeed, these are the minimum specifications that are needed to properly describe a trade. The essential order parameters include

- Order ID
- Ticker
- Buy/Sell indicator
- Order price
- Order quantity
- Visibility
- Validity

Some of these parameters might include additional granularity in the form of conditions, as we will note below. Let us explore the logic a bit further.

- Order ID: This field provides a unique identifier so that its source can be traced to a specific user or OMS. It is auto-generated by the venue and is not therefore an editable field, and is typically set in relation to where the order is meant to reside (e.g., public book versus private book, or integrated book (light and dark) versus dark book (dark only)).
- Ticker: This field provides the unique ticker symbol of the security.
- Buy/Sell indicator: This field is the most fundamental of any order ticket and, as the name suggests, is a flag indicating whether the user is submitting an order to buy or sell securities; the field may be populated by a single character (such as "B" or "S") or selected as a full word.
- Order price: This field specifies the price at which an order is to be executed. In fact, it is likely to have an additional conditional field providing further detail on the nature of the order price and whether any price discretion is possible.
  - In the first instance, an order must distinguish between type, such as market, limit, peg, and so forth:
    - If the conditional field under order price is delimited as "market" no further information is required as the order is designed to execute at the current bid or offer.
    - If the order price is delimited as "limit" then further granularity is required in the message. Specifically, a further sub-condition will be required, such as a valid price that indicates, to the appropriate tick, the amount at which the order should be executed. Thus, an order price delimited as "limit" with a sub-condition of "valid price" might specify, for example, a limit price of $48.15.
    - If the order price is delimited as "peg" then further granularity is again required. Specifically, the sub-condition must identify the specific type of peg and its reference (along with any tick adjustments, if necessary), such as "market peg" and "EBBO" or "alternative midpoint peg" and "NBBO plus two ticks," for example.
  - In the second instance, the field must contain a condition on whether the order is discretionary, meaning the order is executable up to, and including, some nondisplayed price (making it a dark order). It is defined as a number of discretionary ticks against the valid price, and would thus appear as "discretion plus 10 ticks," for example.
- Order Quantity: This field describes the number of shares to be bought or sold, with a round (not fractional) number input under "order quantity," such as 1000 or 5051, for example. An additional condition may be used to indicate the minimum quantity of the order that should be executed (which is useful for FOK, MAQ, and other quantity driven parameters), and how much should be displayed to the public (meaning it serves as a mechanism for creating a reserve order).

- The minimum quantity condition indicates how much of the order should be executed at a minimum. For instance, if the minimum quantity condition is set to the size of the order quantity, then an FOK order is created.
- The display condition sets a maximum amount of the order quantity that should be considered as "public" (or open). When the "public" quantity is less than order quantity, a reserve order is created, where the visible tip of the iceberg is equal to the "public" amount and the nondisplayed portion of the order is the difference between the "public" amount and the order quantity. Through this simple construct, a dark order is created.
- Visibility: This field indicates whether the order is to be displayed in the public markets or remain hidden within the private order book, and where the delimiters may be defined as "light" and "dark." Note that this field is similar to, yet distinct from, the display condition in the order quantity described above. An iceberg can be created only by flagging the visibility as "light" and then adjusting the "public" display order quantity to identify the amount that is to be exposed. A hidden order, which is completely dark, is simply flagged in the visibility field as "dark," meaning that no amount will be shown in the public order book.
- Validity: This field reflects the "time in force" parameters of the order, and can be defined through one or both of the "to" and "from" conditions.
  - The "valid from" condition indicates when the order is due to take effect. In most cases this is flagged as "immediate," which means the order can be executed the moment it enters the venue's matching engine (assuming a match can be found). In other cases it may be delayed by some period such as "market open," "next matching cycle," or a specific date.
  - The "valid to" condition indicates the point at which the order is to be cancelled. Again, this can be defined through a specific date, "next matching cycle," "market close," and so forth.

Consider the examples in Tables 6.3(a) and (b) of how an FOK limit order and a dark peg order with minimum volume might be defined per the parameters above.

Table 6.3(a)   FOK buy limit order at $50.00, 1000 shares

Parameter	
Buy/Sell	**Buy**
Order price	Condition limit = yes
	Condition valid price = $50.00
	Condition discretion = no
Order quantity	Condition order quantity = 1000
	Condition minimum quantity = order quantity
	Condition display = open
Visibility	Light
Validity	Condition valid from = immediate
	Condition valid to = next matching cycle

Table 6.3(b) Dark sell peg order at the midpoint of the NBBO, 2000 shares and minimum quantity 1000 shares, valid market open tomorrow (T + 1)

Parameter	
Buy/Sell	**Sell**
Order price	Condition peg = yes
	Condition valid price = midpoint NBBO
	Condition discretion = no
Order quantity	Condition order quantity = 2000
	Condition minimum quantity = 1000
Visibility	Dark
Validity	Condition valid from = T + 1
	Condition valid to = good till cancel

These essential fields help transform a trader's specific requirements into a common, easily understood, format. We can easily imagine that any mechanism that is able to convert order parameters into a standard form is bound to improve the execution process. Of course, not every order is entered correctly every time, meaning corrections have to be made; in addition, there are times when a trader may wish to change parameters on an existing order. Such changes are a matter of course and quite achievable, but they may result in a change in order priorities. In addition, not all parameters can be changed on an existing order; in such cases the only solution is to cancel the order and resubmit it, which results in a complete change in priority. For instance, parameters that can often be amended via subsequent order messaging without loss of priority include

- Quantity and condition
- Validity

Those that can be changed, but which can result in change of priority, include

- Price and conditions
- Minimum quantity (if added or increased)

Parameters that cannot be changed, and which therefore require resubmission and establishment of a new priority, typically include

- Buy/sell indicator
- Visibility

We have noted at various points in the text that the success of electronic trading in general, and the dark sector specifically, is a direct result of advances in technology and architecture that have emerged over the years. As technological innovations continue to appear it is quite likely that the execution, matching, reporting, processing and other dimensions of the sector will improve in tandem – making the entire process even more efficient and cost effective.

PART III

Environment of the Future

7 | Regulation, Control, and Transparency

Regulation is an essential component of any well-run financial system, and a robust system of rules and controls can add a degree of comfort to all stakeholders – investors, issuers, intermediaries, government authorities, and the public at large. In fact, national markets that feature a strong regulatory framework are generally better placed to attract and mobilize capital and ensure efficient funding and risk management than those lacking such controls.

Of course, no regulatory regime is perfect, and even those that are well regarded suffer occasional mishaps – regulatory missteps or inadequacies tend to be revealed periodically, particularly during times of financial crisis – we need only examine the LDC Debt Crisis of the early 1980s, the US Savings and Loan Crisis of the late 1980s, and the Financial Crisis of 2007–2008, among others, to see that regulatory missteps played a role in losses sustained by financial institutions and investors. In the main, however, regulatory checks and balances may be considered effective and useful, and should be seen as essential to the smooth conduct of financial business. In this chapter we consider how the increasingly significant activity in the dark pool sector is, and should be, regulated. More specifically, we will consider financial regulation in the context of dark pools, the effects of regulatory changes on the development of dark pools, the optimal level of formal regulation (including reporting and transparency), and the potential opportunities for self-regulation.

The Impact of Regulatory Changes on Dark Pools

We noted in Chapter 1 that Regulations ATS and NMS and MiFID were designed, among other things, to create a competitive landscape where trades might be executed through various kinds of venues, rather than strictly through exchanges – subject, of course, to certain minimum standards to ensure fair treatment of clients and transparency on prices (if not necessarily on trading and execution). In fact, the regulations set forth at the beginning of the decade and in the period of 2006–7 (what we referred to collectively as the "first phase" of regulation) appear to have served as a form of deregulation, sanctioning the establishment and expansion of ATSs and MTFs. Some of the effects that have arisen from such measures include

- Increased competition
- Lower costs
- Improved execution
- Enhanced innovation
- Reduced transparency
- Fragmented markets and trades

To begin, we note that first phase regulations in the U.S. and Europe invited the entry of new competitors to the marketplace. These original regulations were central in supporting the creation of new platforms capable of competing directly with regulated, protected markets. The implications of this support have become clear over the past few years: although some venues had been established before the promulgation of these rules, a large number have been established since that time.

A logical by-product of the increased competition has been the trend towards lower fees – including exchange fees, clearing fees, commissions and liquidity charges levied by any venues and institutions supporting the flow and execution of trades. Clients have benefitted from lower fee levels, a process that is likely to continue – until such point that individual platforms can no longer run an economically viable model. When this occurs we may observe instances of consolidation, a halt in fee erosion, or both, and a potential revision of the business model. It is conceivable, for instance, that the execution function may eventually be a free service that is provided by venues that generate revenues from other sources, such as the provision of algorithms, connectivity, OMS/EMS applications, and so forth.

A third effect relates to the quality of execution, which is a by-product of both direct regulatory intervention and increased competition. First phase regulations specifically require authorized venues to provide best execution for clients, and to have policies in place to that effect. Best execution is not limited to price, as we have noted earlier – it may also relate to speed, cost, confidentiality, and other factors. Therefore, it comes as no surprise that venues seeking to gain market share have attempted continuously to improve the quality of their service offerings so that they can, indeed, provide best execution. MiFID, for instance, encourages queue jumping as a way of speeding execution, de facto trading through a similar price in another location that has historically been protected by price-time priority.

Another very important effect of the first phase of regulatory changes has centered on enhancements and innovations related to business models, technological mechanisms, and product/service offerings. In fact, this is a key point for the entire sector, and particularly for exchanges that have historically enjoyed protected market status. The breaking down of barriers has caused these exchanges to refine, and in some cases dramatically alter, their business models, leading them in some cases to pursue multiple channels as described in Chapter 3 (and as we shall revisit in Chapter 8). Thus, it is no longer unusual for an exchange to run a dedicated dark pool in one or more markets, perhaps partner with others on an international crossing network, and so forth. All of these moves have been taken in response to a changing revenue stream that has been affected by the injection of competition and the changing requirements of investors. Of course, not all of these changes relate to business models. In some cases the original regulatory changes spurred venues to enhance their technology and delivery mechanisms, improving connectivity, reducing latency, and facilitating order entry as a way of getting closer to delivering best execution. Indeed, the advancements and sophistication in this area have been so dramatic that something of a "technological arms race" between participants has arisen. There is a strong belief that those offering the most sophisticated, leading-edge technology can gain the upper hand in an important market segment. In fact, technological advances have created the new breed of high frequency traders noted in Chapter 5, who move rapidly in and out of stocks in both visible and dark markets. In other cases innovation has come in the form of new products and strategies, such as advanced algorithms, advanced reporting and analytics, multiple dark pool access points, and so forth. It is possible that many of these enhancements and innovations would have appeared as a matter of course, without the regulatory changes found in ATS, NMS, and MiFID. In fact, the financial sector has a long record of innovation and evolution that comes because of its interest in servicing the needs of clients and maximizing revenues. That said, there seems little doubt that the regulatory "push" that occurred between 2004 and 2008 accelerated some of these innovations, to the ultimate benefit of all parties.

Transparency is a two-edged sword in the world of dark trading, and one where regulators must necessarily walk a very fine line. On one hand, too much transparency eliminates the need for, and benefits of, dark trading. There are very good reasons why opacity is permitted to exist, even thrive, as we have noted at various points in the book. If regulators were to illuminate more of the trading activity that takes places in hidden and reserve books or via crossing networks or internal desks, then the very benefits of confidentiality and reduced market impact would be sacrificed. On the other hand, too little transparency places numerous stakeholders – including investors and regulators – in the uncomfortable position of not really knowing what is occurring: whether all parties are being treated fairly, whether some nefarious activities are taking place, and whether some degree of systemic risk is being injected into the markets. The latter point is particularly relevant in a world where financial crises happen with a fair degree of regularity. Since dark pools and the associated mechanisms of smart order routing, algorithms, and high frequency trading can operate freely, regulators and other stakeholders may be unaware of what could happen during a market disaster (to wit, the "Flash Crash" episode discussed in the Pools in Practice section below). During a period of crisis it may be difficult to be sure whether best execution per NMS and MiFID is occurring, whether settlements are proceeding properly, whether there are increased instances of fraud, whether activity is contributing to volatility and drawing liquidity away from the primary markets, whether the clearing and settlement systems are becoming overly stressed, and so forth. It is worth considering the impact of stress events on dark pool activity to determine whether the sector has the potential of becoming the next "problem area," as we have seen with portfolio insurance, structured notes, complex over-the-counter derivatives, special purposes entities, conduits, asset-backed securities, and so forth.

* * *

Pools in Practice: The Flash Crash

For a few short minutes on the afternoon of May 6, 2010, the U.S. equity markets temporarily plunged, causing more than $1 trillion in market value to disappear. Though the markets quickly rebounded and restored most of the loss, the rapid market fall caught everyone off guard. An ex-post reconstruction of events surrounding the so-called Flash Crash (which had nothing to do with the flash orders we discussed earlier in the book) helps shed some light on a complex set of circumstances that created the perfect environment for the sudden, steep drop – and which appears to have involved both light and dark players.

In the immediate lead-up to the crash, the bellwether Dow Jones Industrial Average (DJIA) of 30 blue chip stocks had been down about 300 points (approximately 3%) in a market that was thinly traded and increasingly volatile. Just before 2.45pm a large mutual fund triggered an automated sell program to hedge its long equity portfolio; the sell program amounted to 75,000 contracts of the S&P 500 e-mini future on the Chicago Mercantile Exchange (CME), worth approximately $4.1 billion in notional terms. High frequency traders initially bought a portion of the e-minis, but as the market continued its downward trajectory they became sellers – adding significantly to the negative momentum. They then began buying and selling contracts amongst themselves, trading 27,000 contracts in only 15 seconds (but only adding a net 200 contract position to the market). Other buy-side institutions became buyers of index futures but sellers of the cash index, which increased overall market pressure on both the S&P and DJIA. To be sure, some dark liquidity participants also helped drive the markets down. Specifically, the internal desks of broker/dealers stopped crossing customer flows with their own proprietary positions, re-routing the client orders directly to the exchanges for execution; this migration from dark to light simply exacerbated the downward moves. In fact, dark trading fell from its normal range of 25%–30% down to a slim 11% during the day, as internalizers re-routed, certain other dark pools rebuffed incoming orders and similarly re-routed, and block traders normally active in dark pools simply pulled back. At this point the DJIA was approaching a 900-point drop, equal to about 9%.

Interestingly, a number of large cap stocks temporarily traded as penny stocks (Accenture and P&G to name but two). This odd phenomenon occurred because of a confluence of two trading mechanisms: "stub quotes" and ISOs. Market-makers sometimes practice "stub quoting," where they place a quote for $0.01 so that a stock they make a book in always has a deep backstop bid – but knowing that a stock should never trade at that level. ISOs (and market orders) are, of course, orders that seek to execute against any available liquidity. During the Flash Crash, these two came together: institutional traders and market-makers placed an excessively large amount of ISO and market orders to execute against all available liquidity – regardless of price. As market liquidity disappeared in some of the large cap names, the flood of orders hit every available bid in a dramatic version of "walking the book" – in some cases all the way down to the stub quote. We can well imagine the shock of seeing a blue chip like P&G temporarily trade for a penny a share.

With no buying interest to halt the self-fulfilling market spiral, the CME decided to stop trading in e-minis for a mere 5 seconds – which was sufficient to stop the spiral. After the 5-second halt "normal interest" returned and stock prices quickly returned to their fair valuations. Most of the 600-point drop that occurred after 2.45 pm was erased, and the markets regained their footing.

Not surprisingly, the massive plunge led to plenty of regulatory and governmental investigations, though the conclusions eventually drawn were not unanimously accepted by all parties. Regulators, for instance, believed that high frequency traders running algorithms played a key role in accelerating the downward pressure through fast outright selling and "quote stuffing" (a practice of sending in, and then quickly cancelling, non-executable orders, generally as a way of examining price trends or testing latency). They also believed that dark pools within the broker/dealer community exacerbated the moves by routing orders to the lit markets for execution. Both findings were rejected by trading professionals. Some market observers noted that the market was already "toxic" before the crash and therefore especially vulnerable: as order flow becomes increasingly toxic (i.e., informed traders adversely selecting uninformed traders), market-makers tend to pull back, causing liquidity to dry up – meaning any subsequent sales place extreme pressure on prices and push the markets down aggressively. After a great deal of analysis and discussion, the main corrective actions set forth were based on tightening up of "circuit breakers," essentially triggering trading halts after small market moves. No additional substantive regulatory steps were taken either for high frequency traders or dark pool operators.

*   *   *

The suite of original regulatory measures attempted to create some basic safeguards, while still preserving the dark characteristics of the market. We know, for instance, that sponsors must create best execution processes that ensure clients cannot be prejudiced, and that a certain amount of high level reporting must occur. In the

U.S., platforms that are considered to be ATSs must register as broker/dealers or self-regulating exchanges, and must therefore adhere to additional regulations. But the result of the original regulations (e.g., ATS and NMS, or MiFID, or the Japan Financial Reform Law) is reduced transparency in the market. Traders and investors can never be entirely sure, ex-ante, that all aspects of the market will work as intended; they have had to take on faith that the market will function properly, and retain some hope that regulators are astute enough to pick up on any problems before they become severe. Reduced transparency is a fact, with all of its attendant benefits and pitfalls.

Finally, and as noted earlier in the book, the advent of so many new platforms has led to a certain amount of sector fragmentation; at a micro level we may also take note of trade fragmentation. Sector fragmentation is, by now, a reality of the marketplace. Traditional exchanges have lost light and dark market share to a host of new electronic competitors and to internalized flows, and have been forced to redesign their business models to face this reality. Most research appears to reflect the fact that conventional trading via exchanges will never again return to its previous levels (unless restrictive regulations are imposed),[1] and that buy-side and sell-side participants will continue to select from among a number of different venues and mechanisms to execute their trades. Trade fragmentation has also appeared, and goes to the heart of our previous discussions regarding block trading, decimalization, and confidentiality. Breaking up large trades into a smaller number of pieces for execution in either dark or light venues has become standard operating practice for many large traders and investors, and it is a trend that is expected to continue. Consider, for instance, one simple example of this phenomenon: with the advent of the regulatory changes we have mentioned, the trading composition on the LSE has changed dramatically, with the average size of a trade falling from £63,020 in 1999 to £14,908 in 2008, and £6,000 in 2012. Similar trends have become apparent on other major exchanges, which surely reinforces the point that slicing trades into smaller pieces is a well-established practice. Of course, this sector and trade fragmentation brings us back to our discussion earlier in the book on the challenges created through multiple pools of fragmented liquidity and the difficulties of sometimes conducting credible price discovery.

We may therefore say that the original regulations promulgated under ATS, NMS, and MiFID created or supported fundamental changes in the traded markets. The issue at hand is whether these regulatory changes have led to certain unintended consequences – in particular, whether these new, and rather opaque, platforms have gained market share so rapidly that the full extent of their activities is not well understood or monitored from a regulatory perspective, and that the possibility of increased systemic risk lurks below the surface. In fact, this issue has emerged at the forefront of regulatory and legislative discussion in various countries and it is against this background that we must consider some of the new regulatory initiatives that have appeared since 2010. Fundamental changes to regulations in Australia,

Canada, the US, UK, and Europe are beginning to alter some of the characteristics of the dark pool environment, as we shall note later in the chapter.

Financial Regulation and Dark Pools

The global regulatory environment related to financial activities must be viewed as a complex and evolving process which is intended to protect consumers and investors. It is also a highly fractionalized process, where individual countries often follow their own paths, and where agencies within individual countries may do the same. Efforts at harmonization and consistency are in place in some areas (e.g., MiFID and MiFID II), and further efforts at internal and cross-border coordination appear to be a common goal. The reality, however, is that a "patchwork" of global financial regulation continues to exist.

The complexity of the regulatory landscape is a direct result of the complexity of the financial markets of the twenty-first century. The broad array of products, markets, and institutions that comprise the financial markets makes it necessary to provide an appropriate degree of oversight related to different dimensions of the system. Such tasks are typically allocated to specific regulators with a given degree of specialized knowledge, resulting in this "patchwork" of controls. This is the case in the U.S., Canada, and Germany, for example, where multiple regulators govern pieces of the system, but not the whole. In some cases national authorities have chosen to create consolidated "super-regulators," which are charged with a holistic view of an entire national system. Regardless of the approach, the main point to bear in mind is that national financial regulators have a responsibility and interest in ensuring that their financial systems operate properly, and that the individual products, institutions, and markets are appropriately controlled – while still being free enough to create widespread innovation and participation.

Regulation in the dark sector

This brings us to the traded financial markets and, in particular, venues that house dark liquidity. Though dark markets have existed in certain financial markets for several decades, true growth, as already observed, is more recent. If we assume that dark liquidity has grown from a relatively negligible amount in 1997 to approximately 40% of all traded volume in the U.S. and approximately 10–15% in Europe in 2013, the issue we must consider is whether the regulatory approach has been appropriate and whether it is sufficient for the future.

We know that financial regulations are designed to ensure a safe and equitable environment for all participants. This becomes more difficult to achieve if activity is opaque, misunderstood, or complex. We might argue that dark trading is characterized by all three elements. As more market share shifts from exchanges to off-exchange platforms and from light to dark, regulators have had to grapple with a very different environment. For all of the requirements imposed by NMS and MiFID on off-exchange trading, certain questions must still be resolved:

- Do the pre-trade and post-trade requirements adequately protect investors?
- Do trade-through rules function properly?
- Are economic incentives for rebates, liquidity fees, and payment for order flow equitable, or are certain participants being disadvantaged?
- Is there a sufficiently adequate picture of the nature of trades being executed in the dark?
- Does reported volume correspond with what regulators expect given overall market statistics?
- Does a standard activity metric need to be imposed on all off-exchange platforms?
- Does gaming need to be explicitly controlled or banned?
- Is high frequency trading/low latency trading in light or dark pools beneficial or harmful?
- Is algorithmic trading beneficial or harmful?
- Does electronic market making via, e.g., high frequency trading, need to be regulated?
- Should certain types of investors be prevented from participating in certain types of "toxic pools?" Is too much market share shifting off-exchange so that the price discovery process is becoming questionable?
- Is the technology underpinning off-exchange trading reliable and can it withstand a disaster?
- How will the market fare in the event of a dislocation, and will dark venues amplify or extend a downward spiral?
- Should dark pools be required to offer price improvement over exchanges?
- Should the volume of an individual security and for securities as a whole that trade in the dark be capped?

The answers to many of these questions are still unknown, or a matter of conjecture. Indeed, the very fact that so many questions remain unanswered has led various national authorities to craft tighter rules around their dark markets. Of course, regulating the dark sector more formally is a balancing act. If regulation becomes too restrictive, the dynamics of the sector might change, perhaps dramatically. The advantages conveyed by the dark sector might be threatened and eventually disappear, leaving market participants operating in a market state similar to that of the 1970s and 1980s. Equally, if there is insufficient regulation – and particularly if there is an inadequate understanding of what individual platforms are doing, and whether they are operating prudently and equitably – we may imagine that the potential for misuse or abuse increases dramatically. Indeed, we might draw a page from the over-the-counter derivatives market, which, while largely successfully and constructive, has also been the source of numerous problems over the years. We recall that the OTC derivatives market is rather loosely and inconsistently regulated, that it features complexity, and that it is extremely opaque[2] – many of the same features characterize the dark pool sector.

Reporting and transparency

Reporting and transparency are important aspects of security and fairness. The issue is especially important in a nascent or developing sector, where a tradition of reporting may not be well understood or established, and where metrics may be ill-defined, subjective, or changeable. Indeed, we need only consider the foreign exchange and over-the-counter derivatives markets, where the earliest years of their respective development were characterized by uncertainties regarding the best way to measure activity, the risks of double-counting or over-estimating volume, and so forth. When the industry and regulators ultimately cooperated on developing reasonable measures, reporting and transparency began to improve – a process that took many years to achieve (and is arguably still not perfect) but which conveys important information about individual and systemic risks.

The same issues apply to the dark pool sector. The market is still arguably in its developmental phase, so it is perhaps no surprise that consistency and transparency are still quite underdeveloped – making it difficult to reconcile the level of activity that is actually taking place. In fact, in many jurisdictions there have been no specific rules requiring trade reporting to reflect dark execution. In the U.S., for example, dark pools have to report trades to the consolidated tapes (as discussed below), but the trades are only identified as being "non-exchange" – not as "dark" or "light," and not as having been executed within a specific dark location. Accordingly, three themes emerge as part of this issue: the use of different metrics; the need to balance transparency with anonymity; and the requirements certain regulators may enforce in order to provide suitable protections.

Reporting metrics

We have noted earlier in the book that no single industry standard has emerged regarding reporting metrics. Some venues must report certain standard information on prints ex-post into a trade reporting facility, consolidated tape, or similar central repository, while others may not be required to do so. Furthermore, what a venue may report into an official facility may be somewhat different than what it chooses to report on its website or convey through its marketing documents to potential clients. Finally, reporting standards can easily vary across national borders. It is clear, then, that different metrics can be employed, giving rise to the possibility of confusion. Recapping our discussion from Chapter 2 there are several ways in which activity in the dark space can be measured:

- Orders touched (or handled): orders that are routed through a pool, but which are not matched in the pool.
- Orders matched: orders that are routed to a pool or contained internally within a pool, where they are matched (totally or partially).

Furthermore, some pools that report matched orders do so by double counting the volume (that is, the buy and the sell orders that cross are both counted) while others report on the basis of a single leg (which corresponds to the way in which exchanges report their volume).

Consider this simple example, which illustrates how venues might report multiple statistics on the same trade. Trade 1 is a dark marketable order to buy 1000 shares of Stock JKL, which routes through Dark Venue A but is not matched; however, the fact that it has been touched is counted as volume by Venue A. Trade 2 represents the same order in JKL, which is routed to Dark Venue B and again remains unmatched; however, Venue B does not report touched volume. Trade 3 is an order in JKL which routes through Dark Venue C and is matched, and where C counts both sides of the trades as volume. Finally, Trade 4 is an order in JKL passing to Dark Venue D, where it is matched, but where Venue D counts only one side of the trade of volume. For each one of these 1000 share transactions passing through four different venues we note the following outcomes:

- Dark Venue A reports "volume" of 1000 shares.
- Dark Venue B reports "volume" of 0 shares.
- Dark Venue C reports "volume" of 2000 shares.
- Dark Venue D reports "volume" of 1000 shares.

It is relatively easy to see the confusion that can arise and why some uniformity in reporting standards can be useful. Let us examine some real examples. Consider the case of LeveL ATS, a consortium platform that crosses continuously. In its monthly marketing reports, LeveL reports its average inflows as well as its average executions, counting both sides as fills. LavaFlow, the ECN owned by Lava (itself owned by Citibank), reported daily single-counted executions including those matched within the ECN and those routed through the ECN.[3] In contrast, Goldman Sachs, operator of the popular Sigma X platform, moved its reporting to single-counted matched trades only, but not making any information available to the public (only to clients). At the same time, the pan-Asian platform BlocSec reported on total volume passing through its platform, whether or not trades were matched. The reporting differences revealed by this small handful of examples, and the resulting challenges in comparability, are quite real.

U.S. reporting

Various reporting standards exist in different jurisdictions, most of which apply to visible trading and some of which are relevant for activity that crosses into the dark sector. In the U.S. we can point to

- Exchange reports
- SEC reports
- Trade reporting facility/consolidated tape system

Consider, for example, that in the U.S. the SEC, exchanges, and/or self-regulating organizations require reporting via the following: Blue Sheets, which includes all proprietary and customer trades that may be subject to potential violations; Daily Program Trading Report, which includes relevant details on all program trades executed on the NYSE (light or dark); NYSE 12B Report, which includes relevant details on orders placed from a proprietary system; and so forth.

In addition, and as indicated in Chapter 1, some degree of reporting uniformity has been injected via SEC Rules 605 and 606 (as an adaptation of Sections 11Ac1–5 and 6 of the Securities Act),[4] which requires market centers that trade NMS securities to provide standard reports that reflect different dimensions of activity.

Rule 605 requires monthly electronic submission by all market centers of relevant information on covered order executions:

- Quality of executions on a security-specific basis (e.g., how market orders are executed in relation to public quotes).
- Effective spreads paid by investors on orders that are routed to a particular market center.
- The degree to which a market center provides executions at prices that are better than the public quotes available to investors using limit orders.

Rule 606 Reporting centers on quarterly electronic submission of the routing of nondirected orders in U.S. equity (and option) trades, including

- Percentage of customer orders that were market orders, limit orders, and other order types.
- Locations of the top 10 market centers to which such orders were routed and any other market center receiving 5% or more of such orders.

Market centers, under the SEC definition, include exchanges, market-makers, and ECNs. The specific form of template is designated in Appendixes A and B of the Rules, and requires that all such information be posted on a freely available website of the submitting party.[5] Note that other ATSs are not required to publish any statistics unless they accumulate more than 5% of U.S. equity volume.

While Rules 605 and 606 deal in aggregate statistics, they do not provide detail and certainly do not reflect the split of light versus dark activity. Some additional reporting for internalized trades and other off-exchange trades must be reported through a trade reporting facility/consolidated tape within 90 seconds of execution. A trade reporting facility may be independently operated by a single entity, or may include the trades of multiple venues; in fact, each trade reporting facility is associated with an exchange or a national securities association and operates under the auspices of the Financial Industry Regulatory Authority (FINRA, the industry's self-regulatory body, which has also promulgated certain new rules, as noted below). The trade reporting facility/consolidated tape allows reporting of transactions executed away from an exchange (under so-called Tape A for NYSE stocks, Tape B for BATS, NYSE Arca and other regional stocks, and Tape C for NASDAQ stocks), and a variety of electronic applications are available to increase the efficiency of the process. For instance, the FINRA/NYSE makes available to FINRA members trading off-exchange a trade reporting application that uses NYSE Arca technology to facilitate the process; the FIX-based application interface focuses specifically on price and volume data. The facility supports block prints, market-maker prints, and early and late prints in all U.S.-listed stocks (not just NYSE stocks). The specific information included in the trade reporting facility data template includes[6]

- Security identification symbol
- Number of shares
- Unit price (excluding commissions or mark-ups/downs)
- Execution time
- Transaction type symbol indicating whether the party submitting the trade report is a reporting member or a nonreporting participant
- A flag indicating whether the transaction is a buy, sell, sell short, or cross
- A flag indicating whether the trade is as principal, riskless principal, or agent
- Clearing broker on the reporting side
- Executing broker on the reporting side
- Executing broker on the contra-trade
- Contra-trade introducing broker
- Contra-trade clearing broker

For information that is used for last sale reporting, the key fields include ticker, number of shares, price, transaction type flag, and execution time. While this information is, again, useful in an aggregate sense, it does not provide specificity with regard to dark execution. In fact, such reporting is still not adequately captured in a holistic sense across exchange and ECN reserve/hidden orders, specialist books, crossing networks, and internal desks.

European reporting

Reporting in Europe focused in the first instance on MiFID's original requirements, and in particular on post-trade transparency reporting. Much of this original reporting was designed to dovetail with market publication and other national regulatory reporting requirements. These initial efforts have since been supplemented by new MiFID II and MiFIR requirements.

When MiFID was being established, regulators used the opportunity to extract a "quid pro quo" from intermediaries: in exchange for breaking the concentration rule and allowing MTFs and systemic internalizers to directly challenge regulated markets, they required them to adhere to pre- and post-trade transparency. Specifically, MiFID imposes certain post-trade reporting requirements under various Articles (i.e., 25, 28, 30, 45) for any equity purchase or sale on an admitted exchange in the European Economic Area.[7] In fact, MiFID requires that all instruments admitted to trading on a regulated market (or prescribed market) be reported, but the information need be supplied to only one regulator under passporting rules (e.g., a branch in one country need not report to both the host country and the home country). We can consider that post-trading reporting features two dimensions: daily transaction reporting to national regulators demonstrating MiFID compliance, and publication to the market.

For any transaction executed via a regulated market, MTF, systematic internalizer, or over-the-counter, basic data must be submitted as quickly as possible, but within the three minutes of execution. The required data, which must go through a quality assurance process, include the following:

- Reporting firm
- Trading day/execution time
- Price
- Volume
- Flag indicating buy/sell
- Trading capacity designation (e.g., principal, principal cross, agency, agency cross)
- Instrument ID/ISIN
- Venue ID
- Customer ID
- Transaction reference number
- Cancellation flag
- For derivatives, additional data are required, including maturity date, put/call flag, strike price, and so forth

Transactions reported to the public tape are based on a subset of the same information, namely ISIN/ticker symbol, price, volume, and execution time. Prints of large transactions can be delayed under MiFID provisions (e.g., so-called deferred trade publication) by up to 60 minutes; similar exceptions exist for program trades and after-hours trades. If the information is not automatically submitted to national regulators ("competent authority") via, for example, the relevant primary exchange or an MTF, then it is incumbent upon the venue to make its own arrangements for proper submission – this can be done via third-party services. Not surprisingly, some exchanges and other venues have begun offering reporting services to other institutions and venues so that they may fulfill their MiFID requirements through existing technologies at minimal cost; in fact, the UK's FSA applies a special "Trade Data Monitor" designation to those reporting services that have the most robust and secure infrastructure.[8] The trade reporting offered by platforms such as LSE, Deutsche Boerse, and Chi-X Europe, for instance, is effected through application program interfaces and feature both quality assurance checks and standardized end-of-day compliance reports to demonstrate adherence to requirements. Other third-party service providers have also begun to offer similar services, such as Markit BOAT,[9] Omgeo (a Reuters/DTCC joint venture),[10] ICMA TRAX 2, and so forth. Fidessa, the architect of OMS/EMS platforms and analytics (such as the fragmentation index noted in Chapter 4), has developed a unique reporting tool that reflects dark and light executions in a stock, ex-post, by specific venue (including MTFs, regulated markets, systematic internalizers, and OTC). This helps provide some indication of which specific securities and platforms are involved in dark executions. Certain other reporting must flow to supranational organizations or other national regulatory authorities, such as the Federal of European Securities Exchanges (FESE).[11] The FESE, for instance, tabulates monthly statistics from both regulated markets and MTFs, including number of trades and turnover; the information is made available via the European Equity Market Report. All national markets also contribute into the CESR's MiFID database, which lists securities that are admitted for trading in regulated markets.[12] More specifically, the database lists all securities deemed to be liquid (per criteria contained in Article 22) and the relevant liquidity band for each; the latter is used to determine whether an order is LIS compared with normal market size (what is also termed "standard market size" or SMS) and is thus eligible for pre-trade transparency waiver, and also the minimum size that qualifies for post-trade deferred reporting, as noted above. It should be noted that all of the original MiFID reporting requirements remain in force despite the fact that MiFID II rules have been created as a supplementary framework.

Future reporting

Though reporting requirements exist in the U.S., Europe, and other jurisdictions, regulators,[13] industry practitioners and even clients[14] have expressed concerns about true lack of transparency in the sector. There is still no single combined regulatory and industry standard regarding the best metric(s) (e.g., single-counted matched volume). Potential proposals for future consistency focus on having regulators require, or institutions volunteer, standardized reporting metrics, identifying each specific print as a dark execution, and include the top names being executed in each venue. The regulatory view of adding more transparency to dark pools appears, in most jurisdictions, to be changing in favor of a more standardized approach, though specific declarations are yet to appear in all national systems; proposals via FINRA and MiFID II are two examples. The preferred, and perhaps most useful, metric may center on individual pool reporting single-counted matched order volume on a periodic basis via a regulator or a self-regulatory organization, identifying dark and light trades.

Naturally, too much information could be detrimental to the sector and arguably defeats the purpose of off-exchange trading (e.g., trading patterns can be detected from such data and can be used to the disadvantage of various classes of clients). That said, as more trading moves from light to dark, regulators and industry groups are correct in attempting to get a better grip on what is occurring, and this can be done only through an agreed series of meaningful metrics. This will ultimately be helpful to regulators, who need to keep closer watch on areas that could generate some degree of systemic risk, and to clients, by allowing them to make more reasoned decisions on the basis of consistent standards – without necessarily sacrificing the benefits of confidentiality that have allowed dark venues to become so important to the trading sector. However, any enhanced reporting is unlikely to occur in real-time[15] (as this could create gaming opportunities) and is unlikely to be made available to the public at large (being reserved for clients and regulators).

The end game of a more robust regime of reporting and transparency is providing stakeholders (including brokers, clients) with security and comfort that the sector is sufficiently well understood and controlled that it will not be the source of future systemic problems, unfavorable treatment, disputes, or noncompetitive behavior. It may also provide venues themselves with additional business flow gained from revealing to brokers and clients their ability to generate minimum levels of activity; to be sure those that are unable to post a critical mass of activity may see their fortunes fade.

Self-Regulation

The financial industry has historically enjoyed the right to a certain amount of self-regulation – that is, adopting certain agreed "self-policing" standards and then ensuring adherence to such standards. Self-regulation of this type is deemed to be an effective layer of control that supplements, rather than replaces, more formalized rules and regulations coming from a financial authority or regulator. For instance, in the U.S., ATSs that choose to register as self-regulating exchanges must adhere to certain self-regulatory standards of control, conduct, and transparency, all of which may be reviewed by the SEC at any time. They may choose to add additional levels of control beyond such minimum standards.

The experience of self-regulation in the financial markets appears to be somewhat mixed. Although such efforts have added additional levels of operating scrutiny to financial markets and instruments, there have been various instances where self-regulation has not been constructive. For instance, the OTC derivatives market, which is largely unregulated, relies heavily on a regime of self-policing. Various industry groups, such as the International Swap and Derivatives Association and the Counterparty Risk Management Group, have created minimum standards of documentation, risk control, and general best practices, and urge members or participants to apply them on a voluntary basis. In fact, such efforts have undoubtedly been helpful in adding some level of control to the marketplace, but they are not infallible. Various problems have arisen over the years in these markets (e.g., corrupt derivatives sales practices in 1995–96, excessively complex and overly leveraged products being sold to unsophisticated customers at various points over the years, and so forth) suggesting that there are limits to what can be accomplished via self-regulation. Similarly, various stock exchanges which are established as self-regulatory organizations have experienced difficulties in the past in terms of questionable or fraudulent practices, including penny-jumping, front-running, spinning, insider trading, and so forth. Again, the system of self-regulation in these markets is far from perfect.

The application of some degree of self-regulation in the dark markets has been posited by some participants as a potential solution for reinforcing controls without exposing the detailed activities of individual platforms. As noted, in the U.S. an ATS can choose to register as a self-regulating organization, and a similar approach may be relevant in other national systems – but perhaps not as a replacement for a more serious regime of regulatory control. The creation of an industry group that can define best practices for the dark sector and represent the unique interests of these platforms might help advance such a process. Potential areas of focus for such a group could, in fact, include

- Establishing a code of conduct regarding trading operations and treatment of clients
- Developing a standardized definition of pool characteristics
- Creating a reporting template that provides sufficient transparency to aid investors and regulators, but which does not jeopardize the advantages offered by the dark sector
- Developing consistent clearing and settlement processes
- Promulgating the FIX Protocol as the single communications standard

These points may be helpful in adding a layer of control and consistency across the sector (and across national borders), though they should not be seen as a substitute for formal regulation.

The Changing Face of Global Regulation

Regulation is obviously intended to provide clients and stakeholders with some appropriate level of clarity and protection. Within the US and global markets exchanges that set primary prices through their matching activities are deemed to be providing a "public service," and thus face a level of regulatory scrutiny (and attendant costs, which can affect the business model) that is greater than those operating dark venues. Indeed, exchanges (and certain financial institutions) that have been subjected to intensive regulatory scrutiny have agitated for more regulations on the dark sector in order to "level the playing field." This has been fuelled by negative light placed on certain other market practices and events that have a tangential relationship with dark trading, such as high frequency trading, flash trading, algorithmic trading, the Flash Crash, and so on. Certain constituents (political, regulatory, financial) have attempted to link all of these issues in with dark trading as a way of justifying the need for increased regulation.

Dark venues are already regulated under the frameworks noted above, and may indeed face stricter requirements in the coming years. However, as we have noted, adding regulation requires some deft balancing, particularly in the market for dark trading where the primary benefits are derived from a certain amount of opacity. Whilst it may be easy for a regulator to demand that dark pools provide greater (and faster) post-trade transparency, offer price improvement over the lit market, adhere to a minimum execution size, or account for no more than a certain percentage of all securities trading, each one of these can have a significant effect on the overall market for dark trading – a market, it should be stressed, that provides considerable economic benefits to those using it. Interestingly, different countries are taking unique approaches in regulating dark trading, suggesting that a "one size fits all" regulatory template is unlikely to develop. To put the regulatory evolution of dark pools in context, let us consider the major regulatory initiatives affecting venues in the U.S., Europe, Canada, and Australia.

U.S. regulatory changes

While NMS and ATS created the foundation for US dark pool regulations, additional initiatives and proposals have been put forth in recent years as a way of strengthening key elements of dark pool trading – hopefully without squelching any of the activity which has been instrumental to growth. In this section we summarize some of the main points put forth by both FINRA and the SEC.

FINRA

FINRA, in its capacity as a self-regulatory organization covering exchanges and broker-dealers, has proposed several enhancements, related primarily to additional reporting requirements. In particular, FINRA has filed with the SEC to adopt FINRA Rule 4552, requiring every ATS to report to FINRA weekly volume information and the number of securities trades occurring within each venue. FINRA has also recommended amendments to various existing FINRA rules requiring every ATS to use a unique market participant identifier in reporting Rule 4552 data to FINRA, so that attribution to the correct hosting venue is clear.[16] The combination provides an additional level of detail (i.e., volume by venue) that wasn't part of the original regulatory construct.

The rationale for FINRA's proposal is to help improve surveillance efforts related to dark trading (with regard to all existing SEC and federal/state securities laws) and to provide end-use clients (who pay a fee for the resulting data) with additional descriptive characteristics of various pools so that they can better direct their trades. It is also intended to facilitate monitoring of the individual ATS volume threshold requirement (that makes an ATS subject to additional SEC requirements once breached), that is, for any volume in a security in excess of 5% (computed as a daily average during 4 of the prior 6 months) the ATS must provide to the national securities exchanges the prices and sizes of the highest buy and lowest sell. Prior to this amendment, the lack of the unique market participant identifier made it difficult to track compliance with the 5% rule.

While much of the FINRA proposal appears logical, it is still limited in its scope. For instance, non-ATS broker/dealers, which we know are important participants in the dark market, need not report under the new rules, meaning the scope of reporting remains incomplete. Furthermore, the data being requested is not entirely comprehensive, i.e., no data is requested or collected on IOIs, order routing, pool participation, or fees/rebates. In addition, the reporting will be subject to a two-week delay, meaning that the usefulness of the information begins to decline with the passage of time. Finally, FINRA charges for the data, rather than making it free to all potential users, meaning that not everyone will trade or execute with the same base level of knowledge. Given these shortcomings, the FINRA approach must be seen as only a modest improvement in gaining additional transparency.

SEC

The SEC indicated in 2013–2014 that it would conduct a thorough review of the dark trading landscape (as well as the activities of HFTs, algorithmic traders, and exchanges) in order to begin developing a new regulatory framework to suit the significant structural changes that have taken place over the past five years. That review is expected to take a year to complete, after which a series of proposals/commentary will be introduced; these will lead ultimately to new rules. Precisely what changes will occur is not known ex-ante, but will presumably focus on creating more detail and uniformity in post-trade transparency, considering the need for price improvement for trades done off exchange, and determining whether to cap dark trading in some manner. This must be seen as an ongoing work in progress.

While the SEC has not made wholesale changes to its NMS and ATS rules, it has offered up certain interim enhancements/amendments. For instance, in August 2012 the SEC adopted Rule 613 under the Securities Exchange Act, requiring national exchanges to submit a consolidated audit trail related to NMS securities. This, by definition, will increase surveillance of at least one segment of the dark market. It is also considering the implementation of a pilot program (strongly supported by NYSE and NASDAQ) that requires off-exchange trades to offer some degree of price improvement (not unlike the Australian and Canadian models, described below); such a pilot program would provide a test case for potential future regulation in this area.

European regulatory changes

As we have noted, the initial regulatory framework for European dark pools came via MiFID, which led to the creation of alternate trading venues, including MTFs, systematic internalizers, and broker crossing networks. While it appears that many regulatory and financial bodies have supported this important market evolution (and the attendant decline in transaction costs, bid-offer spreads, and execution times), some regulators and government officials seem to have been caught off guard by the speed at which alternate venues developed, and the degree to which market share has shifted from light to dark. Some have also expressed concern about the fact that retail flows have been crossed in private networks – which, though not specifically restricted via MiFID, runs contrary to the spirit of the framework.

Accordingly, national securities regulators and other financial authorities have spent the period since 2011 considering how best to amend the process to provide additional investor protections and to place at least some constraints on dark trading. The end result is contained in the new MiFID II (the new directive and amendments to MiFID) and MiFIR (associated regulations), approved in January 2014 after a lengthy period of proposal and consultation.[17] The directive gives EU states some amount of flexibility in converting to local law, while the regulations are binding on all EU states. The directive itself touches on three critical aspects of the financial system:

- Organizations, including investment firms, broker-dealers, corporate finance companies, market operators, data service provides, and so forth.
- Activities, including receipt/transmission of orders, execution, own account/proprietary dealing, investment advice, portfolio management, exchange and market structure operation, underwriting, custody/safekeeping
- Financial instruments, including securities, money market and fixed income instruments, trust funds, derivatives (including commodity derivatives) and contracts for differences

The scope is thus quite comprehensive. The primary themes of MiFID II and MiFIR include:

- Ensuring continued competition within the European securities market sector, whilst strengthening the requirement that all trading flow must through some regulated venue (e.g., exchange, MTF/ATS, systematic internalizer, organized trading facility)
- Increasing transparency, including standardized pre- and post-trade requirements and post-trade trade detail to public authorities
- Reducing data fragmentation
- Lowering transaction costs
- Enhancing investor access to different markets and marketplace structures, as well as clearing facilities

- Improving investor protections
- Harmonizing cross-border differences and third country access, and creating a single European "rule book"
- Ensuring the marketplace features no unfair advantages or disadvantages
- Reducing the possibility of systemic dislocations

Naturally, some aspects of MiFID II related to trading in derivatives, commodities, OTC bond market transparency, and so forth, are not directly applicable to our discussion and will thus be ignored. Within the dark pool sector specifically, the main thrust has been on who can offer dark liquidity, how orders should interact within the dark space and how taxes and transparency should best be handled. Those primarily impacted by the changes include broker-dealers, investment banks/ securities firms, buy-side asset managers, wealth management firms, custodians, and market infrastructure providers. The main beneficiaries must be seen as investors and those seeking to minimize systemic risks.

To better understand some of the processes involved in creating the new framework, let us briefly consider some of the views held by the main actors on the essential points of trading caps, price improvement, transparency, and market structure.

- Trading caps: The Council of the European Union and the European Commission recommended the imposition of caps through limits to the reference price waiver (RPW) and negotiated price waiver (NPW) equal to 8% on the total consolidated amount traded in any stock during a trading day in the dark and 4% of total trading per stock on a single dark venue. Not surprisingly, market participants (including the vast majority of polled institutional investors) and at least a few national regulators (along with the European Parliament) disagreed with this position fearing potential competitive disadvantages versus marketplaces with no such caps (e.g., U.S., Canada, Australia). While some have viewed the cap scheme as a way of moving trading back on to the traditional exchanges (to the detriment of all those who benefit from stronger competition), at least some have expressed concern that caps would not necessarily lead to executions returning to lit venues, with attendant scrutiny, but to some alternate, equally opaque, mechanism that may not be subject to any regulation at all.
- Price improvement: The European Commission recommended requiring dark pools to offer price improvement over trading in light markets, giving clients at least a one tick improvement (following the model adopted by both Canada and Australia, noted in the section immediately following). Whilst generally supported by registered exchanges, it was roundly criticized by many other market participants.
- Transparency: The European Commission was in favor of only granting large in size (LIS) waivers (allowing pools to trade blocks larger than average market size), effectively abandoning or capping any other waivers (including the RPW (allowing pools to match orders to the midpoint of the EBBO), the NPW (permitting

orders to be negotiated at the VWAP), the order management system (OMS) waiver (allowing the creation of icebergs on exchanges or MTFs), and so forth. Naturally, each one of these waivers is important in defining dark trading, so there was again considerable industry pushback. Industry participants were in favor of standardized pre- and post-trade consolidated data with FIX tags and regulators supported a requirement for all trading venues to publish post-trade data by close of business and to publish annual data on execution quality. Disclosure regarding risk controls, particularly for those involved in HFT, algos, and DMA, were strongly recommended by both regulators and most industry participants.

- Market structure: Various regulators proposed tighter market structure requirements for certain market participants. As we have already discussed, MiFID provided for three classes of venues: regulated exchanges, MTFs (to cross buyers and sellers in a non-discriminatory way), and systematic internalizers (to cross in-house trades with some degree of pre-trade transparency). Broker crossing networks, essentially private brokers comingling proprietary order books with customer orders (and which can discriminate which clients are able to participate) were not recognized as trading venues under MiFID, and were thus exempt from the original set of regulations. Not surprisingly, a number of BCNs have developed over the past few years in response to this "market opportunity," accounting for approximately 5% of total European volume in 2013. Regulators (as well as a number of industry participants) were in favor of moving BCNs into organized trading facilities (OTFs[18]), systematic internalizers, or MTFs in order to have a well managed, level playing field.

With differing opinions surrounding this complex topic, it took some time for final conclusion to be reached. After more than three years of consultations the European Parliament, Council of the European Union, and European Commission released the final agreed draft of the new regulations in January 2014, covering all of the areas mentioned above. With regard to dark trading, the EU Commissioner noted that "The MiFID II reform means that organised trading of financial instruments must shift to multilateral and well-regulated trading platforms. Strict transparency rules will ensure that dark trading of shares and other equity instruments which undermine efficient and fair price formation will no longer be allowed."[19] The apparent view of the EU is that dark trading creates fragmentation, which hampers the price discovery mechanism, themes we have touched on earlier in the book.

With the tri-party agreement in hand (reconciled by a parliamentary vote) responsibility shifted to the European Securities and Markets Authority (ESMA) to create the detailed rules – in essence, to translate the high level regulatory aspirations into the mundane practice of daily business. The process calls for industry comment, followed by drafting of technical standards and final implementation of those standards (estimated to begin in 2016–17, with a multi-year phase-in). Detailed rules will thus be formulated for the following summary framework:

- Caps are placed on dark trading, as noted above, at 4% and 8%, de facto changing the RPW and NPW. No change is enacted to LIS and OMS waivers under MiFID, and no price improvement is needed to trade in the dark.
- All trading will be conducted on regulated platforms, meaning either a regulated exchange or an MTF/SI (or, for non-equities, an OTF). BCNs will be required to convert.
- Post-trade transparency is required for all transactions, though the possibility of deferred publication or volume masking exists.[20]
- Trading controls and algo testing must be in place for firms engaged in HFT/ algo trading, including formal regulations and liquidity obligations when acting as market maker. Risk control systems must be in place for those that provide clients with some form of DMA.

These are substantial regulatory changes designed to strengthen the market whilst keeping alive the dark activity that has become so central to the marketplace. Of course, the true effects will become clearer following the ESMA technical rule drafting and with the passage of time and the accumulation of trading experience.

Other regulatory changes

Whilst the U.S. and Europe have the most active dark markets and have consumed most of our discussion, we would be remiss in not considering regulatory changes that have been put in place for various other regional markets, including Canada, Australia, and Singapore. These countries have mature, active, and generally liquid equity markets and have promoted dark trading for the past few years. Yet, in 2012 they decided to "tighten up" local practices through their national regulatory frameworks.

Use of dark pools in Canada has historically been small compared to the U.S. (e.g., circa 5–10% of all equity trading) and new regulations promulgated by the Canadian Securities Administrators and the Investment Industry Regulatory Organization of Canada (IIROC) may put additional pressure on future growth. In particular, the new rules (enacted in October 2012) give visible orders priority over dark orders that are traded in the same marketplace at the same time, meaning that a dark execution must offer price improvement if it is to take priority. More specifically, this means that a dark trade must offer at least a 1 trading increment improvement for any security that has a spread greater than 1 trading increment, or ½ a trading increment if the spread is less than 1 increment. In addition IIROC can designate a minimum order size for non-displayed (hidden) orders and it can do the same with exchange iceberg orders. It further provides that an order in a market must trade with visible orders at the same price before trading with dark orders.

Australia has also made changes to its regulatory framework, focused on both price improvement and transparency. With regard to the first point, the Australian

Securities and Investment Commission (ASIC) introduced in 2013 Rule 4.2.3, which requires that all trades in the dark market that are below block size must offer the trader or investor a price improvement over what is available in the lit market (e.g., higher than the best bid or lower than the best offer by at least one tick); this is, of course, similar to what the Canadian markets have introduced (but what the European markets rejected). Prior to the introduction of the rule, dark trading accounted for approximately 25% of all local volume; following implementation of the rule in May 2013, volume shifted back towards the visible markets (i.e., the Australian Securities Exchange). Regarding the second point, ASIC implemented its "Market Integrity Rules" following an extensive consultation period; these rules focus on additional disclosure and monitoring of conflict of interest. Accordingly, every crossing network must disclose in a public manner the nature of the platform, the products traded, date of operations, types of orders accommodated, nature of obligations, fees, and so forth. The crossing networks must also disclose as soon as practicable which orders have been executed as principal and which have been matched against another system, and must disclose ex-post transaction information details. From an integrity standpoint, no crossing network can discriminate against users (i.e., any trader or investor must be welcome to execute) and users must be able to opt out of any system. Every crossing network is required to closely monitor all trading and notify ASIC of any breaches or suspicious activities, or any malfunctions in the matching engine. Finally, crossing networks must always give priority to client orders (rather than proprietary orders) and cannot pay more for order flow than commissions received for those orders.

Other countries are in the process of (re)defining their own regulations for controlling dark trading. Singapore, for example, has chosen a very different approach to the one favored by Canada and Australia: rather than opting for price improvement, authorities have set minimum order/value size before a trade can move off the Singapore Exchange (SGX) into a dark pool. Specifically, in 2012 the Monetary Authority of Singapore (MAS) passed regulations banning any trade smaller than S$150,000 (or 50,000 shares) from moving from light to dark. This requirement has effectively kept retail trades out of the dark market, and has hindered certain pools from building up a necessary mass of critical liquidity. In fact, the Chi East joint venture between Chi-X and SGX closed down after a year of operation as a result of insufficient liquidity, largely attributed to the MAS regulation. In addition to the size requirement, the MAS has also passed a post-trade transparency rule requiring all dark trades to report into the local exchange within 10 minutes of execution.

Knowing that regulation is a dynamic process, and that the landscape for future rules will continue to change with market progress, it is worth stressing a key point regarding "regulatory overreach." It is incumbent upon regulators (and self-regulation organizations) that wish to foster dark trading to remain prudent about introducing new "heavy handed" regulations. We know that dark pools are all somewhat unique and that they truly add value to participants. Accordingly, regulators must take care not to impose new conditions and rules that would compress or even eliminate the value-added. For instance, if regulators in future demand more pre-trade transparency, we may easily imagine that large institutional investors that regularly execute block trades, and who frequent dark pools, would be penalized through market impact and would sacrifice what might be as much as 100 bps of market impact savings. That lost savings would ultimately be borne by retail customers on whose behalf the institutional investor is likely to be dealing. Regulation brings with it intended and unintended consequences.

Toward a Practical, Uniform Regulatory Framework

The creation of the right kind of regulatory framework in a marketplace that is intended to be freely tradable, flexible, mobile, and confidential is complex. Regulations like NMS and MiFID already address many of the essential points of the marketplace, but it is quite clear that when these regulations were being developed and designed the market share of dark venues was still relatively small. Growth since that time has been considerable and the trajectory is equally impressive, meaning that regulations in various countries will have to be revisited on a periodic basis to keep pace. For instance, when these two broad frameworks were being created, little or no attention was paid to algorithms, smart order routers, flash trading, high frequency trading, gaming, ping pools, and so forth. Each one of these mechanisms has the potential of changing the client experience and the business environment, and must at least be considered in the next round of regulatory reform. While Europe is addressing some of these points through MiFID II, the U.S. has not yet weighed in via SEC rule changes. It is also becoming quite apparent that while NMS and MiFID have rightly sought to spur competition, the sponsoring regulators must surely be somewhat surprised at the speed with which new ventures have been created and old business models have been abandoned. Again, MiFID II seeks to harmonize market structure issues, but countries such as the U.S. and Japan have not yet adapted their regulatory frameworks.

Adding regulations for the sake of simply doing so is counterproductive, burdensome, and costly – indeed, the economics of any market can be destroyed by heavy-handed regulation. However, avoiding helpful regulation most likely means waiting for a disaster to occur – the history of the financial markets shows us that lack of regulation or the delay by regulators in recognizing the riskiness of a market or product leads ultimately to some amount of financial damage to intermediaries, clients, or both. In fact, regulators are often criticized, and rightly so, for being several steps behind the marketplace, playing "catch up" rather than anticipating areas of potential disaster.

This problem seems almost certain to arise in a market where opacity is a primary characteristic, and where ultra-sophisticated institutions stand ready to take advantage of the uninitiated or unsophisticated – not necessarily through illegal activities, but by capitalizing on the construct of the market and by employing advanced technologies and analytics that may not be available to all. Knowing this, it seems sensible to consider what a potential dark pool regulatory framework might look like in the coming years – one that avoids or minimizes problems before they happen. Again, some (though not all) of these points have been addressed in Europe through MiFID II, but are still missing in most other countries with dark trading.

- Client risk disclosure: The framework should establish additional "buyer beware" risk disclosure. While clients that buy and sell securities are aware of the fact that they are committing capital and that the capital may be subject to market risks that create losses, it is probably fair to say that at least some of those executing trades that route to dark pools do not necessarily know the nature of the pools or their specific construct. Standardized disclosure should be provided to all investors dealing in the sector noting that each pool must abide by regulatory standards regarding pricing and execution, but that each pool has the potential of attracting clients with very different goals (leading to pool toxicity) or informational asymmetries (leading to adverse selection) – either of which can lead to bad fills.
- Conflicts of interest: The framework should examine the business models and relationships of sponsoring institutions to ensure that no conflicts of interest exist or can develop. We have noted that it is possible for any single institution to be involved in handling dark flow in any number of ways, often simultaneously, for example, by running an internal proprietary book, operating a crossing network, serving as a liquidity provider in other dark pools, acting as a partner in a consortium platform, paying agency brokers for flow, and so forth. Given these multiple channels, regulators should periodically review the intra and intercompany relationships and the treatment of clients against this landscape to ensure that best execution is occurring and that potential conflicts of interest are properly managed from a compliance perspective, for example, via Chinese walls (recalling from earlier in the book that at least a few firms have been sanctioned and fined over roles that put them in conflict with client interests).
- Reporting: The framework must establish a minimum standard of reporting – as noted above, one that is helpful and consistent, but which is not anticompetitive. Reporting should be performed on a daily basis, ex-post, into the national regulator, and indicate such items as total volumes matched in a pool and how much was dark, along with the top 10 securities matched and the crossing prices of each trade; trades matched outside of normal market hours should be appropriately flagged. The regulator should not make details of this information public, but should use it to monitor compliance with pricing rules and to determine whether increasing market shares are being passed through mechanisms that are not directly involved

in price discovery. Of course, if individual pools want to publish some of these statistics for marketing purposes, they should be free to do so.

- Infrastructure: The framework must establish minimum standards of technological execution speed (to ensure a client has an opportunity to achieve best execution) and redundancy (to ensure a client is adequately protected in the event of infrastructure disruption or collapse). While these standards also happen to coincide with the desires of individual platforms, it is still possible that some platforms may be willing to sacrifice investment in execution and redundancy at the expense of clients.

- Clearing and settlement: The framework must also provide for minimum standards in clearing and settlement, ensuring those that provide such services have the proper technological processes and can handle significant volumes, even during periods of market stress. The fact that some regions feature clearing and settlement that is split among a number of providers means that there is a potential quality differential, suggesting that certain minimum characteristics should be applied for the safety of clients.

Self-regulation can also play a role in the overarching regulatory framework, per the points described in the section above. Although these can be helpful additions to the process, we must remember that there are limits to what can be expected from such self-policing.

It is also interesting to think about what a regulatory framework should not include. In other words, it is worth considering what parts of the sector should be left to the free market to resolve. This may mean some clients or other investors may be damaged financially, but only when they enter into a business relationship or deal in a pool without being sufficiently educated to the risks, and not because they are being treated unfairly or a venue is operating in contravention of rules.

- Pool Toxicity: The framework should not control pool toxicity. The fact that a pool attracts a certain set of core clients which then help shape its profile by sending in a particular type and quality of order flow is certainly not illegal and should not be regulated. Thus, apart from helping alert potential traders/investors that a pool may feature certain characteristics (e.g., a ping pool, a statistical arbitrage pool, a high frequency pool, a long-only pool, and so forth), regulators should not prohibit flows from routing where they may.

- Algorithms: The framework should not specifically control, define, or even catalog algorithms (though it should require certain minimum standards of client disclosure for users of algorithms). Though algorithms are by now widespread and have become very sophisticated, there should be no specific limitations imposed by a regulatory framework on what algorithms can or cannot do, and they should not be banned for specific sets of clients. Indeed, it should be the responsibility of the broker or adviser dealing with a client interested in algorithms to provide proper screening, education, and advice.

- Gaming: The framework should not define specific measures to control gaming within pools, nor should it mandate that every pool establish its own gaming safeguards. While gaming is certainly an annoyance for some investors, and especially those moving large blocks, it should be the responsibility of the management of individual pools to decide whether gaming should be permitted. Pools that choose to allow gaming are known in the market and those routing to such pools will be fully apprised ex-ante of such risks.

Ultimately, the right degree of regulation and transparency can help foster further safe growth in the dark sector, without giving away "trade secrets" which are part of the appeal of the business model – and which ultimately benefit both clients and providers. We might also argue that it is better to revisit the current framework of regulation in light of rapidly changing market circumstances now, rather than in a few years, so that potential problems can be addressed before they become more damaging.[21]

8 | The Future of Dark Pools

Throughout this book we have discussed the micro and macro issues of the dark pool sector by reflecting a bit on history, development, evolution, structure, practice, and architecture. In this concluding chapter we will look ahead, speculating on what the future may hold by considering the pros and cons of dark pools and how these might affect the future of dark pools in the marketplace. We will follow this with a discussion of some of the potential trends that might impact the dark sector in the coming years.

Pros and Cons of Dark Pools

We have noted in the text that the global equity trading markets of the millennium are characterized by falling average trade size, shrinking margins, and intense competition. Despite these challenges, new venues with new dark trading techniques have emerged to take market share from the established primary markets. In fact, the dark pool sector features many "pros" which should propel future growth; equally, there are some "cons" which could hinder, or at least slow, expansion. Let us summarize these to gain some insight on what aspects might be reinforced or altered in the coming years.

Pros

Based on our previous discussions we know that a dark pool can

- shield large blocks of stock from market exposure and reduce market impact
- preserve confidentiality/anonymity
- lower fees/costs associated with execution
- provide investors/traders with access to dark liquidity at no incremental cost
- make use of smart order routing so that orders are not stranded
- use base reference pricing/pegging to add transparency
- create partnerships with other dark platforms to increase chance of match/fill
- interact with visible liquidity to increase chance of match/fill

- give sponsoring institutions a chance to develop additional client business and revenues without using risk capital
- analyze trading patterns to prevent gaming
- ban pinging/IOC to prevent gaming
- bar participants with different trading characteristics/profiles/time horizons to reduce the chance of pool toxicity

The advantages are thus quite clear for both traders/investors as clients and for sell-side institutions active as sponsors, partners, or intermediaries.

Cons

However, we also know that no venue or business model is perfect. In fact, a dark pool can

- fail to cross orders when liquidity is not plentiful
- lead to bad fills from gaming and fishing
- lead to bad fills if information leakage is not halted
- create information asymmetries from IOIs posted on advertising/ negotiation platforms, or from IOIs sent by broker/dealers to liquidity partners
- strand orders in venues without proper pool partnerships
- "spin" its performance metric because of lack of commonality
- create investor confusion due to a multiplicity of venues, business models, and restrictions
- expose unwary investors to toxic order flow
- fractionalize liquidity across venues
- absorb liquidity from markets responsible for price discovery, leading to questions about the solidity of a security's price
- support only truly standardized and liquid securities/assets
- create confusion and uncertainty about what might occur during a time of market crisis/dislocation

Dark pools clearly are not perfect, but they still offer very compelling advantages for those choosing to use them. In fact, by virtually any measure the benefits that they can provide – particularly to investors aware of potential perils like adverse selection and gaming – seem strong enough to outweigh any particular problems. While this may be true conceptually it is also borne out by volume figures, which demonstrate increasing market share moving into the dark sector. The sector is beyond the phase of having to "prove itself" – indeed, with estimates reflecting that dark trading is approaching 30%–50% of all trading activity in global equities, there can be no doubt that this phenomenon is here to stay – so long as regulatory authorities do not apply excessively restrictive regulations in the future. In fact, the dark sector is now in the mode of refining and adapting to become an even more integral part of daily trading activities – not only in equities, but also in other asset classes and instruments.

Potential Future Trends

Given the importance of electronic trading and dark trading in supporting second-ary market activity, it seems likely that both will endure over the medium term. After several years of transformation and strong growth, it is interesting to hypothesize on what the dark sector might look like in the next five years. To do so let us consider some of the future macro trends which might appear within the dark sector, noting also some possible changes that might appear to help counteract the cons mentioned above. In particular, we focus on

- Continued migration of market share from light to dark
- Increasing consolidation across existing pools
- Further multi-channel structures from established exchanges
- Greater distinctions between pools
- Greater migration from risk-taking to agency
- Continued migration from "high touch" to direct access
- Greater expansion in select regional markets
- Deeper penetration into select non-equity asset classes
- Growing sophistication and use of algorithms
- Faster processing and execution times
- Greater use of automated processes/STP
- Further regulatory enhancements

Continued migration of market share from light to dark

We have already reviewed the benefits of operating in the dark, and have summarized some of the key pros in the section above. As trading and investing have evolved from "high touch" processes with higher costs to more efficient "low touch" processes with efficiencies and cost savings, the appeal of the electronic trading sector has become very well entrenched, and will not revert to "old style" trading/execution. Furthermore, the ability to preserve confidentiality and reduce or entirely eliminate market impact is a very powerful motivation to deal in the dark sector, and certainly are the key reasons why the trend of migration from light to dark will continue. As noted in the beginning of the book, dark trading in stocks appears to account for approximately 40% of all trading in the U.S., and between 8 and 15% in Europe. By various market estimates, U.S. dark trading is expected to account for between 50% and 60% of all turnover in the next three years; growth estimates in Europe also reflect strong trends in the coming years. Whether dark market shares will emerge above or below these forward estimates is difficult to predict, but it is clear that this form of trading has been embraced by investors, regulators, and the operators of the largest visible markets, and the migration trend should remain strong.

The arguments in favor of moving to the dark sector are particularly compelling for asset managers that are managing increasingly large investment portfolios on behalf of clients, and where the need to effect multibillion dollar program trades or slice up large blocks is by now almost routine. As capital and wealth accumulate, the investment process becomes increasingly focused on both efficiencies and execution without impact, both of which can be achieved via the dark sector. To reinforce the argument and propel the trend, it is interesting to note that every major visible marketplace also operates separate dark channels – as we have discussed, visible marketplaces such as NYSE Euronext, NASDAQ OMX, BATS, LSE, Deutsche Boerse, and others have moved aggressively into the dark space in recent years, recognizing the inevitability of the tilt toward dark execution. In fact, there is, and will continue to be, more "blurring of the lines" between the exchange and off-exchange business models, as noted below.

Of course, none of this should be taken to mean that the visible markets will be forever abandoned or will cease to exist from one day to the next. Quite the contrary: the visible markets and the price discovery process they support are essential anchors for the dark sector. It is quite reasonable to suppose that the two can coexist over the medium term, even as volume and fill rates begin to favor dark venues.

Increasing consolidation across existing pools

After years of rather dramatic expansion in the number of dark venues (particularly during the period of 2000–11), the stage is set for consolidation. There is little reason to believe that the marketplace can support such a large number of venues, even those that attempt to offer a different suite of services, or which try to create unique inter-pool relationships. We recall that in the 1990s the ECN phenomenon took the financial world by storm, with literally dozens of platforms developing in a few short years because of technological advances and client interest. Consolidation inevitably followed, with a large number of ECNs bought up by stronger competitors and even established exchanges. As noted, Archipelago, Instinet, Island and Brut, key ECNs of the period, ultimately ended up as part of either the NYSE or NASDAQ.

The consolidation seen in the ECN sector seems very likely to replay in the dark sector, as economies of scale prove to be an important factor in a fragmented market where pricing wars are common and overcapacity may be an issue. The consolidation phase should play out both in the U.S. and Europe, where ATSs and MTFs have multiplied rapidly and where the degree of liquidity fragmentation is becoming significant. Individual platforms face formidable competition from each other and from established exchanges, suggesting that a "roll up" is likely to occur. This is inevitable if business models are predicated primarily on large and increasing trading volumes. However, since financial markets regularly experience financial crises that force investors to the sidelines and cause volumes to dry up, every platform must analyze its ability to sustain operations if volumes were to fall by 25% or 50% or more, for periods of one to two years (such as the world experienced in 2007–2009).

Exchanges themselves have lost market share over the past ten years because of the forces that we have described in the book. The major exchanges have sought to change their business models to embrace, rather than bar, the new world of execution; regional exchanges have been in consolidation mode, and will very likely cease to exist as a standalone force in the sector. Even global exchanges have merged with one another, to wit NYSE and Euronext (the merged company then purchased by the Intercontinental Exchange, or ICE), NASDAQ and OMX, LSE and Borsa Italiana, and so forth. The evolutionary changes in the exchange business model have led to reduced charges/fees, greater rebates, cost-cutting, development of multiple channels to deliver executable services, and renewed emphasis on "name brand" recognition – all as a means of survival. The future may well include cross-asset product offerings through these established platforms, including foreign exchange, commodities, and certain other highly standardized instruments.

Consolidation is certain to be a major force in reshaping the sector in the coming years. In fact, the process is already underway, and looks to continue over the coming years as the strongest individual platforms seek to develop a larger market presence and as the weaker players give way by selling out. As we might expect, exchange or non-exchange platforms that can attract more dark liquidity will fare better, and serve as consolidators; once a platform covers its fixed costs, growing volume generates revenue that drops heavily to the bottom line. The commoditized nature of execution (and the advent of decimalization) means that this is ultimately a high-volume/low-margin game. Those that cannot generate enough interest will necessarily cease to exist (see Pools in Practice for further examples). Of course, until the full physical consolidation occurs, it is quite likely that smart order routers, aggregators, and specific algorithms will continue to play the role of "virtual consolidators."

* * *

Pools in Practice: Not every pool makes it ...

The reality of the dark sector is that it is competitive and dynamic, and subject to the forces of free market competition, including the battle for profits and market share. Though we've seen that different business models are available to those seeking a role in the sector, simply choosing one is not a guarantee of success. Indeed, there have been winners and losers, as in any industry. The first two decades of electronic dark trading have been evolutionary and fluid, with venues sometimes changing course radically in order to remain relevant: ATSs have converted into registered exchanges, exchanges have acquired technology and analytics firms as well as ECNs, banks have expanded their dark venues to include additional geographic markets, and so forth. Unfortunately, not every dark pool has managed to succeed, even after adapting business focus. Let's look at a few examples of those who failed to create enduring businesses.

First up is Kabu, the Japanese PTS launched in 2006 by Mitsubishi UFJ, the large financial conglomerate. Though the intent behind Kabu was to provide off-exchange electronic trading (including dark trading) to the retail sector, the platform was never able to attract a meaningful market share, accounting for less than 0.1% of Japanese equity trading in 2011. Lack of in-roads into the off-exchange trading sector and the enormous competition from the Tokyo Stock Exchange (with its newly designed Arrowhead electronic trading platform) caused Mitsubishi UFJ to abandon its efforts in late 2011.

Next we have NASDAQ OMX's NEURO European dark MTF, proving that even a well-established exchange can't always make a go of it. NEURO was launched in May 2009 as the exchange's dark pool, providing crosses on approximately 800 large cap European stocks. After failing to build critical mass in the highly competitive European marketplace, the exchange decided in early 2010 (relatively quickly in the pool's life-cycle) to shut down NEURO, transferring relationships to other parts of the NASDAQ OMX group. Despite the closure, the exchange continues to run its Nordic@Mid platform and its reserve order books.

We find another exchange-related example in Axe-ECN, which was for a time the New Zealand Exchange's answer to off-exchange trading in Australian stocks. The ECN, which was set up by a consortium including NZX (50%) and several international banks (10% each) in 2006 to trade in Australian equities, faced a series of delays before being allowed to enter the marketplace. However, in 2011 the NZX conducted a review and concluded that it would be unable to compete against the very powerful Australian Securities Exchange on an economically rational basis, and opted to close the ECN.

Next up is Pipeline Trading. The U.S. ATS was founded in 1999 and launched its popular Pipeline Block Board, which served as a hidden book supporting blocks, in 2004; the platform also acquired 3D Markets in 2009 to commence block options dealing. Pipeline was sanctioned and fined by the SEC in 2011 for directing customer orders to Milstream Securities, a wholly owned subsidiary, rather than crossing them with other client flow as had been disclosed. The SEC action hit Pipeline's business sharply and, though it tried to rebuild by rebranding itself as Aritas in early 2012, it was ultimately unable to maintain its business and shut down its dark order crossing in 2012.

Moving to Asia we note the example of Chi East, a dark pool created in 2010 as a joint venture between Chi X Global and the Singapore Exchange. Originally designed to offer dark liquidity in both Hong Kong and Singapore stocks, the platform failed to create a sufficient critical mass of liquidity and was forced to shut down in May 2012 – marking the end of a high profile venture by two of Asia's most advanced exchange players.

Last in our examples is the NY Block Exchange (NYBX), created in 2009 by the NYSE Euronext and BIDS Trading as a dark block venue that had access to NYSE's *dark books and its icebergs. Despite high expectations resulting from the trading pedigree of the partners, NYBX was unable to generate sufficient interest in its platform to justify the use of resources, and after about three years in operation NYSE and BIDS decided to abandon the venture and focus on their other dark ventures.*

It is worth noting that in these brief examples (just a sampling of total market closures) all four parent companies were, and are, well-resourced, experienced financial players who decided objectively that they couldn't create enough value to pursue their dark ventures. This helps demonstrate just how competitive is the marketplace. Of course, it goes without saying that this theme will play out in the future as well: other dark venues will ultimately fail to generate a critical mass of market share or returns to justify the use of shareholder/stakeholder resources, and will end up shutting down.

* * *

Further multi-channel structures from established exchanges

Structural change appears to be a constant in the world of securities trading, and exchanges, the main fora for such trading, are likely to be active when it comes to changing and refining their own business models. The largest global securities exchanges have approached the dark trading phenomena in different ways and at different speeds, though it is fair to say that by now all of them realize the importance of dark trading in the financial environment of the twenty-first century.

Accordingly, we should not be surprised to see the large venues continuing to find the best ways to participate in dark trading. This may come in different forms: some may choose to create and/or expand their standalone dark pools (similar to what we have seen via LSE/Turquoise/Baikal or NASDAQ OMX/Nordic@Mid), others may opt for liquidity partnership agreements (such as demonstrated by DAX/Xetra and Liquidnet), others may choose outright acquisitions of other platforms (in the spirit of BATS/DirectEdge/Chi-X Europe) and others may wish simply to offer up hidden/reserve order functionality where none existed before. In fact, some exchanges may choose to pursue multiple channels simultaneously. There is no single "correct" strategy or template that all established exchanges should or must follow, as each must deal with unique national, competitive, and regulatory realities. However, there should be little doubt that some form of strategic expansion will be an element of exchange business plans.

Greater distinctions between pools

As noted, the execution dimension of dark trading is a highly commoditized affair. Indeed, there is nothing particularly special about a trade that is submitted and executed, and which is then cleared and settled. More interesting is the environment in which the execution occurs – here there is great opportunity for every venue to display its characteristics and profile. As we have noted in Chapter 3, understanding the profile of a given pool ensures that the requirements of any single trader/investor can be aligned with those of other participants in the same pool, to avoid or minimize pool toxicity.

As we know, venues have the option of pursuing different kinds of business models. We have presented a number of the most common ones earlier in the book, stressing the point that only those creating a viable business proposition for investors will succeed. It appears that the most significant evolutionary developments have already occurred: ELOBs versus crossing networks, buy-side versus sell-side, call auction versus continuous crossing, and so forth. What we may expect to see next is further refinement in the characteristics of the surviving pools, so that the distinctions become greater; this should ultimately help investors route their orders with even greater precision. In the coming years we may therefore expect to see pools with additional distinguishing factors. For instance

- Some pools will enforce antigaming very strictly while others will not.
- Some pools will be known to attract "low-quality" liquidity (e.g., flows from market-makers, day traders, high frequency traders, algo traders, proprietary desks, smart order routers, pool IOIs, and so forth), while others will attract "higher-quality" liquidity (e.g., natural flows from active and passive funds, retail flows).
- Some pools will be known as broad-based regional generalists (covering a multitude of stocks in many countries, on a cross-currency basis) while others may be focused as true national specialists.
- Some pools will be known for having the best/fastest technology while other pools may be regarded as slight laggards (though still competitive).
- Some pools will be known for significant flexibilities in accepting order types and algorithms, while others will be viewed as more restrictive.
- Some pools will be known to accommodate passive investors and others will attract active investors.
- Some pools will operate integrated (dark/light) books while others will operate only dark books, and so forth.

We should not regard any of these distinguishing characteristics as "good" or "bad" – simply different. These types of features will appeal to different segments of the investing population, and may thus find success in a consolidating sector. Some of the offerings may create slightly higher costs – for investors who value the services on offer, the premium may be worth paying.

Greater migration from risk-taking to agency

The provision of liquidity through market-making activities, dealing activities, and proprietary activities is ultimately a function of risk capital availability (itself a function of new regulatory requirements), decimalization, and market volatility, some or all of which have caused at various providers of risk capital to pull back on their support of trading liquidity in recent years. In reality, these forces are not going to disappear – they are part of the permanent landscape of trading, meaning that the number of parties willing to provide risk capital on the back of very thin margins is not going to increase in the medium term, and is actually more likely to decrease. In addition, the experience resulting from any financial crisis or dislocation (to wit 1997, 1998, 2001–2, 2007–9) causes at least some risk intermediaries to become even more risk averse (perhaps permanently), shrinking the pool of available risk capital further. History has shown that any time a risk profile becomes misbalanced – that is, when returns are not sufficient to compensate for the risks being carried – any negative dislocation will cause a rapid, and sometimes very prolonged, loss of risk appetite. Greater regulatory capital constraints appearing in the aftermath of a crisis (e.g., Basel III) simply makes the allocation of capital to such businesses even more unappealing.

All of this means that business models that have already migrated in the direction of agency brokerage will continue to do so, and some of those that were previously willing to act as liquidity providers on a risk basis may choose to convert their models. Naturally, there will always be some providers of risk capital in the market – sophisticated and well-diversified brokers/dealers and hedge funds that have a broad range of trading mechanisms and platforms may choose to support low-margin equity trading through risk capital, knowing that additional revenues can be generated through, for example, high volume algorithmic flows, crossing of blocks with concessions, high frequency trading, and so forth. Under such a scheme, we may consider that the risk capital supporting decimalized and commoditized equity flows may be a form of "loss leader," to be compensated through other aspects of the business platform. However, the agency broker model will emerge as perhaps the most sensible approach for the vast majority of institutions over the coming years.

Continued migration from "high touch" to direct access

The traded financial markets were founded on close interaction between clients and brokers (or sales traders) regarding strategies and execution – a relationship that we define as "high touch." The advent of electronic trading began to change that relationship, to the point where the execution element has given way to a variety of technology solutions embedded in ECNs, crossing networks, DMA, and algorithms. Brokers and sales traders have been steadily disintermediated from the execution dimension of the process – this is certainly the case among sophisticated buy-side investors who prefer to take more direct control over their executions. Of course, some investors continue to rely on brokers or sales traders for executions; these, however, are typically smaller or more passive investors that tend not to generate the same amount of flows or the same degree of block trades. As technology continues to improve, it is quite likely that even some of these investors will move from high touch to direct access.

Such a trend means that the role of the broker or sales trader will continue to evolve. Brokers have value to add and, per our comments in the section above, agency brokerage will continue to play a role in the sector – particularly with regard to advisory services, where brokers will find themselves increasingly occupying the role of trusted advisor related to trading strategies, algorithmic offerings, opportunities for finding latent liquidity, and so forth; sales traders at major banks are likely to migrate in a similar direction, meaning the focus of the role will be on advice rather than execution. But pure execution via direct access, sponsored access, or naked access is set to expand further.

Greater expansion in select regional markets

Migration of more trading to the dark side is set to emerge as an important theme in the Asia/Pacific financial markets in the coming years. In fact, at least one research study predicts that up to 15% of Asian trading will be dark in the coming years, up from less than 5% in 2009.[1] Individual markets within Asia operate on very different dynamics, which leads to different trading styles and requirements. Unlike the U.S. and European markets, which feature reasonably homogenous characteristics and comparable states of financial market development, the Asian markets are quite heterogeneous and segmented, meaning that growth is unlikely to occur at an even pace. In fact, we can view the region in two broad segments: domestic financial markets that are mature and advanced, comparable in many ways with what we might find in the U.S., UK, and continental Europe; and, financial markets that are in a relatively early stage of development with regard to products, innovation, depth, and breadth – such markets may be considered truly "emerging." In the first category we can include Australia, New Zealand, Japan, Korea, Taiwan, Singapore, and the Hong Kong component of China. In the latter category we would add the rest of the major Asian markets, including ex-Hong Kong China (e.g., Shanghai and Shenzhen), Thailand, Malaysia, Philippines, Indonesia, India, and Vietnam.

The move toward greater dealing in nondisplayed liquidity has already begun in the advanced Asian economies, and should expand over the coming years. And while the types of venues and mechanisms described in Part I will be central to this growth, the powerful established exchanges, such as the Tokyo Stock Exchange, Osaka Stock Exchange, Hong Kong Stock Exchange, Australian Securities Exchange, and the Singapore Exchange will surely remain the dominant players. As investors seek the best possible execution, more competition via dark liquidity will certainly be a feature of the landscape. As the regional markets move to match their peers in the U.S. and Europe, such offerings will be expected by domestic and foreign investors.

Within the emerging Asian sphere (i.e., the smaller markets) the future trends are likely to be rather different. As noted earlier in the book, one of the chief issues relates to the "premature arrival" of crossing networks and other dark mechanisms that could remove a critical mass of liquidity from nascent exchange structures that are in the process of trying to serve as the nexus of liquidity. Such markets are still building visible liquidity, and any undue emergence of nondisplayed platforms could simply lead to a market structure where securities are very thinly traded and for which the price discovery process might prove very questionable. Without a robust price discovery mechanism, it is obviously very difficult for traders/investors to know when to participate as buyers or sellers, and could hamper both the formation and transfer of capital.

Ultimately, of course, further expansion of nondisplayed liquidity in the Asian sphere will need to have the proper review and sanction of each national regulator. These regulators will have to ensure that they have the proper controls and oversight in place to monitor activity in the dark space, perhaps even through the passage of specific regulations that lay down the essential ground rules (not unlike Regulation NMS or MiFID/II, for example).

Of course, there are other emerging markets that we might consider as part of this discussion. The Latin American financial markets, like the Asian ones, reflect varying degrees of development and sophistication, ranging from the most advanced (Mexico, Chile, Brazil) to the most rudimentary (Peru, Bolivia) and the most uncertain (Argentina, Venezuela). Like Asia, the region is characterized by different currencies, investor profiles, and so forth. Accordingly, the same argumentation noted above applies: certain countries will benefit from a move to dark trading in the near term (as already demonstrated in Brazil, for example), while most others are many years away from such a market structure. The Eastern European/Near East sphere is in much the same state of play, with Russia, Turkey, and Poland emerging as the most likely candidates for such mechanisms in the medium term, and most other nations not needing or requiring any such mechanisms for at least several years.

Deeper penetration into select non-equity asset classes

Our discussion in this book has centered on the dark sector in relation to equities. Equities have been at the forefront of this pioneering effort, for all the reasons we might expect: the securities are highly standardized and commoditized, and are thus able to attract a great deal of liquidity; the simplicity of the instrument lends itself to electronic handling with a minimum of intervention, definition, or confusion; investors of all types have small or large exposures to the equity markets through their portfolios, and thus a have natural interest in participating; a great deal of equity trading still occurs in the visible markets on formal exchanges, so the portion that can migrate to the dark is still relatively large; and, competition among intermediaries to provide services is very high, meaning friction costs payable by investors/traders are low.

If we look at these defining characteristics and apply them to other asset classes and their tradable instruments, it becomes clear that some are well suited for the same handling, while others are not. Let us first focus on those markets where dark trading is unlikely to occur in the medium term. In the first instance we may include all instruments that lack uniformity sufficient to create a mass of tradable liquidity and fungibility. In the second instance we may consider all instruments that are very complex, and whose pricing is dependent on negotiation. In the third instance we can consider all instruments that are already de facto trading in the dark by virtue of their construct. Finally, we can consider instruments that are being subject to greater regulatory scrutiny or specific structural rules, for which migration to the dark is unlikely to be a credible option.

- Lack of uniformity: Assets that lack uniformity include various classes of asset-backed securities, loans, corporate bonds, structured notes, complex options, and complex swaps. These assets are either completely bespoke, or are launched/ structured heterogeneously through multiple issues.
- Excessive complexity: Assets that feature a high degree of complexity include convertible bonds, asset-backed securities, and complex options and swaps. Valuation issues surrounding such contracts or securities mean there can be a sometimes wide divergence in quoted prices.
- Already trading grey/dark: Assets that have historically traded grey or dark via over-the-counter mechanisms (away from formal exchanges and marketplaces) include asset-backed securities, vanilla and complex derivatives, physical commodities, and spot/forward foreign exchange. While they may not trade through the formalized dark pools we have described in the book, they already reap some of the advantages of off-exchange trading.
- Subject to increased regulation: Assets that are subject to increased regulation, such as swaps, are almost certain to remain in lit markets, or to move partially or totally from grey/dark markets to lit ones. For instance, trading in standard interest rate swaps, currency swaps, and credit default swaps has historically occurred via OTC dealers and to some degree via broker screens, suggesting some possibilities for standard dark trading in the most liquid structures. However, regulatory rules enacted via the Dodd Frank Act and MiFID II, for example, now require certain standard swaps to flow through so-called swap exchange facilities (SEFs) or organized trading facilities (OTFs) which are characterized by appropriate pre-trade transparency and standardized clearing and settlement. While this does not apply to all swap trading, it is not unreasonable to suppose more liquidity will migrate to these (partially) lit markets, moving in the opposite direction of dark trading.
- Subject to structural rules: Some assets, such as exchange traded derivatives, work efficiently because they are subject to structural rules that govern the mechanics

of trading. Since replicating such structural rules off exchange is not possible or desirable, then it stands to reason there is little likelihood of migration to dark trading. For instance, with exchange traded derivatives, all parties must post initial and variation margin to mitigate the effects of counterparty risk, and must clear and settle through approved clearinghouses. These structural rules define the trading protocol of the marketplace and underpin the regulatory framework that is in place.

The need for dark mechanisms in these asset classes may thus be limited.

Perhaps more interesting is to consider assets which may indeed benefit from the advantages of the dark sector. Here we necessarily focus on assets and associated instruments which are liquid, relatively standardized, and relatively easy to understand and price; those that might be more widely held by a broad group of investors/traders; and those that currently trade very visibly, through formal exchanges or marketplaces (or which may trade in such a manner in the near future). For example, benchmark government bonds and bellwether corporate bonds that trade through formal exchanges or visible dealer markets may indeed benefit from dark trading; however, as we have noted earlier in the book, even these securities require willingness by participants to focus their buying and selling efforts on benchmark issues in order to create critical pools of liquidity – there are otherwise too many individual issues to properly conduct liquid trading. Exchange-traded funds (ETFs) are another candidate and have indeed commenced an early migration to the dark.

Iinstitutions supporting trading in bonds and ETFs are varied, and can include agency brokers, interdealer brokers, market-makers, proprietary desks, as well as the entire range of buy-side investors. In each case there is enough formal, visible, and regulated activity occurring to leverage the benefits of dark trading mechanisms.

Demand for dark trading cannot be forced upon the investing/trading community. Rather, participants must feel that the mechanism can add value, per some of our discussion above. Under such a scenario, intermediaries will gradually start making available such offerings, perhaps adapting OMS/ EMS and algorithms to accommodate these new instruments.

Growing sophistication and use of algorithms

We know from Chapter 5 that algorithms have been very popular with both buy-side and sell-side institutions. Indeed, algorithms have been instrumental in supporting electronic trading, benchmarking, black box strategies, and routing and execution, and are surely a permanent part of the traded market landscape – both visible and dark. This trend is likely to continue in the future, as sell-side financial institutions, sophisticated buy-side entities and technology advisory firms continue to push the frontier of algorithmic trading. Growth may center on new strategies to take advantage of market opportunities, and additional efficiencies within algorithms themselves to speed the process along. In fact, like other technological progress noted below, advances in algorithms must be seen as part of the trading "technology arms race" – a continuing escalation of intellectual resources and investment poured into the development of the "next generation" of trading tools, and institutions and venues that are able to deliver on such advances first stand to gain a competitive edge. In addition to increased sophistication, it is entirely possible that the universe of users will expand, moving from the current focus of large- and medium-sized buy-side investors, to smaller funds and even retail investors – a process which is gathering momentum.

One note of caution to be added to this topic relates to the number of algorithms available in the market. The traded sector currently features thousands of discrete algorithms that are designed to achieve particular goals. Although having choices is clearly beneficial, there is also likely to be a natural saturation point, after which it becomes difficult for buy-side clients to reasonably evaluate all of the available options and the performance that might be expected of each. Algorithms are part of the quality-versus-quantity tradeoff, where any single high-performance algorithm is much more valuable than dozens of mediocre ones. The risk in this future trend is that the sell-side will continue to develop algorithms at a pace that is much faster than the buy-side's ability to evaluate, absorb, and select. In fact, algorithm providers can do themselves and their clients a service by being much more discriminating in their offerings, while clients should be stricter in considering, evaluating, and using them. Regulators appear likely to add greater discipline to the process (e.g., MiFID II). That said, the development of new offerings should provide for interesting results and potential new efficiencies in the light and dark markets.

Faster processing and execution times

The world of electronic trading is built upon processing and execution, and venues that provide the fastest speed are in a better position to capture market share (all other things being equal). Best execution rules promulgated by regulators emphasize price as the top priority, but also make reference to the need for fast execution times – a point which many platforms have followed in earnest. In fact, the race to create engines with the ability to process and execute in milliseconds (and microseconds) is a serious matter. Sell-side financial institutions and technology firms have invested large amounts of capital in the pursuit of this effort, with each platform competing for bragging rights. At stake is the business flow of large institutional investors, including hedge funds, program trading funds, statistical arbitrage funds, index arbitrage funds, and high frequency trading funds, which seek maximum execution speed in support of their trading and investing strategies. If they cannot be assured of the fastest execution in their preferred venues, they may redirect their flows elsewhere – and in a business where volume trumps margin, capturing as much of this flow as possible is essential.

There are, of course, signs that the trend toward accelerating these processing and execution times even further will continue. Just as the producers of microchips have sought to develop chips with greater and faster computing capabilities, the same is true in the electronic trading space. We might well imagine that hundreds of millions of dollars (or more) will be spent in the coming years to continue shaving more microseconds/milliseconds off the time required to analyze, route, match, and execute. In fact, this endeavor may begin to favor the well-established, well-capitalized exchanges and financial institutions, which can generally afford to support the increased capital investments the effort will require – barriers to entry are becoming almost too expensive for smaller ventures/funds. Indeed, this may ultimately cause certain independent or marginal players to become part of the consolidation process.

Greater use of automated processes/STP

Automation has been central to the success of electronic trading and its associated strategies, and has also spilled into the dark sector. Though such automation has existed for the past three decades, it has clearly become more sophisticated and comprehensive in recent years, a trend that is likely to continue as technology allows for additional breakthroughs. In fact, the advent of truly automated execution has radically changed the face of trading and liquidity – from the perspective of not only trading and investing clients, but also of sell-side operators offering services. As noted earlier, virtually every major sell-side institution participating in the marketplace has been forced to change the supporting business model in order to address the changes and to capture business.

It is interesting to note just how little "human interaction" is now required in the trading process – for those who choose to follow such a route. The idea of STP has long been touted as the ultimate "end game" for investors and traders, as it reduces the specter of human error and operational risk, increases efficiencies, and lowers costs. STP is achievable in certain financial products and markets, primarily those with very standard characteristics; those with a greater degree of customization or negotiation do not necessarily lend themselves to the same processes. However, for trading of equities, currencies, and government bonds in the dark and light markets, STP is readily available. Consider, for instance, the example of a large institutional investor executing a buy program trade covering 100 stocks. The investor's computer model, based on proprietary analytics, generates a purchase signal on the program; an algorithm within the platform analyzes the program in relation to the market state at various venues and develops an order execution strategy, which is conveyed via the OMS/EMS into a series of dark pools based on a routing sequence; as the program is filled, a message is sent back to the OMS/EMS in real-time to confirm the executions; once completed the filled orders are routed into the clearing and settlement flow, which confirms details and ultimately settles, through electronic book entries, the relevant debits/credits to securities and cash accounts, reverting with appropriate messaging. This simple example demonstrates how, in theory, human involvement can be completely removed from the process – all because of technology.

Clearly, many investors are still uncomfortable relinquishing all aspects of trading to the "machines." At a minimum, many still want to interact with their trading and investment strategies, and continue to take at least some form of "hands on" role, even if it relates to monitoring while the execution is underway. But technology makes it possible to automate the entire process, and it is not difficult to imagine more investors eventually following this trend – regardless of whether the executions occurs in the dark or light sectors.

Further regulatory enhancements

We have noted in Chapter 7 the nature of both original and new regulation and the potential changes that might yet occur to keep pace with a continually evolving trading environment. While NMS and MiFID spelled out the original ground rules to protect markets, electronic operators and internal platforms and subsequent amendments via FINRA, MiFID II, and other national regulations have attempted to address additional issues, the process is not yet complete. Accordingly, the enhancement opportunities suggested in Chapter 7 appear likely to emerge in the future, though it is unclear when. Briefly restating these, we note the potential for further focus on client risk disclosure, conflict of interest management, reporting uniformity, infrastructure standards, and clearing and settlement consistency. These may be supplemented by certain self-regulatory initiatives, such as a code of conduct, FIX promulgation, and cooperation on reporting and clearing and settlement. Each one of these initiatives could help in ensuring that the dark market remains prudent and under control, and does not become a locus of systemic risk and the site of the next financial disaster.

One fundamental issue which is worth exploring is whether regulators might reverse themselves at some future point, bringing dark trading back into the light; in other words, whether regulators (either nationally or en masse) might seek to undo the evolution of the past two decades. While not a strict parallel, some precedent may be found in the over-the-counter derivatives market, which was the subject of scrutiny during the credit crisis of 2007–9. These previously unregulated contracts, some of which were deemed to have been a factor in compounding massive losses in the financial system (e.g., credit default swaps), have since become more tightly regulated, with standardized versions of the product being routed through centralized clearing mechanisms (as well as the SEFs and OTFs noted above). Of course, the parallel is not perfect, and differences do exist – but this action reveals the fact that regulators can sometimes radically change a market structure that has been in operation for years.

Such an action, were it to occur in the dark sector, would have to be driven by significant problems within the marketplace. In particular, there would likely have to be deep, widespread, and continuing problems with regard to client discrimination on best execution; pervasive problems related to front-running, gaming, or information leakage; large instances of outright fraud; or significant liquidity dislocations during the next major market crisis. Short of such problems, it would seem unlikely that regulators would reject the benefits of dark trading by reversing course. Regulation is ultimately designed to protect stakeholders, and as long as the industry conducts itself in a prudent and fair manner (under existing regulations and self-regulatory initiatives), it seems implausible that dark trading will be abolished.

Concluding Thoughts

For all of the advances that have occurred in the dark sector in the past decade, and in expectation of those that have yet to arrive, it is clear that the fundamental focus remains on the needs of the investors and traders. Dark liquidity exists to give investors and traders the best possible opportunities to execute their desired transactions efficiently, cost-effectively, and confidentially. If they are not being properly served, they will cease to support the sector.

The best way of ensuring that such needs are met is by

- Delivering the best technology platforms, and allowing traders and investors to link into the most appropriate dark pools.
- Creating the most flexible business models for delivering client requirements – ones that are adaptable to a dynamic environment, and which allow sponsors to generate sufficient revenues to justify the allocation of resources.
- Adhering to sensible regulations that promote confidence and security, but which still support the very features that have made the dark sector so popular.

If these essential elements can be preserved, we may expect that dark pools will continue to be an important, and growing, element of the financial marketplace for years to come.

Appendix 1

Listing of Dark Pool Sites

The following is a sample listing of sites supporting dark liquidity, reflecting the "state of play" in existence in 2014.

VENUE	WEBSITE
ASX Centre Point	www.asx.com.au
Bank of America Merrill Lynch MLXN	www.gmi.ml.com/electronictrading
Barclays LX	www.barx.com
BATS, BATS Europe	www.batstrading.com, www.batstrading.co.uk
BIDS Trading	www.bidstrading.com
Bloomberg Tradebook	www.bloombergtradebook.com
Bloc Sec	www.clsa.com
BNP Paribas BIX	www.bnpparibas.com
BNY ConvergEx	www.covergex.com
Burgundy	www.oslobors.no
Chi-X Global	www.chi-x.com
Citadel Securities Apogee	www.citadelsecurities.com
Citibank Citimatch	www.icg.citi.com
Credit Suisse Cross Finder	www.credit-suisse/investment_banking.com
Deutsche Bank Super X	www.autobahn.db.com
Deutsche Boerse/Xetra Midpoint	www.xetra.com
Direct Edge	www.directedge.com
Equiduct	www.equiduct.com
Fidelity Cross Stream	www.capitalmarkets.fidelity.com
GETCO Execution Services/Knight Trading	www.kcg.com
Goldman Sachs Sigma X	www.gset.gs.com
Instinet	www.instinet.com
ISE Midpoint Match	www.ise.com
ITG POSIT	www.itg.com
Japannext	www.en.japannext.co.jp
JP Morgan	www.jpmorgan.com
Lava	www.lavatrading.com

VENUE	WEBSITE
LeveL ATS	www.levelats.com
Liquidnet	www.liquidnet.com
London Stock Exchange	www.lseg.com
Morgan Stanley MS Pool	www.morganstanley.com
NASDAQ OMX,	www.nasdaqomx.com,
NYSE Euronext Match Point	www.nyse.com
Perimeter Financial Block Book	www.pfin.ca
Pragma Trading/Onepipe	www.pragmatrading.com
River Cross	www.riverx.com
SmartPool	www.tradeonsmartpool.com
Swiss Exchange/SLS	www.six-swiss-exchange.com
Tokyo Stock Exchange Tostnet	www.tse.or.jp
TriAct Canada Match	www.triactcanada.com
Turquoise	www.lseg.com
UBS PIN/Cross	www.ubs.com
Wells Fargo Liquidity Cross	www.wellsfargo.com

Appendix 2

Listing of MiFID Regulated Markets, Systematic Internalizers, and Multilateral Trading Facilities

REGULATED MARKETS	COUNTRY
AB NASDAQ OMX VILNIUS	LT
AIAF – MERCADO DE RENTA FIJA	ES
ATHENS EXCHANGE DERIVATIVES MARKET	GR
ATHENS EXCHANGE SECURITIES MARKET	GR
BADEN-WUERTTEMBERGISCHE WERTPAPIERBOERSE (REGULIERTER MARKT)	DE
BATS EUROPE REGULATED MARKET	GB
BATS EUROPE REGULATED MARKET	GB
BOERSE BERLIN (BERLIN SECOND REGULATED MARKET)	DE
BOERSE BERLIN (REGULIERTER MARKT)	DE
BOERSE BERLIN EQUIDUCT TRADING (BERLIN SECOND REGULATED MARKET)	DE
BOERSE BERLIN EQUIDUCT TRADING (REGULIERTER MARKT)	DE
BOERSE MUENCHEN (REGULIERTER MARKT)	DE
BOLSA DE BARCELONA	ES
BOLSA DE BILBAO	ES
BOLSA DE MADRID	ES
BOLSA DE VALENCIA	ES
BOND VISION MARKET	IT
BONDSPOT SECURITIES MARKET	PL
BOURSE DE LUXEMBOURG	LU
BRATISLAVA STOCK EXCHANGE	SK
BUDAPESTI ÉRTÉKTOZSDE (BUDAPEST STOCK EXCHANGE)	HU
BULGARIAN STOCK EXCHANGE – SOFIA JSC	BG
CYPRUS STOCK EXCHANGE	CY
DERIVATIVES REGULATED MARKET – BMFMS	RO
DERIVATIVES REGULATED MARKET – BVB	RO
DUESSELDORFER BOERSE (REGULIERTER MARKT)	DE
DUESSELDORFER BOERSE QUOTRIX (REGULIERTER MARKT)	DE

REGULATED MARKETS	COUNTRY
ELECTRONIC BOND MARKET	IT
ELECTRONIC OPEN-END FUNDS AND ETC MARKET	IT
ELECTRONIC SECONDARY SECURITIES MARKET	GR
ELECTRONIC SHARE MARKET	IT
EUREX DEUTSCHLAND	DE
EURONEXT BRUSSELS	BE
EURONEXT BRUSSELS DERIVATIVES	BE
EURONEXT COM – COMMODITIES FUTURES AND OPTIONS	NL
EURONEXT EQF – EQUITIES AND INDICES DERIVATIVES	NL
EURONEXT IRF – INTEREST RATE FUTURE AND OPTIONS	NL
EURONEXT LISBON	PT
EURONEXT PARIS MATIF	FR
EURONEXT PARIS MONEP	FR
EUROPEAN ENERGY DERIVATIVES EXCHANGE N.V.	NL
EUROPEAN ENERGY EXCHANGE	DE
EUROPEAN WHOLESALE SECURITIES MARKET	MT
FISH POOL ASA	NO
FRANKFURTER WERTPAPIERBOERSE (REGULIERTER MARKT)	DE
FRANKFURTER WERTPAPIERBOERSE XETRA (REGULIERTER MARKT)	DE
FRANKFURTER WERTPAPIERBOERSE XETRA INTERNATIONAL (REGULIERTER MARKT)	DE
GXG OFFICIAL LIST	DK
HANSEATISCHE WERTPAPIERBOERSE HAMBURG (REGULIERTER MARKT)	DE
INTERCONTINENTAL EXCHANGE – ICE FUTURES EUROPE	GB
INTERNATIONAL MARITIME EXCHANGE ASA	NO
IRISH STOCK EXCHANGE – MAIN SECURITIES MARKET	IE
ISDX MAIN BOARD	GB
ITALIAN DERIVATIVES MARKET	IT
LJUBLJANA STOCK EXCHANGE OFFICIAL MARKET	SI
LONDON INTERNATIONAL FINANCIAL FUTURES AND OPTIONS EXCHANGES (LIFFE)	GB
LONDON STOCK EXCHANGE – REGULATED MARKET	GB
LONDON STOCK EXCHANGE DERIVATIVES MARKET	GB
MALTA AUTOMATED TRADING SYSTEM	MT
MARKET FOR INVESTMENT VEHICLES (MIV)	IT
MEFF EXCHANGE	ES
MERCADO CONTINUO ESPANOL	ES
MERCADO DE DEUDA PUBLICA EN ANOTACIONES	ES
MERCADO DE FUTUROS DE ACEITE DE OLIVA – S.A.	ES
MERCADO ESPECIAL DE DÍVIDA PÚBLICA	PT
MERCADO REGULAMENTADO DE DERIVADOS DO MIBEL	PT
MTS CORPORATE MARKET	IT
MTS GOVERNMENT MARKET	IT
NASDAQ OMX HELSINKI (ARVOPAPERIPÖRSSI)	FI
NASDAQ OMX STOCKHOLM AB	SE
NASDAQ OMX TALLINN	EE

REGULATED MARKETS	COUNTRY
NASDAQ OMX COPENHAGEN A/S	DK
NIEDERSAECHSICHE BOERSE ZU HANNOVER (REGULIERTER MARKT)	DE
NORD POOL ASA	NO
NORDIC GROWTH MARKET NGM AB	SE
NYSE EURONEXT – EURONEXT AMSTERDAM	NL
NYSE EURONEXT – MERCADO DE FUTUROS E OPCOES	PT
NYSE EURONEXT LONDON	GB
NYSE EURONEXT PARIS	FR
OMX NORDIC EXCHANGE ICELAND HF.	IS
OSLO AXESS	NO
OSLO BØRS ASA	NO
POWER EXCHANGE CENTRAL EUROPE	CZ
POWERNEXT DERIVATIVES	FR
PRAGUE STOCK EXCHANGE	CZ
RIGAS FONDU BIRŽA (RIGA STOCK EXCHANGE)	LV
RM-SYSTEM	CZ
SECURITISED DERIVATIVES MARKET	IT
SPOT REGULATED MARKET – BMFMS	RO
SPOT REGULATED MARKET – BVB	RO
LONDON METAL EXCHANGE	GB
TRADEGATE EXCHANGE (REGULIERTER MARKT)	DE
WARSAW STOCK EXCHANGE	PL
WARSAW STOCK EXCHANGE/BONDS/CATALYST/MAIN MARKET	PL
WARSAW STOCK EXCHANGE/COMMODITY DERIVATIVES	PL
WARSAW STOCK EXCHANGE/ETPS	PL
WARSAW STOCK EXCHANGE/FINANCIAL DERIVATIVES	PL
WIENER BOERSE AG AMTLICHER HANDEL (OFFICIAL MARKET)	AT
WIENER BOERSE AG GEREGELTER FREIVERKEHR (SECOND REGULATED MARKET)	AT
ZAGREB STOCK EXCHANGE	HR

SYSTEMATIC INTERNALIZERS	COUNTRY
CITIGROUP GLOBAL MARKETS LIMITED	GB
CITIGROUP GLOBAL MARKETS U.K. EQUITY LIMITED	GB
CREDIT SUISSE SECURITIES EUROPE LTD	GB
DANSKE BANK	DK
FINECOBANK S.P.A.	IT
GOLDMAN SACHS INTERNATIONAL	GB
KNIGHT CAPITAL EUROPE LIMITED	GB
NOMURA INTERNATIONAL PLC	GB
NORDEA BANK DANMARK A/S	DK
SOCIETE GENERALE	FR
UBS AG (London Branch)	GB
UBS LTD	GB

MULTILATERAL TRADING FACILITIES	COUNTRY
AIM ITALIA – MERCATO ALTERNATIVO DEL CAPITALE	IT
AKTIETORGET	SE
ALTERNATIVA FRANCE	FR
ALTERNEXT	BE
AQUIS EXCHANGE LIMITED	GB
ATHENS EXCHANGE ALTERNATIVE MARKET	GR
BADEN-WUERTTEMBERGISCHE WERTPAPIERBOERSE (FREIVERKEHR)	DE
BALTEX FREIGHT DERIVATIVES MARKET	GB
BATS TRADING LTD	GB
BATS TRADING LTD	GB
BETA MARKET	HU
BGC BROKERS LP	GB
BLINK MTF	GB
BOERSE BERLIN (FREIVERKEHR)	DE
BOERSE BERLIN EQUIDUCT TRADING (FREIVERKEHR)	DE
BOERSE MUENCHEN (FREIVERKEHR)	DE
BOND VISION CORPORATE	IT
BROKERTEC EUROPE LIMITED	GB
BUCHAREST STOCK EXCHANGE S.A.	RO
BURGUNDY	NO
CANTOR SPREADFAIR	GB
CANTORCO2E	GB
CREDITEX REALTIME	GB
DUESSELDORFER BOERSE (FREIVERKEHR)	DE
DUESSELDORFER BOERSE QUOTRIX (FREIVERKEHR)	DE
EASYNEXT	BE
EASYNEXT LISBON	PT
EMERGING COMPANIES MARKET	CY
E-MID REPO	IT
E-MIDER	IT
ENERGIEFINANZ TRADING PLATFORM	DE
EQUILEND EEUROPE LIMITED	GB
ETC/BROKERTEC PLATFORM	GB
EUREX BONDS GMBH	DE
EUREX REPO GMBH	DE
EURO MTF	LU
EUROBENCHMARK TRES. BILLS	GB
EUROCREDIT MTS	GB
EUROGLOBAL MTS	GB
EUROMTS	GB
EUROTLX	IT
EXTRAMOT	IT
FIRST NORTH	IS
FIRST NORTH	DK
FIRST NORTH ESTONIA	EE
FIRST NORTH FINLAND	FI

MULTILATERAL TRADING FACILITIES	COUNTRY
FIRST NORTH LATVIA	LV
FIRST NORTH LITHUANIA (ALTERNATIVE MARKET)	LT
FIRST NORTH STOCKHOLM	SE
FRANKFURTER WERTPAPIERBOERSE (FREIVERKEHR)	DE
FRANKFURTER WERTPAPIERBOERSE XETRA (FREIVERKEHR)	DE
FRANKFURTER WERTPAPIERBOERSE XETRA INTERNATIONAL (FREIVERKEHR)	DE
GALAXY	FR
GFI AUCTIONMATCH	GB
GFI BASISMATCH	GB
GFI CREDITMATCH	GB
GFI ENERGYMATCH	GB
GFI FOREXMATCH	GB
GFI MARKETWATCH	GB
GFI RATESMATCH	GB
GXG FIRST QUOTE	DK
GXG MAIN QUOTE	DK
HANSEATISCHE WERTPAPIERBOERSE HAMBURG (FREIVERKEHR)	DE
HI-MTF	IT
ICAP ELECTRONIC BROKING LIMITED	GB
ICAP ENERGY	NO
ICAP ENERGY TRAYPORT PLATFORM	GB
ICAP ISWAP PLATFORM	GB
ICAP SECURITIES	GB
ICAP TRUEQUOTE	GB
INSTINET BLOCKMATCH	GB
IRISH STOCK EXCHANGE – ENTERPRISE SECURITIES MARKET	IE
IRISH STOCK EXCHANGE – GLOBAL EXCHANGE MARKET	IE
ISDX GROWTH	GB
ISDX SECONDARY MARKET MTF	GB
JP MORGAN CAZENOVE	GB
LATIBEX	ES
LIQUIDNET EUROPE	GB
LMAX	GB
LONDON STOCK EXCHANGE – AIM	GB
LONDON STOCK EXCHANGE – MTF	GB
MARCHÉ LIBRE	BE
MARKETAXESS EUROPE LIMITED	GB
MERCADO ALTERNATIVO BURSATIL	ES
MERCADO ALTERNATIVO DE RENTA FIJA	ES
MONETARY-FINANCIAL AND COMMODITIES EXCHANGE – SIBIU S.A.	RO
MTS AUSTRIA	GB
MTS BELGIUM	BE

MULTILATERAL TRADING FACILITIES	COUNTRY
MTS DENMARK	BE
MTS FINLAND	BE
MTS FRANCE SAS	FR
MTS GERMANY	GB
MTS GREECE	GB
MTS IRELAND	GB
MTS ISRAEL	GB
MTS SLOVENIA	GB
MTS SPAIN	GB
MULTILATERAL SYSTEM FACILITY ALTERNEXT	PT
MULTILATERAL TRADING FACILITIES ORDER DRIVEN	IT
MY TREASURY	GB
NASDAQ OMX NLX	GB
NAVESIS-MTF	GB
NEW EUROMTS	GB
NEWCONNECT	PL
NIEDERSAECHSICHE BOERSE ZU HANNOVER (FREIVERKEHR)	DE
NORDIC MTF	SE
NX	GB
NYSE ARCA EUROPE	NL
NYSE BONDMATCH	FR
NYSE EURONEXT – ALTERNEXT AMSTERDAM	NL
NYSE EURONEXT – ALTERNEXT PARIS	FR
NYSE EURONEXT – MARCHE LIBRE PARIS	FR
OSLO CONNECT	NO
PEX	PT
POSIT	IE
PRAGUE STOCK EXCHANGE – START	CZ
REUTERS TRANSACTION SERVICES LIMITED	GB
RM-SYSTEM CESKA BURZA CENNYCH PAPIRU A.S.	CZ
SHAREMARK	GB
SIGMA X MTF	GB
SISTEMA ESPAÑOL DE NEGOCIACION DE ACTIVOS FINANCIEROS	ES
SL-X TRADING EUROPE	GB
SMARTPOOL TRADING LIMITED	GB
SPECTRONLIVE TRAYPORT	GB
SWAPTEAM	GB
TOM MTF CASH MARKETS	NL
TOM MTF DERIVATIVES MARKET	NL
TPFORWARDDEAL	GB
TRADEBLADE (SECURITIES)	GB
TRADEBLADE (TREASURY & DERIVATIVES)	GB
TRADEGATE EXCHANGE (FREIVERKEHR)	DE
TRADEWEB / THE TRADEWEB SYSTEM	GB
TRADING AFTER HOURS (TAH)	IT
TRADING FACILITY	BE

MULTILATERAL TRADING FACILITIES	COUNTRY
TRADITION ENERGY	GB
TRADITION-VOLATIS	GB
TRAD-X	GB
TULLETT PREBON ENERGY (TREASURY & DERIVATIVES)	GB
TULLETT PREBON ENERGY (UK)	GB
TULLETT PREBON PLC – TP CREDITDEAL	GB
TULLETT PREBON PLC – TP REPO	GB
TULLETT PREBON PLC – TP TRADEBLADE	GB
TULLETT PREBON PLC – TULLET PREBON ENERGY	GB
TURQUOISE GLOBAL HOLDINGS LTD	GB
UBS MTF	GB
VEGA-CHI	GB
VENTES PUBLIQUES	BE
VOLBROKER	GB
WARSAW STOCK EXCHANGE/BONDS/CATALYST/ BONDSPOT/MTF	PL
WARSAW STOCK EXCHANGE/BONDS/CATALYST/MTF	PL
WCLK PLATFORM	GB
WIENER BOERSE AG DRITTER MARKT (THIRD MARKET)	AT
ZAGREB STOCK EXHANGE MTF	HR

Notes

1 Introduction to Dark Pools

1. No set parameters define a block trade – different market conventions exist, though most center on the absolute number of shares (e.g., 10,000 shares in the U.S.) rather than market value or percentage of trading volume. Although simple to measure, this makes comparisons a bit difficult and somewhat less practical. Indeed, traders often prefer to think in terms of a percentage of trading volume; for instance, traders may note that regardless of the number of shares traded, blocks that consume 25% or more of daily trading volume are, indeed, significant transactions.
2. Odd-lot or "retail" size trades are also an important part of the equation – since they represent a relatively steady flow of business they have become an important feature of many dark business models. However, we must first consider the effect of block trades.
3. Of course, locating the opposite side of block interest is sometimes challenging; such liquidity suppliers are often "latent" or hidden from view, not advertising their interest in absorbing or providing a block. It often takes the efforts of brokers or sales-trading desks with extensive relationships in the asset management sector to uncover such pockets of latent liquidity.
4. Consider, for instance, that in 2013, approximately 40% of total U.S. equity trading, traded in the dark; of that figure, approximately 35% came via dedicated dark venues, while the rest came from internal proprietary crossings.
5. This has long been a rather manual process, much of it based on sales/trading contacts at major dealers working with clients to arrange these customized trades – possible, but somewhat time consuming, and highly manual. The process made the early days of off-exchange trading perilous from an information leakage perspective – protecting anonymity was difficult. That said, the process continues to be used to varying degrees to the present time.
6. It is worth noting that some of the U.S. regulations also reference amendments to the Securities Act of 1934 (Regulation of Securities Information Processors); we will inject some of the most relevant definitions from this regulation throughout the book, as appropriate.
7. Prior to NMS, market practices were regulated through a series of rules related to trade-through restrictions, locked/crossed market rules, the Intermarket Trading System rule, and so forth.
8. A European parallel exists in the European Best Bid Offer.

9. For instance, rather than using the Intermarket Trading System for quote links, venues are encouraged to create linkages through other private facilities, such as NYFIX, Radianz, SAAVIS, and so forth.
10. The regulation also called for the conversion of NYSE to full electronic operations.
11. This includes 30 states, including the 27 members of the European Union plus Ireland, Norway, and Liechtenstein.
12. In fact, the Investment Services Directive created an overarching framework for financial services harmonization, particularly with regard to investment and markets, but national implementation varied greatly – meaning that a consistent approach to the matter was lacking until the advent of MiFID.
13. See http://mifiddatabase.ceru.eu.
14. See, for example, the MiFID Implementing Regulation, Annex II, Table 2.
15. See, for instance, http://www.osc.gov.on.ca/en/SecuritiesLaw_orders_index.htm.
16. Consider, for instance, that the average quoted spread on a NASDAQ stock was an average of 6.6 cents per share before decimalization, and declined to below 1.9 cents per share after the change.
17. Note that the same phenomenon occurs through a splitting of time. Some markets match on a continuous basis while others do so at discrete periods (a so-called call auction). The continuous matching permits less pooling of orders at any point in time and can thus lead to the same lack of critical mass at any point in time. We will consider continuous versus call auction markets in Chapter 2.
18. Consider, for instance, that in asset management surveys in 2011–2013 assets under management of major institutional investors were significant including pension funds with $31.0 trillion under management, mutual funds $23.8 trillion, insurance portfolios $24.4 trillion, real estate $10.0 trillion, central bank currency reserves $7.3 trillion, sovereign wealth funds $4.0 trillion, hedge funds a further $1.8 trillion, and private equity funds $1.6 trillion; private wealth not managed through these channels consisted of a further $33 trillion.
19. Hedge funds are also significant users of prime brokerage services offered by major financial institutions. Such services, which are by now well established, include execution, position management, securities financing/margining, reporting, collateral management, and custody.
20. SOES is governed by various rules, including a maximum trade size of 1000 shares in any stock, no trading in stocks with a price above $250, no multiple trades in the same stock until a five-minute window has passed, short selling done on a zero plus tick basis, and affirmative obligations for market-makers to fill at displayed prices, as long as the volume corresponds with the amount market-makers are seeking.
21. Level I provides for real-time bid/ask quotes for securities trading on NASDAQ, but does not disclose who is buying or selling, or the amount of shares at stake. Level II provides real-time access to the quotations of individual market-makers registered in a NASDAQ stock, and the size being offered or bid, along with the name of the market-maker seeking to trade the stock. This allows subscribers to see which market-makers are showing the strongest book in a stock. Level III allows for all Level II services plus the ability to enter quotes and execute orders, and is thus restricted to members of National Association of Securities Dealers (NASD) that operate as registered market-makers.
22. Consider, for instance, that by some estimates approximately 50% of the activity on Euronext Paris takes the form of icebergs.

23. Chi-X was launched as an MTF in March 2007 and saw its share of market matching increase rapidly and dramatically by early 2008, when it became a market leader among MTFs. Chi-X was purchased by BATS in 2011 and is now organized as a Registered Investment Exchange rather than an MTF.
24. The original participating banks included Citibank, Goldman Sachs, Merrill Lynch, Morgan Stanley, UBS, Credit Suisse, Deutsche Bank, BNP Paribas, and Societe Generale, some of which also operate crossing networks or systematic internalizers.

2   Market Liquidity and Structure

1. In fact, in mid-2009 the SEC responded favorably to the NASDAQ's request to amend the exchange's rules through the creation of the so-called collared order, which is any market order that is cancelled if it is trading $0.25 or 5% away from the midpoint of the NBBO at the time the order is received by the exchange. The change excludes market-on-open, market-on-close, and unpriced orders flowing through NASDAQ's crossing offers. See, for example, http://www.sec. gov/rules/sro/nasdaq/2009/34–60371.pdf.
2. "Testimony Concerning Dark Pools, Flash Orders, High Frequency Trading, and Other Market Structure Issues," William O Brien, DirectEdge, Senate Banking, Housing and Urban Affairs, October 28, 2009.
3. In fact, if a market is trading fast, meaning bids and offers are of such significant size that specialists cannot keep pace, a customer cannot be guaranteed a fill at the best prices.
4. Since a market-maker must stand ready to quote two-way prices and fill orders, it requires a certain amount of capital to support its risk positions, however fleeting they may be. Though many market-makers attempt to neutralize positions taken on as quickly as possible, this can sometimes take minutes, hours, or days to complete (depending on the nature of the security that has been acquired or sold); in that intervening period, enough risk capital must be on hand to support the exposure. If a market-maker suffers from a dearth of capital, its ability to bid or offer aggressively is certainly diminished. The same applies to dealers, who are in the business of taking risk positions and warehousing them until they are flattened. A block dealer, specializing in providing the kind of depth that clients need on large trades, must have even more capital to support its positions.

3   Dark Pool Structure

1. For instance, exchanges such as NASDAQ OMX, NYSE Euronext, and BATS all feature hidden order books, which they operate in parallel with their dedicated crossing networks.
2. Though individual exchange mechanics can differ, orders are routed to specialists via order matching systems (applicable for electronic exchanges) or through order book officials or directly to specialists (for physical exchanges).
3. Securities and Exchange Commission, "Regulation of Exchanges," 1997.
4. Note that in addition to the standard MTF business model, a new breed of micro-MTFs have developed; these tend to be structured as market neutral MTFs offering access to cheap liquidity.

5. See "Directive 2004/39/EC of the European Parliament and of the Council of 21 April 2004 on markets in financial instruments," amending Council Directives 85/611/EEC and 93/6/EEC and Directive 2000/12/EC of the European Parliament and of the Council and repealing Council Directive 93/22/EEC.

6. See Financial Services Authority, 2006, "Implementing MiFID for Firms and Markets."

7. Note that in 2003, Instinet split its ECN activities from its agency brokerage activities. The Instinet brokerage was sold to Nomura Securities in 2007.

8. In the U.S., the best orders on an ELOB are also backward integrated into NASDAQ Level II feeds, and are thus visible to the entire market; note that this applies only to visible orders, not reserve orders.

9. The only real chance for market impact arises through gaming, which we discuss in Chapter 5.

10. In fact, from the perspective of confidentiality and order priority, the hidden orders on an exchange and the orders an exchange might hold through a crossing network are identical – simply housed in different legal structures, and accessible through different technologies and interfaces.

11. That said, sponsors of certain of these buy/sell side pools may still restrict access on particular clients or client segments, depending on the nature of the pool and the characteristics of the flows entering the pool.

12. In fact, there is an argument to be made that, under MiFID, there is sufficient incentive to transform from a systematic internalizer to an MTF.

13. If a third market dealer accepts agency limit orders for listed stocks then it must follow a strict protocol. If the limit order bids a better price than the dealer bid, the dealer will adjust its bid to reflect the limit order price and size. If the bids are equal but the limit order bids for more size, then the dealer will increase its bid size to the limit order size. When the limit price equals the best bid in the market, the dealer will match marketable sell orders with the limit buy order; if a trade happens at a price below the limit order price, the dealer can fill the limit order for its own account. The same approach applies for sell limit orders.

14. For instance, Bank of America acquired Direct Access Financial, Bank of New York bought Sonic Trading, Citibank bought Lava Trading, Goldman Sachs bought Redi Plus (through Spear Leeds Kellogg), and so forth.

15. See, for example, http://reports.celent.com/PressReleases/20080313/DMA.asp.

16. For instance, Instinet, as a pioneering ECN, creating its own crossing network, to capture flows that it would have otherwise missed.

17. This includes customer crosses at volume weighted average price and time weighted average price levels.

18. In fact, this process is very similar to ITG POSIT's 12-time crosses.

19. Since the LSE is a primary exchange it must, under MiFID, adhere to the LIS rules noted in Chapter 1, meaning that hidden orders must be of a minimum size in order to remain dark; to protect such orders from being "pinged" by gamers, the exchange has Minimum Execution Size (MES) requirements.

20. While most flow is, logically, institutional in nature, some retail houses, such as Schwab, have established relationships with certain broker/dealer crossing networks to route retail flows as well. This has a certain advantage for passive institutional orders in the pool, which can cross piecemeal against retail flows as they enter the pool, often at a much better level.

21. The systems may be structured as auction systems, interdealer systems, single dealer systems, and multidealer systems.

4 Topics in Pricing and Execution

1. Consider the example of U.S. exchange Direct Edge, which offers a rebate model via its EDGX platform and a "free/free" model via its EDGA platform (i.e., there is no fee levied on either a maker or a taker of liquidity).

2. In one study, Liquidnet has estimated a cost savings of 1.7 cents per share because of price improvements coming via execution against nondisplayed liquidity.

3. See Celent's research of July 2009, for example.

4. Consider, for instance, that the LSE announced a rebate program in late 2008 to capture a greater amount of high frequency trading in its light and dark offerings, but discontinued the practice less than a year later.

5. Interestingly, some exchanges that have opted not to aggressively pursue one of the hybrid model channels we discussed in Chapter 3 have used this theme as a marketing pitch, claiming that clients opting to deal through a dark pool may be subject to potential abuse or mistreatment with regard to pricing, execution, gaming, and so forth. As more trading moves dark and as more dark venues convert to exchanges, this strategies appears increasingly questionable.

6. Note that some markets begin the trading day with a single price auction to clear the market, and then switch to a continuous two-way market for the balance of the trading session.

7. Dealers can compete against order flow in a displayed market by filling market orders on the same terms. As dealers capture this flow, the market becomes less appealing to limit order traders, causing them to send limit orders to another market, or to switch to market orders. Electronic markets that support nondisplayed orders (and physical markets with floor brokers or specialists holding nondisplayed orders) can therefore get traders to come deal with them.

8. This argument, however, is still reserved for securities that are relatively illiquid or marketplaces that are in a nascent state of development. In practice, the prices of large capitalization, liquid stocks (and other securities) cannot be influenced to any degree by the activities of crossing networks, and are unlikely to be able to do so even in the medium term.

9. Consider, for instance, that POSIT crosses 8 times per day, choosing a price at random from within a 7-minute period after a call; the random selection helps eliminate any possibility of price manipulation.

10. In the main, securities prices cannot be directly impacted by orders routed via crossing networks as they are pegged to a base reference. However, there is a theoretical argument to be made that as a primary market becomes more fragmented, crossing networks can have some pricing impact. We will expand on this concept in the section that follows.

11. We note that a pure increase in the number of dark pools and associated mechanisms need not necessarily lead to an increase in the amount of available block liquidity – on the contrary, it may actually lead to a decrease in such liquidity, as orders are increasingly atomized and allocated across pools. However, certain microstructures do appear to attract more liquidity – dedicated crossing networks, for instance, seem to be able to concentrate more block liquidity than other venues, helping reduce some of the negative implications of fragmentation.

5 Trading in Dark Pools

1. Certain other factors appear to influence spreads, including the differences between commissions on limit orders and market orders, volatility, time to cancel, and so forth.
2. For instance, when uniformed investors use limit orders, the orders fill quickly if bids are overpriced or offers are underpriced as informed investors quickly take advantage of the situation. If both uniformed and informed investors are on the same side of the market, limit orders supplied by the uninformed investors will not get filled, meaning an opportunity loss.
3. For instance, in the U.S. markets, a size precedence rule applies when a cross of 25,000+ shares is made. In such cases, the cross can jump the time queue, but not the price queue. Any limit order with a better price has to be incorporated in the block trade, and may displace some parts of the previously matched block.
4. In order to combat the possibility of information leakage, the investor may give a broker general parameters about the size of the portfolio, the number of stocks, and the general liquidity characteristics of the stocks (or groups of stocks), and the broker will submit a bid for the entire portfolio at some theoretical discount to market that is based on these general characteristics.
5. With order slicing via algorithms established as a regular practice, it comes as no particular surprise that the share of the NYSE Euronext's block trading volume is on the decline.
6. FIX has been instrumental in supporting the growth of algorithms as it has allowed for quick and consistent messaging. The FIX Algorithmic Trading definitional language, which entered beta-testing in 2006/2007 and is rapidly becoming the algorithm standard, is central to the process. Not surprisingly, messaging traffic has increased dramatically as a result of the penetration of algorithms in the trading world.
7. Some standard algorithms actually remove a dimension of control by automating the scheduling, that is, as in a VWAP or implementation shortfall routine. However, algorithms are intended to give the user greater control than might be found in a standard market order or limit order.
8. The growth in algorithm volume has come partly as the expense of DMA smart order routed trades, which appear to have declined slightly in recent years.
9. Note that further decomposition into "grandchild orders" is also possible.
10. For an in-depth mathematical discussion of a VWAP model, see Kakade et al. (2004), as an example.
11. A trader can also grant an order to a broker/dealer who will guarantee a forward VWAP fill; this shifts the price execution risk from the trader to the broker/dealer.
12. Tactical adjustments can take various forms, for example, adjustments to trading speed, discretion in capturing opportunities, ability to instantly redirect to alternate platforms, and so forth.
13. For instance, the algorithm may perform an analysis of a pool's volume, inside spread, average order size, internal order fill, and so forth, to find the best match for a client's circumstances.
14. See, for example, http://online.wsj.com/article/SB124908601669298293.html.
15. Barriers to entry are quite limited – those with limited capital and who are clients of a sponsoring broker can enter the market. Whether they can sustain their activities over the medium- and long-term is, of course, a separate matter.
16. See, for example, http://online.wsj.com/article/SB124908601669298293.html.

6 Aspects of Technology and Architecture

1. Though we illustrate this framework in the context of an equity trade, similar processes can apply to foreign exchange, government bonds, listed derivatives and so forth, with perhaps only minor differences related to any particular stage.
2. Some exchanges and electronic platforms lease out space proximate to their own operations to reduce the physical distance; in an era where execution performance is measured in milliseconds or microseconds, the distance between transmitting an order from afar and from an exchange's premises can make a difference.
3. OMS platforms for buy-side clients are typically delivered in the form of virtual infrastructure so as not to create additional hardware demands.
4. For instance, firms such as SunGuard, Fidessa, NYFIX, and many others offer a range of product offerings.
5. In fact, off-the-shelf OMS platforms often include an order router as part of the standard architecture. Such capabilities are available, for example, in buy-side systems such as Bloomberg Tradebook, IOE Bridge, Lava Colorbook, REDIplus, SunGard Smart Brass, and so forth.
6. The costs of an OMS/EMS platform can vary dramatically, from less than $100,000 up to several millions of dollars.
7. Connectivity to broker execution services, prime brokerage, and custodians are all relevant factors.
8. A rule of thumb regarding messaging capacity that must be supported by the user's infrastructure is estimated as number of users times number of connected brokers/venues times total daily orders times 10.
9. A disaster recovery process is also essential, so that the user has proper backup in the event of problems with some aspect of the OMS or its connections.
10. If the intent was to wait for contra-liquidity rather than immediately verify the existence of, and execute against, a contra-trade, the IOC instruction could be replaced with a "time out" restriction, allowing the rump order to remain in a pool for a matter of time, for example, 10 seconds, 30 seconds, 1 minute. This is, of course, a different form of routing strategy.
11. Note that in addition to the logical sequence noted above, the router must have software and hardware capabilities that support the steps above and allow for efficient processing and communications. These, for instance, may comprise the following:
    a. An OMS/EMS or other API that can accept the order parameters noted in Step 1, and which has the capability of converting a submitted order into FIX Protocol.
    b. A ping processor that is capable of deriving and aligning the "ping sequence" as it evolves through the routing chain. This is required when the "ping sequence" is dynamic and derived from changing parameters, for example, volume statistics.
    c. A dark pool router that can pass remaining unfilled IOC orders to the next dark pool in the sequence determined by the ping processor.
    d. A status processor that can reflect back to the dark pool router the status of the IOCs and the remaining balance of units/shares to be filled, including completion once the entire order is done.
    e. A processor that can compare the bid price or ask price of the order with the price currently available in an exchange/ECN.

12. The FX market, for instance, relies on FpML, while the fixed income market is migrating toward FIX.
13. See, for instance, the main resource databank maintained by the FIX Protocol Organization, at www. fixprotocol.org.

7 Regulation, Control, and Transparency

1. Consider, for instance, that NYSE purchased Archipelago for $3 billion in an attempt to revive its fortunes and boost market share; that, of course, has not proven to be the case, though Arca has delivered other advantages related to electronic execution and trading. The same occurred with NASDAQ, which purchased the Instinet/Island combination but still lost ground.
2. In the aftermath of the Credit Crisis of 2007, certain aspects of the OTC derivatives market – centering primarily on credit derivatives, clearing arrangements and pre/post-trade transparency – are in the process of being brought under stronger regulatory control (e.g., Basel II, Dodd-Frank Act).
3. See, for example, https://www.lavatrading.com/solutions/lavaflow.php.
4. The reporting requirement came into force in November 2000.
5. See, for instance, http://www.sec.gov/interps/legal/slbim12rappxa.htm, and http://www.sec.gov/ interps/legal/slbim12b.htm.
6. For more detail, see http://www.finra.complinet.com/en/display.
7. See, for example, http://www.cesr-eu.org/data/document/07_043.pdf.
8. See, for example, http://www.fsa.gov.uk/pubs/international/guidelines_tdm.pdf.
9. For instance, BOAT reports real-time trade reported volumes from MTFs, dark pools, and brokers.
10. For instance, through Omgeo's Transaction Reporting, counterparty, client, security type, identifier, price, quantity, currency, and dates are sent to a host for validation; once validated, the client receives confirmation and a batch run sends the report to the relevant regulatory body.
11. See, for example, http://www.fese.be.
12. See, for example, http://mifiddatabase.cesr.eu.
13. See, for example, http://www.sec.gov/news/speech/2009/spch052009jab.htm.
14. See, for example, the CESR's study and associated responses, "Call for evidence on the review of the scope of the MiFID transaction reporting obligation" which suggests that one year after the implementation of MiFID institutional clients still had significant concerns about transaction reporting and transparency.
15. Industry commentary appears to favor weekly or monthly reporting to ensure there is no possibility of gaming.
16. More, specifically, FINRA has stated: "Rule 4552 to require each alternative trading system ('ATS') to report to FINRA weekly volume information and number of trades regarding securities transactions within the ATS; and (ii) amend FINRA Rules 6160, 6170, 6480, and 6720 to require each ATS to acquire and use a single, unique market participant identifier ('MPID') when reporting information to FINRA."
17. Though MiFID II/MiFIR stands as a new initiative, the overall goals of the MiFID framework remain the same, that is, reinforce management controls, create a safe trading environment, improve transparency, and emphasize the "know your client" practice. We

recall that the impetus behind MiFID was to make financial firms bring their operational risks under control, to handle client orders and transactions in a proper and prudent way, segregate customer and proprietary activities and to document and report all relevant transactions and relationships. None of this changes with the second iteration of the rules and regulations.

18. For instance, as noted in Proposal for a Regulation of the European Parliament and of the Council on markets in financial instruments and amending regulations [EMIR] on OTC derivatives, central counterparties and trade repositories – COM(2011) 652 final 2011/0296(COD), an "Organised trading facility (OTF) means any system or facility, which is not a regulated market or an MTF, operated by an investment firm or market operator, in which multiple third-party buying and selling interests in financial instruments are able to interact in the system in a way that results in a contract according to the provisions of the MiFID Directive."

19. See, for example, http://europa.eu/rapid/press-release_MEMO-14-15_en.htm?locale=en

20. During the discussion phase the Commission of European Securities Regulators recommended the identification of "dark trading" with a "D" flag in post-trade transparency reports (including trades on registered markets and MTFs under the reference price waiver and the large in scale waiver). That said, where a dark order executes against a lit order, the transaction should be reported according to the status of the resting order in the order book. More generally, trade reporting (which contains ex-post details on actual trades, including names/types and number of instruments, quantity, date, time, price, client designation, algorithm designation) will be directed only to European Securities and Markets Authority (ESMA) and relevant authorities; from a flow perspective, information goes from the investment firm to the trading venue to the consolidated tape provider to the national authority to ESMA. Transparency reporting (which contains high level, but not detailed, information on execution quality, pool access, and so forth) will be directed to the public at large. For algorithms, which may interact with either dark or light pools, the proposed focus is on testing and monitoring systems constantly to ensure resiliency and to make certain that algorithmic functions do not contribute to market volatility.

21. We need only look at the largely unregulated credit default swap market to understand the problems that can be created when an insufficient level of transparency exists, and when a pure self-regulatory approach is taken. Credit default swaps were at the center of some of the significant financial losses that occurred within the banking and insurance sector during the credit crisis of 2007–9: the market grew dramatically during the early part of the decade, even as participants and financial regulators failed to properly take account of the enormous amount of leverage and volatility that was being injected into the market. The result was a series of massive losses and an ex-post agreement with regulators to move the standard portions of the market under a regulatory umbrella, including standardized clearing and settlement as a way of removing counterparty risk.

8 The Future of Dark Pools

1. See, for example, Aite Research, 2009, "The Rise of the Asian ATSs: The Waiting Game."

Glossary

Agency brokerage Intermediaries that link buyers and sellers (without committing capital), in exchange for a fee. Agency brokers are important players in directing client order flow to specific exchanges and off-exchange venues.

Aggregator crossing network A crossing network, which may be independent or owned by a consortium, that links with the broadest range of existing dark pools, directing flows to platforms where established arrangements exist.

Algo *See* Algorithm.

Algorithm A decision rule applied to trading strategies and incorporated into algorithmic trading platforms. Algorithms are employed for short-term trading and execution, and can be designed to perform a variety of functions, including searching for dark liquidity, parceling trades into small orders to reduce market impact cost, executing trades at specific levels or against benchmarks, and so forth.

Algorithmic trading The use of computer-driven algorithms to execute financial transactions in the marketplace. The process is designed to be highly automated, with minimal need for manual intervention. Algorithmic trading is popularly used in the equity markets, but it is also found in the foreign exchange and commodities markets.

All-or-none (AON) order A designation on an order indicating that the entire amount of an order should be filled or else not at all; the order remains in force pending future execution (e.g., resting, awaiting arrival of the full amount of the contra-trade) unless it is specifically cancelled.

Alternative midpoint peg order A peg order that pegs to the "less aggressive" side of the midpoint of the best bid offer by a small fraction.

Alternative Trading System (ATS) An electronic venue that serves as an alternative to a traditional exchange, providing trading services by matching buyers and sellers directly, without the use of a broker or dealer.

Average latency The average amount of time it takes for an order to travel from the trade entry interface into a marketplace, typically measured in milliseconds.

Benchmark order Any type of order that is submitted for execution at a price that is different than the base reference price, but which is still permissible under regulatory rules.

Block crossing A crossed trade in an institutional block of shares, either on an exchange or through a dark pool.

Block crossing network In Europe, a crossing network that only crosses, on a discriminatory basis, institutional sized blocks, leaving retail flow and sliced institutional orders to other networks. Ventures established by broker/dealers (as broker crossing networks) were not regulated under MiFID and therefore operated as private over-the-counter markets. Changes from MiFID II have caused these pools to convert into MTFs or systematic internalizers.

Blotter scraping The process of examining the trading blotters of participating broker/dealers to find matches for incoming order flows/IOIs. This business model is used by a small number of liquidity aggregation venues that deal with buy-side, rather than sell-side, flows.

Breadth The cost of completing a trade, and another term for the bid-offer spread on a security. In general, the less liquid a stock, the greater breadth, or bid/offer, and vice versa.

Broker/Dealer crossing network A crossing network that is owned and operated by a broker/dealer (e.g., investment bank, universal bank, or other international commercial bank). The broker/dealer crossing network commingles external flows with internal flows captured by the sponsoring institution.

Brokered market A market where agency brokers bring together interested buyers and sellers to arrange a trade. There is no dealer risk capital supporting or creating liquidity in such instances, simply an agency function that arranges execution on a negotiated basis.

Call crossing network A crossing network that accepts confidential bids and offers into the pool and holds them until a call auction is declared, at which point the matching engine performs its matching routines to cross as many orders as possible. Though the number of calls performed each day can vary by platform, in practice it ranges from once a day to once per hour.

Call market A marketplace that trades only when a "market" is specifically "called." This means that buy and sell orders are gathered at discrete points during the day and are matched or exchanged according to particular rules during each call session.

Cash neutrality In portfolio or program trading, the process of balancing buys and sells so that as trades are executed in one market, they are offset by opposing trades in another market (through a process known as "legging"). This reduces open market risk and the possibility of a loss.

Child order A portion or slice of a parent order that is executed independently, but according to price and/or time considerations embedded in the logic of an algorithm.

Concentration rules In Europe, rules existing before the introduction of MiFID which required all securities transactions to be executed through a regulated market or primary exchange. These have been abandoned through MiFID.

Conditional order Any type of order that is submitted for execution (in limit or market form) once a specific event occurs. The named condition can relate to price, volume, time, and so forth.

Consolidated display In electronic trading, the minimum information that must be displayed according to regulation, including prices, quantities and tickers of the best bid and offer of a given security, along with consolidated information on last sales.

Consortium crossing network A crossing network that is owned by a number of partners, such as banks, brokers/dealers, independent crossing networks, and exchanges, and which is managed by an independent management team.

Continuous crossing network A crossing network that accepts confidential bids and offers into the pool and, through a matching engine, crosses them on a continuous basis.

Continuous market A market that trades on an ongoing basis during the trading session (e.g., 9am to 4pm for markets in stocks and listed derivatives) or throughout the day (e.g., 24/7 for markets in foreign exchange and certain electronically traded securities and derivatives).

Contra-liquidity The opposing side of a trade, often considered in the context of block trades. Algorithms and smart order routers handling an order attempt to detect contra-liquidity in dark pools and on exchanges to try to get the best execution price and the quickest fill.

Contra-trading The practice of buying and selling shares within the same settlement period so that no payment need be made. Contra-trading is typically found in day trading, where a speculator purchases shares during the day and closes out the position before the close of business; since both transactions settle on the same day (e.g., T + 3), the speculator has no gross cash outflow.

Cross The process of executing a trade that has been matched, often used in the context of off-exchange trading.

Cross order An order to buy and an order to sell the same security at a specific price that is better than the best bid and offer on an exchange, and equal to or better than a base reference price.

Crossing network An electronic venue that matches orders confidentially on a continuous or predefined time schedule. The base price used to cross trades is generally the midpoint of the bid and offer on an exchange, meaning that the platform does not contribute to price discovery. A crossing network, which is a form of alternative trading system attempts to minimize costs and market impact, while preserving client anonymity.

Dark algorithm An algorithm that is specifically designed to detect, and interact with, a dark pool.

Dark liquidity *See* Nondisplayed liquidity.

Dark pool An electronic venue or mechanism that accumulates nondisplayed liquidity and provides matches of bids and offers. A dark pool can take the form of an alternative trading system, internalized order flow, or exchange reserve/hidden orders, and is designed to minimize costs and market impact while preserving client anonymity.

Day order A limit order that is valid until the exchange closes, for example, 4pm, at which point it is cancelled.

Decimalization The market practice, enforced by regulation, of quoting stocks in 1 cent increments.

Depth The amount of a trade that can be done at a particular price, and a reflection of buying and selling interest in a security. The greater the depth, the greater the ability for investors to clear their books at a given price; the shallower the depth, the lesser the ability to clear the books.

Derivative order A form of limit order where the limit price is derived from, or related to, a particular variable, such as the midpoint of the bid and offer, the last sale, the last sale less one tick, and so forth.

Direct market access (DMA) A process where a buy-side client makes use of a broker's electronic trading systems to access a securities market directly, without any direct involvement by the broker; executed trades flow through the broker's books and records for the account of the client. DMA can result in faster execution at a lower cost, and provides a greater degree of anonymity.

Directed order An order placed by a client with a broker or dealer that instructs routing to a specific venue or exchange.

Discretionary order A limit order that features a working visible price and a hidden discretionary price, which increases price flexibility to improve the chances of execution. The discretionary price spread may be triggered by a broker or through an order management system or trading interface.

Displayed liquidity Trading volume that is visible to the market at large, and which reflects available market depth. Displayed liquidity excludes reserves orders, hidden orders, positions held in the books of specialists/floor brokers, as well as orders residing in off-exchange dark pools.

Displayed market A market in which offers to trade are made visible to the public.

Distributed/electronic market A market that operates in the electronic sphere, through use of advanced technologies; the ability for participants to network into these markets from afar gives rise to the term "distributed." Such markets do not rely on physical interaction between participants to establish prices or effect purchases and sales—all dealing occurs through a variety of electronic mechanisms.

Do-not-route order Any type of order that is submitted for execution in a single exchange or venue and cannot be sent to any other exchange or venue should a fill not occur. In such cases the order rests in the order book as a working order until it is filled or specifically cancelled.

Downtick order An order that leads to the purchase or sale of securities if the market moves down by a tick.

Electronic communications network (ECN) An electronic system that disseminates to third parties any orders entered by a market-maker, and permits such orders to be executed. ECNs exclude any systems that cross multiple orders at one or more specified times at a single price set by the system and those that do not allow orders to be crossed or executed against by participants outside of such times, as well as any system operated by a market-maker that executes customer orders primarily against the market-maker's proprietary book.

Electronic limit order book (ELOB) An electronic platform that operates as a form of electronic exchange, posting standard limit orders and, in some instances, also managing hidden orders. An ELOB aggregates bids and offers submitted by buyers and sellers, posting varying degrees of price and volume information without attribution to the buyer or seller; as bids and offers are queued in the ELOB, price assumes priority, followed by time.

European best bid offer (EBBO) In Europe, the best available bid and offer on a quoted stock, which must be made available to any buyer or seller.

Exchange crossing network A crossing network that is wholly or majority owned by a stock exchange, generally as a way of bringing more liquidity into the exchange itself. An exchange crossing network operates in parallel with traditional exchange activities.

Execution rate The number or value of trades that are matched compared with the number or value of trades routed to a venue, typically expressed as a percentage.

Exposed to the market A purchase or sale order in the securities markets that must be shown to the market at large before it can be internalized or crossed on an alternative venue.

Fill-or-kill (FOK) order A designation added to an order indicating that the entire amount of the order should be filled and, if it cannot, should be cancelled.

Fisher *See* Shark.

Flash trade An order that is exposed to fee-paying participants for a matter of milliseconds so that they can determine whether or not to provide a cross. Flash trades have been discontinued by many venues, in part due to criticism that the structure creates a "two tier" market that can disadvantage certain investors.

Fragmentation The splitting of a market into a number of separate submarkets. Each submarket possesses its own liquidity supply and demand forces which interact to fill orders to the greatest extent possible.

Gaming The act of taking advantage of information gained through pinging to position an order to take advantage of a known large bid or offer residing in a dark pool. While not illegal, certain dark pool operators attempt to guard their pools from pinging and gaming, often by establishing minimum order size and tracking trading patterns of participants.

Good after date order An order that comes into force after a specific time.

Good till date order An order that is valid until the end of a defined period, at which point it is cancelled.

Good till cancelled order An order that remains valid until it is specifically cancelled.

Grey market The market for orders that straddles the dark and lit segments, e.g., reserve orders on exchanges, MTFs, ATSs or a combination strategy involving a dark order that re-routes a portion to the lit markets under certain conditions

Hidden order An order that is not exposed to the market, but which is embedded in a venue's dark book. In general, a hidden order is a limit order that assumes a lower priority than visible orders and reserve orders for the same price level.

High frequency trading Tick-by-tick, high turnover buying and selling that is based on real-time data analysis and fast execution times, and which accounts for increasing amounts of exchange, and off-exchange, turnover.

Iceberg *See* Reserve order.

Immediacy The degree to which a trade can be executed in the current moment, and a key measure of liquidity.

Immediate-or-cancel (IOC) order A designation on an order indicating that any unfilled portion of an order that exists shortly after it has been submitted is to be cancelled.

Independent crossing network A crossing network that is broadly held by public investors or which is entirely private; independence from exchanges and other financial institutions is sometimes viewed as a competitive advantage, as the chances of any conflict of interest are nonexistent.

Indication of interest (IOI) A form of message conveyed by an investor to a broker or dealer which indicates interest in executing a trade under certain size and price parameters. The IOI is not generally binding and is not typically considered an order, but may lead to the creation of an order or some other actionable instruction.

Information leakage The degree to which knowledge of an order or trade is known to the market, which can lead to market impact.

Intermarket sweep order (ISO) An order type unique to the U.S. markets and promulgated under U.S. price protection regulations. The ISO can be viewed as a limit order with an immediate-or-cancel designation, which ignores the National Best Bid Offer and does not route to other venues. This means that the order executes in a designated market center, even if better prices are available elsewhere, and is thus specifically exempted from trade-through rules.

Inside spread The difference between the best bid and best offer on a traded security.

Inverse pricing The practice of rebating more for posting liquidity than charging for taking liquidity, generally as a short-term mechanism to gain a critical mass of order flow.

Latency A time delay involved in the processing or execution of a trade.

Latency jitter The variance, or variability, in the average latency of execution, measuring the degree to which a low latency platform is reliable. The greater the jitter (variability) the less reliable the platform.

Latent liquidity Blocks of stock held by institutional investors in their portfolios that may be available for sale, but which are not actively advertised or marketed. Latent liquidity may be brought to market through the efforts of brokers, who communicate with investors and ascertain their willingness to sell portions of their positions.

Legging The process of entering or exiting a long/short position in increments in order to minimize or eliminate open market risk. This is typically done by executing one buy against one sell, or vice-versa, until the total order is complete.

Light liquidity *See* Displayed liquidity.

Limit-if-touched order An order to buy or a sell a security at a limit price, which is held until a trigger is touched; once touched, it is submitted as a limit order.

Limit-on-close order A limit order submitted to execute at the closing price if it is at, or better than, the specified limit price.

Limit-on-open order A limit order submitted to execute at the opening price if it is equal to, or better than, the limit price.

Limit order An order to buy or sell a particular number of securities at a desired price (or better).

Marketable limit order An order that can be executed immediately; a buy order is at or above the best offer, while a sell order is at or below the best bid.

Marketable order An order that can be executed immediately, such as a market order or a very aggressively priced limit order.

Market by price A full range of bids and offers in a security as reflected through a limit order book; the market by price features the best bid and offer, as well as all other quotes that are away from the market.

Market depth The number of shares in a company's stock that are bid and offered, ranked by price. Market depth contributes to the displayed liquidity that all investors can see.

Market-if-touched order An order to buy a security below the current market or sell a security above the current market, which is held back until a trigger (or touch price) is reached; once touched, it is submitted as a market order.

Market impact The effect of information transfer from an order on the market price of a quoted security.

Market impact cost The deviation of the price of a transaction from the market price that would have existed had the transaction not been executed. This approach disregards the bid-offer spread, which is assumed to be an explicit cost. Market impact cost may be temporary (as related to the incremental liquidity required to execute a trade) or it may be permanent (as related to the new price demanded by the market once it becomes aware of the trade).

Market-not-held order *See* Discretionary order.

Market-on-close order An order submitted to execute as close to the closing price as possible, though there is no guarantee of a fill.

Market-on-open order An order submitted to execute as close to the opening price as possible, though there is no guarantee of a fill.

Market order An order to buy or sell a particular number of securities at the current available market price.

Market peg order A peg order that pegs to the opposite side of the base reference (e.g., to the offer for a purchase, or the bid for a sale).

Market-to-limit order An order that is submitted as a market order and is cancelled if it can only be partly filled, with the balance resubmitted as a limit order (where the limit price is equal to the price of the original fill).

Markets in Financial Instruments Directive (MiFID) A pan-European legislative directive enacted in 2007 within the European Economic Area to protect consumers/investors and increase competition. MiFID rules center on systems and controls, client management, best execution, and reporting.

Match The process of matching a buyer and seller of an asset, typically stock, away from a conventional exchange.

Matching cycle The process of gathering open orders and attempting to match them according to one or more defined rules (typically price and time). The matching cycle may be performed continuously or at discrete intervals (e.g., hourly, daily, and so forth).

Midpoint peg order A peg order that pegs to the precise midpoint between the bid and the offer of the base reference.

Microsecond 1/1000th of a millisecond, and a metric that is used by the most advanced matching engines to measure execution performance.

Millisecond 1/1000th of a second, and a common metric used in evaluating the execution performance of a matching engine.

Minimum acceptable quantity (MAQ) order A designation on an order indicating that at least a minimum amount of a full order size must be filled.

Multilateral trading facility (MTF) An alternative trading system used for electronic trading, permissible under MiFID. An MTF may be designed as a form of electronic order book, or as a crossing network/price reference system.

MiFID *See* Markets in Financial Instruments Directive.

MiFID II The new European regulatory framework for traded financial instruments, approved in 2014. MiFID II builds on the original MiFID, imposing additional requirements in a number of sectors, including dark trading, commodities, and derivatives. With regard to dark trading, MiFID II imposes volume caps on dark trading (per venue/total), eliminates broker crossing networks and requires additional post-trade reporting.

Naked access The most independent form of direct market access, where a client's own systems are co-located at the exchange through the broker's membership, and trades are cleared through the broker's clearing account.

National best bid offer (NBBO) In the U.S., the best available bid and offer on a quoted stock, which must be made available to any buyer or seller under Regulation NMS.

Negotiated crossing network A crossing network that permits a degree of price negotiation between participants. Through indications of interest and electronic messaging, buyers and sellers can anonymously agree to cross a particular amount of shares at a price that they establish.

No touch Any trading and execution mechanism that eliminates direct intervention of a broker or sales desk, e.g., direct market access, sponsored access or naked access.

Nondirected order An order placed by a client with a broker or dealer without any specific instruction on the routing to a specific venue or exchange.

Nondisplayed liquidity Trading volume that is not displayed to the market, but which is available for execution. Nondisplayed liquidity, which in total comprises the dark pool sector, may be held within exchanges in the form of hidden orders and reserve orders or on the books of specialists or floor brokers, or within dedicated venues, such as electronic communications networks, crossing networks, and proprietary desks.

Nondisplayed market A market in which offers to trade are not visible to the public.

Open order A limit order that has not yet been filled, and which remains "open" for a fill.

Order-driven market A market in which prices of securities are determined through the publication of offers to buy and sell particular quantities, which are conveyed via orders. Buyers and sellers are permitted to execute with each other (and need not use a market-maker or dealer), but all trades must follow the order precedence rules established by the marketplace.

Order generation logic The mathematical instructions embedded in an algorithm that dictate how a parent order is to be parceled into separate child orders for individual execution over a specific time horizon.

Order placement logic The mathematical instructions embedded in an algorithm that indicate how each individual child order in a parent order should be executed, for example, as a limit order, a market order, a limit order than converts to a market order after a period, and so forth.

Organized trading facility A new trading mechanism created under MiFID II that is designed for off-exchange trading in non-equity instruments.

Parent order An overarching order to execute a particular transaction that can be divided up into smaller child orders. A parent order is commonly used as a fundamental starting point in various algorithmic trading strategies.

Pass-through-order Any type of order that remains in a designated venue for a single matching cycle (where a matching cycle may be continuous, discrete, or end-of-day), after which any unfilled portion is rerouted to alternate venues.

Peg order An order to buy or sell a particular number of securities based on a price that is pegged to a base reference, such as the NBBO or EBBO.

Physical market A marketplace with a central physical trading floor where floor brokers, floor traders, specialists, and other exchange personnel gather to conduct business, and where buying and selling is conducted via open outcry or negotiation.

Ping venue A crossing platform sponsored by a hedge fund or electronic market-maker that operates "black box" trading strategies. The ping venue only accepts immediate-or-cancel orders from clients (who are primarily from the sell-side), and these orders interact directly with the sponsor's own liquidity. The models under-pinning the venue determine whether any single order entering the venue should be accepted or rejected.

Pinging The act of sending small orders into a dark pool as a way of discovering whether a large bid or offer exists in a particular stock. If the small orders are executed the pinging is said to be successful and can lead to gaming of the pool.

Portfolio trade *See* Program trade.

Post only order An order that is not routed and is cancelled it if is marketable against a contra-order in the venue; post only orders are intended to amass liquidity in a particular pool.

Post-trade transparency The process of providing authorities and other interested parties with general, though not specific, information about executed trades. In certain jurisdictions dark pools and other off-exchange venues must supply to the consolidated tape ex-post data on shares crossed by ticker, with associated prices.

Pre-routing order *See* flash trade

Pre-trade transparency The ability to visibly see the top of book for traded instru-ments, including bid and offer prices and market depth. Pre-trade transparency is the key element that distinguishes light from dark markets.

Preferencing A process where an agency broker directs order flow to a dealer or market-maker in exchange for payment.

Price concession The discount a buyer of a large block of stock will demand from the seller as a way of compensating for the risk of market impact.

Price improvement The savings generated when a trade is executed at a price that is superior to the base reference price at the time the order reaches the market, typically measured in terms of ticks or fractions of ticks. In some markets dark venues must offer at least a one tick price improvement to take precedence over lit markets.

Price reference system The equivalent of a crossing network under MiFID.

Primary peg order A peg order that pegs to the same side of the base reference (e.g., to the bid for a purchase, or the offer for a sale).

Private trading system (PTS) In Japan, an automated trading system that offers off-exchange trading, including after-hours trading, in stocks and bonds.

Program trade A single trade comprised of an entire portfolio of stocks, typically developed and executed through computerized models.

Protected bid A bid quotation on a stock that is displayed via an electronic trading center, is disseminated via a national market system and is the best bid available in the market.

Protected offer An offer quotation on a stock that is displayed via an electronic trading center, is disseminated via a national market system and is the best offer available in the market.

Quote stuffing A practice used by certain high frequency traders that centers on sending in and immediately cancelling orders, often to test system latency or detect pockets of liquidity.

Quote-driven market A market in which prices of securities are determined through quotes supplied by market-makers or dealers, which they alone are allowed to adjust in relation to relative supply and demand. In general, any party trading via a quote-driven market must execute through a market-marker or dealer, rather than via another trader/investor.

Rebate An amount paid to a trader or investor providing liquidity to an exchange or electronic platform, as a way of amassing sufficient critical mass to effectively cross orders. Rebates are typically computed as fractions of a basis point on the amount of the order.

Regulation ATS In the U.S., Regulation Alternative Trading System put forth by the Securities and Exchange Commission, which defines the nature of electronic trading systems and requires that any such platform be registered as a broker/dealer or a self-regulated exchange. Regulation ATS also indicates that the platform must provide to a national securities exchange or national securities association, for inclusion in the public quotation system, the prices and sizes of its best priced buy and sell orders that are displayed to more than one person.

Regulation NMS In the U.S., Regulation National Market System put forth by the Securities and Exchange Commission, which seeks to consolidate and strengthen the framework for trading and execution on exchanges and electronic platforms. The key elements of the regulation focus on order protection (via protected bids and offers and trade-through restrictions), order access, pricing increments, and market data/information display.

Reserve order A form of limit order that is only partly exposed to the public. The reserve thus combines a visible limit order and a hidden order and, while the total amount is available for execution, only a portion is displayed. As each visible portion is executed, the next portion becomes visible, and so forth until fully executed. However, from a priority perspective the reserved portion of the order is third in priority for the same price, ranking behind visible orders and ahead of hidden orders.

Resident order A dark or light order that rests in a venue.

Resiliency The degree to which the price of a security reverts to its previous level following a trade. The more resilient the security, the quicker the price will return to the pre-trade price.

Resting The act of allowing an unfilled order to remain in situ in a particular venue for multiple matching cycles, in hopes of achieving a fill.

Router logic The mathematical instructions embedded in an algorithm that indicate where to route each individual child order in a parent order to take advantage of available trading liquidity.

Rules-based trading *See* Algorithmic trading.

Shadow order A client order resident in a broker-dealer's internal book with a duplicate that can access external pools; execution of either order leads to an instantaneous cancellation of the second order.

Shark An individual or institution that is able to detect any single strategy being used within the dark pool sector and use that knowledge to front run or position itself to profit. This is typically done through algorithms that are specifically designed to identify revealing trading patterns.

Ships passing in the night A characteristic and disadvantage of order routing without pre-trade transparency, where orders seeking contra flow may not find each other due to the large number of dark venues in operation.

Shotgunning The process of using an aggregator or algorithm to send in multiple IOC orders into multiple dark venues to find liquidity.

Slicing The process of dividing a large order, such as a block trade, into a number of smaller orders, so that potential market impact is reduced.

Smart order router (SOR) A coding mechanism that divides an order according to the rules defined in an algorithm and then selects the proper destination(s) so that execution can be fulfilled. An SOR maintains compliance with order protection and best execution requirements and generally permits prioritization of venues based on transaction costs.

Sniffer An algorithm that is used for pinging and, ultimately, gaming, of a dark pool.

Sponsored access A form of direct market access where the client connects directly to an exchange or other marketplace using the broker's membership; however, the client does not use the broker's technology or accounting mechanisms as in standard DMA.

Spray The process of sending out multiple orders to multiple venues to fill a position as quickly as possible, typically up to a level dictated by the limit price parameter.

Standing order *See* Open order.

Step-up order *See* Flash trade

Stop limit order An order that creates a limit order to buy or sell some quantity of securities if a trigger price is attained.

Stop order An order that creates a market order to buy or sell some quantity of securities if a trigger price is attained.

Stub quote A place holder quote used by a market maker for a stock, typically set at 0.01, to make sure a stock does not trade at 0 in any circumstance.

Sunshine trade A large trade that is deliberately exposed to the market as an invitation to deal, and which will therefore generate some degree of market impact.

Sweep-to-fill order An order that seeks to execute as quickly as possible at the best available prices, regardless of venue. The order is submitted to the first location with the best price and is filled to the extent possible; it then sweeps to the next venue with the next best price for further fills, and so forth, until complete.

Sweeper *See* Sniffer.

Systematic internalizer An internal crossing book or proprietary desk that crosses incoming client orders and/or proprietary positions, which can operate under MiFID through the same pre- and post-trade transparency and best-execution rules as multilateral trading facilities and primary markets.

Tape A In the U.S. markets, the portion of consolidated tape reporting related to stocks listed on the NYSE.

Tape B In the U.S. markets, the portion of consolidated tape reporting related to stocks listed on BATS, NYSE Arca and regional exchanges.

Tape C In the U.S. markets, the portion of consolidated tape reporting related to stocks listed on the NASDAQ.

Top of book The best bids and offers in a security, shown with associated market depth.

Top of market The best bid and the best offer on a security, as reflected in a limit order book.

Touch price The "at best" price of a security.

Toxic pool A dark pool that features order fills with prices that tend to be slightly worse than other venues, generally by hosting aggressive traders or those with rapid execution strategies that may be able to take advantage of investors with a more passive approach.

Trade through The purchase or sale of a stock during regular trading hours, either as principal or as agent, at a price lower than a protected bid or higher than a protected offer. In the U.S., trade-throughs are prohibited under Regulation NMS.

Trading fast A market environment where bids and offers are of such significant size that specialists cannot keep pace, suggesting that a customer cannot be guaranteed a fill at the best prices.

Trailing stop limit order A form of stop limit order that carries an attached trailing amount that moves with the market price of the security.

Trailing stop order A form of stop order that carries an attached trailing amount that moves with the market price of the security.

Twilight pool A pool that conducts most of its business in the dark but exposes its book to the light at certain times of day or when certain conditions are met. The twilight pool's specificity is still not the same as in a lit market, i.e., the pool won't flash a full set of bids and offers or market depth as in an ELOB, but it may provide information on the stocks being traded.

Transaction cost analysis (TCA) A framework for analyzing the costs and relative performance of executing a strategy through a particular venue or mechanism. The TCA process allows traders/ investors to ensure they are getting best execution treatment.

Ultra low latency trading A form of trading that relies heavily on fast execution times in order to generate profits.

Upstairs market An off-exchange gathering of buyers and sellers of large blocks, so named as it developed above the exchange floors.

Uptick order An order that leads to the purchase or sale of securities if the market moves up by a tick.

Visible market Any securities market that provides complete transparency with regard to order books and execution. Exchanges and various types of electronic communications networks/multilateral trading facilities are the main examples of such markets.

Visible liquidity *See* Displayed liquidity.

Walking the book The process of sweeping a buy or sell order through a book at increasingly worse prices in order to complete the cross.

Working order *See* Open order.

Selected Bibliography

Aite Group, 2007, "Rise of dark pools and rebirth of ECNs: death to exchanges?" September.

Anand, A. and Weaver, D., 2004, "Can order exposure be mandated?" *Journal of Financial Markets*, 7(4), pp. 405–26.

Biais, B., 1993, "Price formation and equilibrium liquidity in fragmented and centralized markets," *Journal of Finance*, 48(1), pp. 157–84.

Black, F., 1995, "Equilibrium exchanges," *Financial Analysts Journal*, 51(3), pp. 23–29.

CFA Institute, 2012, "Dark pools, internalization and equity market quality," CFA Review, November, Charlottesville, VA: CFA Institute.

Commission of European Securities Regulators, 2007, "Consultation paper on improving MIFID databases," December, Paris.

Commission of European Securities Regulators, 2007, "Publication and consolidation of MiFID transparency data," February, Paris.

Commission of European Securities Regulators, 2008, "Call for evidence on the review of the scope of the MIFID transaction reporting obligation," November, Paris.

Commission of European Securities Regulators, 2009, "Waivers from pre-trade transparency obligations under MiFID," August, Paris.

Commission of European Securities Regulators, 2010, "Post-trade transparency standards," August, Paris.

Conrad, J., Johnson, K., and Awahal, S., 2003, "Institutional trading and alternative trading systems," *Journal of Financial Economics*, 70, pp. 99–134.

Conroy, R. and Winkler, R., 1986, "Market structure: the specialist as dealer and broker," *Journal of Banking and Finance*, 10(1), 21–36.

Degryse, H., Van Achter, M., and Wuyts, G., 2005, "Dynamic order submission strategies with competition between a dealer market and a crossing network," Working Paper.

DeWinne, R. and D'hondt, C., 2007, "Hide and seek in the market: placing and detecting hidden orders," *Oxford Review of Finance*, 11(4), pp. 663–92.

Domowitz, I., 1990, "The mechanics of automated trade execution systems," *Journal of Financial Intermediation*, 1(2), pp. 167–94.

Domowitz, I. and Yegerman, H., 2005, "Measuring and interpreting the performance of broker algorithms," ITG Working Paper.

Esser, A. and Monch, B., 2004, "The navigation of an iceberg: the optimal use of hidden orders," Working Paper, University of Frankfurt.

European Union, 2004, "Directive 2004/39/EC of the European Parliament and of the Council of 21 April 2004 on markets in financial instruments," Brussels.

Fidessa, 2013, "European dark trading analysis," London: Fidessa.

Financial Services Authority, 2007, "Implementing the markets in financial instruments directive," January, London.

Financial Services Authority, 2007, "Transaction reporting users pack" July, London.

Foucault, T., Moinas, S., and Theissen, E., 2007, "Does anonymity matter in electronic limit order markets?" *Review of Financial Studies*, 20(5), pp. 1707–47.

Gresse, C., 2006, "The effect of crossing network trading on dealer market's bid-ask spreads," *European Financial Management*, 12(2), pp. 143–60.

Gsell, M., 2006, "Assessing the impact of algorithmic trading on markets: a simulation approach," Johnann-Wolfgang Goethe University Working Paper.

Handa, P. and Schwartz, R., 1996, "Limit order trading," *Journal of Finance*, 51(5), pp. 1835–61.

Harris, L., 1993, "Consolidation, fragmentation, segmentation and regulation," *Financial Markets, Institutions, and Instruments*, 5, pp. 1–28.

Hatstand Ltd, 2013, "Mifid II Trading Venues, Release 2," London: Hatstand.

Hendershott, T. and Jones, C. and A. Menkveld, 2011, "Does algorithmic trading improve liquidity?" *Journal of Finance*, 1, pp. 45–69.

Investment Industry Regulatory Organization of Canada, 2012, "Dark pools, dark orders and other developments in market structures in Canada," Consultation paper 23–404, Ottawa, Canada: IIROC.

Investment Industry Regulatory Organization of Canada, 2013, "Provisions respecting dark liquidity," Ottawa, Canada: IIROC.

Investment Technology Group, 2008, "Cul de sacs and highways: an optical tour of dark pool trading performance," August.

Kakade, S., Kearns, M., Mansour, Y. and Ortiz, L., 2004, "Competitive algorithms for VWAP and limit order trading," University of Pennsylvania Working Paper.

Lepone, A. and Mistry, M., 2006, "Transparency and information content of undisclosed orders: evidence from the Australian market," Working Paper, University of Sydney.

Madhavan, A., 2000, "Market microstructure: a survey," *Journal of Financial Markets*, 3, pp. 205–58.

Mittal, H., 2008, "Are you playing in a toxic dark pool?" *Journal of Trading*, 3(3), Summer.

NYSE Euronext, 2011, "Universal trading platform for cash market trading CCG FIX 4.2," August.

O'Hara, M., 1995, *Market Microstructure Theory*, London: Blackwell.

Pardo, A. and Pascual, R., 2004, "On the hidden side of liquidity," Working Paper, University of Valencia.

Parlour, C. and Seppi, D., 2003, "Liquidity based competition for order flow," *Review of Financial Studies*, 16, pp. 301–43.

Securities and Exchange Commission, 1997, Regulation of Exchanges, Washington DC: SEC.

Securities and Exchange Commission, 2000, Regulation ATS, April, Washington DC: SEC.

Securities and Exchange Commission, 2005, Regulation NMS, August, Washington DC: SEC.

Smitdt, S., 1979, "Continuous versus intermittent trading on auction markets," *Journal of Financial and Quantitative Analysis*, 14(4), pp. 837–86.

Sussman, A., 2005, "Institutional equity trading 2005: A buy-side perspective," Tabb Group Research Report.

Wagner, W., ed., 1989, *The Complete Guide to Securities Transactions*, New York: John Wiley.

Wall Street Journal, May 18, 2009, "Dark pool battle intensifies."

Index

Printed and bound by CPI Group (UK) Ltd, Croydon, CR0 4YY